Early American Rebels

Early American Rebels

Pursuing Democracy from Maryland to Carolina, 1640–1700

Noeleen McIlvenna

The University of North Carolina Press CHAPEL HILL

This book was published with the assistance of the Fred W. Morrison Fund of the University of North Carolina Press.

The University of North Carolina Press has been a member of the
Green Press Initiative since 2003.

Library of Congress Cataloging-in-Publication Data
Names: McIlvenna, Noeleen, 1963– author.
Title: Early American rebels : pursuing democracy from Maryland to Carolina,
    1640-1700 / Noeleen McIlvenna.
Description: Chapel Hill : The University of North Carolina Press, 2020. |
    Includes bibliographical references and index.
Identifiers: LCCN 2019044426 | ISBN 9781469656052 (cloth) | ISBN 9781469656069
    (paperback) | ISBN 9781469656076 (ebook)
Subjects: LCSH: Representative government and representation—
    United States—History—17th century. | Insurgency—United States—
    History—17th century. | Democracy—United States—History—
    17th century. | United States—History—Colonial period, ca. 1600-1775. |
    Great Britain—Colonies—America—History.
Classification: LCC E188 .M17 2020 | DDC 973.2—dc23
LC record available at https://lccn.loc.gov/2019044426

Cover illustrations: *Top*, Christopher Browne, *A New Map of Virginia, Maryland, and the Improved Parts of Pennsylvania and New Jersey* (courtesy of the Library of Congress Geography and Map Division); *bottom*, John Speed, *A New Description of Carolina* (courtesy of the David Rumsey Map Collection, http://www.david rumsey.com).

To Lance

Contents

Figure and Maps

Acknowledgments

My thanks go first to Stephen Jenkins and to Billie Jenkins, genealogists who provided essential leads at the beginning of my research. I hope they understand why the book became much more than the story of John Jenkins.

I am truly grateful for the financial support from the North Caroliniana Society, who awarded me an Archie K. Davis fellowship. Wright State University support also proved crucial; funding from the College of Liberal Arts allowed travel to archives from Annapolis to London. During those travels, archivists at the Maryland State Archives, Maryland Historical Society, and the Edward H. Nabb Research Center for Delmarva History and Culture were consummate professionals. Librarians at Duke University and North Carolina's State Archives, at the Alderman Library, University of Virginia and the National Archives in London also eased the pain of research.

Readers improved the book a great deal, and I am thankful for their thorough feedback. The UNC Press editorial staff are patient with me, and Chuck Grench's relentless positivity sustains a writer over the long, long years of writing a book.

Good colleagues make everything possible. My writing group, a troop of dedicated women, sat at tables with me for years, ensuring I never gave up. Carol Mejia-Laperle, Sirisha Naidu, Marie Thompson, Nimisha Patel, Sarah Twill, and especially Deborah Crusan, who fed me nearly every week while I slowly produced these pages, have my undying loyalty. And while I tried to describe the struggles of the Gerard network for self-rule, I learned in real life what it took to maintain a coalition against power. My fellow AAUP-WSU officers reminded me why the work of academics matters so much to a free society, and the faculty's collective struggle for the soul of the university over the last several years illuminated the truth that perseverance is militancy. I am forever inspired.

My family's faith in and patience with me through the production of three books deserves a major award. Tess models scholarly discipline for me, instead of the other way around. My partner, Lance Greene, taught at universities in other states while I wrote this one. He came back though, and as always, made the figures and formatted the text. But his ongoing contribution is so much more. His intellectual company challenges my thinking. His steadfastness and love allow me to work from a firm foundation. The book is dedicated to him.

Early American Rebels

Introduction

We are about to meet some of the most determined egalitarians in American history. The household of the first Susannah Gerard of St. Clement's, Maryland, would nurture both ideas and action profound for their time. Informed by experiences, and demanding some say in their own destiny, men and women moved around the Chesapeake region, looking for a means to build a political system that would serve their needs. That they maintained the struggle over a half century, spread over at least three colonies, and managed to be elected again and again by their neighbors allows us to see that they were not a fringe movement, but in fact, leaders who brought modern ideas into the mainstream, only to face repression. Yet they won battles, and some seemed to win the war in their own lifetimes. This story of political radicals in the seventeenth-century colonies might have been told as an intellectual history, tracing the shifts in thought over time between republicanism, democracy, and equality before the law, while disentangling the knots between religious theology and the spectrum of political radicalism. But because these people were not intellectuals in the normal usage of the term, but in fact activists, this is a political history—a history of class struggle.

The struggle occurred at a particular moment in the development of global capitalism, a stage economists usually call "primitive accumulation." In sixteenth- and seventeenth-century England, the lords of the manor were enclosing their lands in high hedges, forcing peasants to the cities and replacing them with more lucrative sheep. For a century, an unemployed rural proletariat—landless laborers—existed in England. In time, the wool constituted the raw materials and the unemployed peasants the labor that joined together in the workshops built by early industrialists. The profits their work generated would become the capital that could finance the ever larger factories, mills, and mines generating ever more capital for ever more development. In the American colonies, however, the process differed. Europeans violently expropriated the land not from feudal peasants but from Indians. Then, unfree workers—at first indentured servants bound for years to work without pay, and later enslaved people kidnapped from Africa and their children born into slavery—performed the labor. The system did not match our normal vision of an urban working class toiling for poverty wages in a textiles factory. These laborers performed their work instead in tobacco and cotton fields, on rice and indigo plantations. But the result—the creation of massive capital and political power in the hands of a few—was the same. This process took about a century in the area around the Chesapeake Bay.

At this primitive accumulation stage, the term "class" was not what it became after the Industrial Revolution. In the British realm of 1600, the dominant concept was blood or kinship hierarchy. Accident of birth determined the limits of the possible. The child of the king, the child of the country squire, the child of the yeoman, and the child of the peasant knew their place. The top 5 percent, nobility and gentry, expected that all in society would behave accordingly, accepting without protest the parameters of power for their social rank. Every institution in society undergirded this reality, not least of all the Church of England. A glimpse at a wedding of an heir to the British throne takes us back to a time when the monarch's position at the front of the church reflected their position in society, and the rest filed into their pews in the social order of their birth. This hierarchy thus seemed to an uneducated populace to be endorsed by God, and the church/state censorship ensured that any critical thinking of the premise would not find an audience. It had been this way for centuries, and the trappings of pomp and mysticism encouraged all to believe that no alternative existed.

"Religion Is but Policy"

But by 1600, there was also no way for some to unknow that the Reformation had fundamentally changed everything. The previous century had witnessed the overthrow of the pope and all his trappings of mysticism in England. And while the Tudors sought to marginalize the devotees of Luther and Calvin, and the concept of the "priesthood of all believers" with its inherent need for literacy (people must be able to read their own Bible rather than have priests tell them what Scripture said), those who sought to purify the Anglican Church of the last remnants of Roman Catholicism remained. The questioning of any power source often leaks into other sources, however. In a place with no separation of church from state, any effort to reform the Church automatically threatened the state.

The English Civil War became the English Revolution because of this spillage. When Parliament challenged royal authority, the entire framework of English political, legal, and social structures began to shake. When an army based on merit defeated one based on lineage, it shuddered. And when that victorious army put Charles I on trial and executed him, the edifice might have collapsed. The lifting of censorship in the 1650s widened the cracks. But too many powerful people had too much to lose to allow that to happen, so they quickly rebuilt the entire structure. They felt that they must bring back a king, for it seemed like that symbol was the lynchpin of the whole. And so, in 1660, the upper classes brought Charles II to the throne.

But the questions and some of the answers did not evaporate completely. As low-born English people sailed the Atlantic to the New World, they carried visions of a New World order. Sometimes embedded in their religion, but sometimes not, their ideas could thrive in wilderness colonies absent the instruments of state repression. Where some confronted a Catholic proprietor, the threat of arbitrary power loomed particularly close. Yet, even in colonies like Virginia and North Carolina, free of Catholicism, the people of this revolutionary generation fought for representation. People of privilege, then and now, might look upon these visionaries as barbarous for their lack of decorum. But from a different perspective, they appear as the vanguard of American principles: Why do "they" alone have the right to decide? If my fate is affected, why can I not have some say?

Tens of thousands came to America during the decades surrounding the English Revolution. Ideologically, they occupied a full spectrum of political thought, from the William Berkeley types who loudly proclaimed that breeding determined abilities and opportunities and rights, to the Ann Hutchinsons who understood that such announcements about genetics justified, indeed cloaked, a plan to ensure that others did the hard and dirty work for nothing. The spectrum incorporated those who could question one kind of authority (perhaps religious) but not others (class, race, or gender) and could fight for political equality for the group to which they attached their identity, but not others. As the leading historian of democratic thought explains, "The discourse of democracy, over time and across cultures, has lacked the consistency or coherence of philosophical systems," and because these colonial settlers are everyday people in search of the best solution in the specific moment, not intellectuals in a library, we see their ideas through their political decisions in motion.[1] Over the course of a lifetime, people shifted their place on the spectrum. Among the most radical, there was a great range of confidence in the plausibility of altering ancient systems. And at least for a while, they succeeded in North Carolina, lending that state a different culture than those around it. But even the most faithful to the dream of an equal society might falter when faced with setbacks. The old guard did not abandon their positions easily, and they had most of the weapons. The historical ladder of progress often looks more like a roller coaster.

I build on the excellent work of others, many of whom have taken an Atlantic perspective of the English Revolution or the Glorious Revolution, such as Carla Pestana, John Donoghue, Peter Linebaugh and Marcus Rediker, and David Lovejoy.[2] These historians have highlighted the back and forth nature of Atlantic ideas, with special attention to the Puritans of New England, whose ties to the Puritans of the English Civil War led them to play very active roles. Other historians of the colonies have examined closely various upheavals in the colonies in this era, notably Tim Riordan's study of Ingle's Rebellion, James Rice's work on Bacon's Rebellion, and Lois Carr and David Jordan's investigation of the Protestant Associators of Maryland.[3]

"For in All These Parts They Correspond Very Much One with Another"

Early American Rebels seeks to combine these two lines of research and then go beyond them, to see how revolutionary ideas spread beyond New England and the Caribbean and how popular politics played out in the Chesapeake. The narrative crosses colonial lines, and shows Ingle's Rebellion, Fendall's Rebellion, Bacon's Rebellion, Culpeper's Rebellion, and the Glorious Revolution as one piece. They are of one piece, *because they were organized by a connected group of people.*

My story is not that of elite planters. Small farmers in the Chesapeake sought a republic of equals in the half century prior to the imposition of the slave society. Their stories have been mostly lost or misunderstood. The preservation of historical papers favors the rich, favors the white, favors the male—in the ownership and use of colonial pen and paper, in the official government records, in the decisions of whose history is worth preservation. A historical record that includes everyone is tough to write, but hidden in the genealogies and the topographical maps lie some of the stories of the powerless.[4]

The genealogy, despite the difficulties created by the loss of women's names by marriage, reveals the relationships. Just as the gentry on both sides of the Atlantic maintained their networks through intermarriage, so did those who sought to topple inequality. Recent work in the digital humanities has brought to light the crucial part played by women in the maintenance of radical networks, precisely because of the need for both secrecy and network-building.[5] Relationships between the women who carried the messages, hosted the meetings, and communicated with family members kept the struggle alive, especially when it had to be sustained behind closed doors, fearing repression. Teaching their daughters and their sons through their words and by example, women like the elder Susannah Gerard constituted the backbone of the movement. We cannot say for certain that she was the font of the radical ideology, for we have not a single record of her words. We can only lay out all the evidence of this two-generation network and ponder the roles of the women at the center. Perhaps that women comprised a small minority of the colonial settlements worked to their advantage at times; their rarity helped men view them as more valuable than back in England, and thus they were more likely to listen to women's opinions.[6]

The maps reveal the lines of communication in a world lived along water. We see the friendships that genealogy does not reveal. We see the communities of another time, lost now, as settlement patterns shift from a farming economy to an industrial and postindustrial landscape. Homes and communities divided more by land than by water, built along the edges of peninsulas jutting into the Potomac or Albemarle Sound, served as safe places far from the prying eyes of power, where activists could talk through and teach others about alternative structures of government.

The songs and ballads reveal the discourse of another time, when speeches were not recorded, when newspapers were not available everywhere. We see some of the speech in the trial transcripts, of course, when dissidents faced charges of slander or blasphemy or sedition. But this popular seventeenth-century drinking song shows how widespread alternative narratives were.

> There's many men get store of treasure
> Yet they live like very slaves:
> In this world they have no pleasure
> The more they have the more they crave
> Hang such greedy-minded misers
> That will ne'r contented be.[7]

Despite the political instability inherent in semi-constant struggle for representation, we should not confuse such instability with barbarity. There is something noble in facing off against those more powerful than oneself in a quest for a more equal society. Yet in paying close attention to political struggle, we cannot ignore the economic structures forming in the same era. The real barbarities of the colonial era started with masters subjecting teenagers to years of servitude without pay, subject to violence in a land offering little hope for escape, and later became those masters' sale of other people's children and the unlimited brutality necessary to keep them enslaved. This book closes as southern slavery became the dominant economic system.

Many who would proclaim their right to representation had no compunction in withholding that right from others. Still, it is worthwhile to acknowledge the general pattern that the more slaves one owned, the more likely one fought against the equality even of one's fellow white man.[8]

Equality of representation for all Americans seems now a principle that no one can contend. Thomas Jefferson declared it "a self-evident truth" centuries ago, although he clearly thought it self-evident that he meant that only white men were born equal. Our story here will be one part of the saga of the push for equality, the part played by poor and middling white men in an era when family lineage guaranteed privilege or curtailed opportunity. Some radicals of the seventeenth century might appear terribly conservative by today's standards, but they represented a significant stepping-stone on the path toward equality. Thus the story of those who fought for the incremental extension of the principle of equality does not merely constitute a quaint tale or nostalgia for our ancestors. It has the potential to unlock a strategy for the full accomplishment of that American dream, the level playing field: the level classroom, the level courtroom, and the level credit line. It reminds us that when we look for leadership in the quest for American principles, we should look down to those below, not up to those already enjoying power and privilege.

CHAPTER ONE

Ingle's Rebellion, 1638–1650

The Hierarchy is out of date
Our Monarchy was sick of late
But now 'tis growne to an excellent state
Oh God a mercy Parliament

The settlement of Lord Baltimore's colony occurred in a revolutionary era. Historians often explain the early decades of Maryland's colonial past in the context of religious tensions, but serious political tensions also simmered, carried over from England. Religion and politics were so entangled in the seventeenth-century Atlantic world that one might say that the churches, rather than court factions, anticipated political parties. As the Roundheads and Cavaliers clashed on the fields of England, important philosophical differences emerged about who should govern. Was "the Hierarchy . . . out of date?" How much power should Parliament have, and how widespread should the franchise be for that Parliament? These arguments played out around the Chesapeake Bay as well as in London.[1]

The *Ark* and the *Dove* sailed across the Atlantic in the winter months of 1633–34 to settle the coastal region north of Virginia. The passengers had left an England full of the disgruntled. Puritans seeking more local control from the Church of England were flooding into Massachusetts, and now Lord Baltimore looked to find a place that would allow Catholics to practice their faith free of harassment. In the eyes of the Puritans, Charles I's direct rule from the throne, aided by his henchman Archbishop Laud, had made England's state church more Catholic-friendly, with altars and prayer book, but the changes did not include bringing Catholics back in from the cold. So for dissenters of all stripes, the brand-new colonies along the water's edge of North America beckoned with toleration. Many dissented as much from an unchecked monarchy as they dissented from the Anglican Church, although this particular monarch's religious policies helped that political questioning along.[2] That the Americas offered a chance to remake the political landscape was rarely articulated in any of the tracts and other promotional literature. To write such was treason. And the promoters, successful men on the whole, tended to favor an English political system in which they had succeeded, anyhow. This was certainly true of anyone with the title "Lord."

The first Lord Baltimore (actually named George Calvert) had traveled to Newfoundland and Virginia in the 1620s, looking for lands that might serve both his religious and entrepreneurial bents. He was granted a charter for Maryland months after his death in 1632, and his son Cecilius inherited both the Baltimore title and the almost seven million acres in the Americas. A proprietorship guaranteed him as "the source, within the province, of office and honor, the fountain of justice, the commander of the military, the recipient of the provincial revenue. . . . They were in kind the power of the English monarch." This new Lord Baltimore occupied a moderate wing of Catholicism, seeking only toleration, rather than fostering any plot to retake England for the pope. When it came to politics or any other decisions, he consistently voted for his wallet rather than adhering fundamentally to any core principles. So his new colony happily welcomed Protestants and Catholics. As long as they paid their rents and everyone could practice their faith in peace, he had no further ambition for Maryland's settlers.[3]

Baltimore carefully planned his colony to resemble a little England with lords of the manor and plenty of servants and a few of the middling sort in between. Unlike today's sprawling "middle" class, in the seventeenth-century Chesapeake region, at least 70 percent and perhaps as many as 85 percent of the population were servants.[4] Maryland's elaborate shoreline made for a scattered colony of riverine plantations, but a small town also developed in St. Mary's City. The manorial lands—averaging 2,000 acres—were granted to gentlemen who should employ servants to raise tobacco and corn. This country squirearchy would run local courts, but defer in more important matters to the governor, Baltimore's younger brother, Leonard Calvert. Although they were the elite of these early days in Maryland, this group should not be confused with the great aristocrats depicted in *Downton Abbey* or *Brideshead Revisited*, nor even with eighteenth-century Virginia planters, who might scoff at 2,000 acres.

However, Baltimore's charter also contained a clause detailing the need for the "Advice, Assent, and Approbation of the Free-Men . . . or of their Delegates" in any legislation. Thus from the beginning, Maryland had a General Assembly, and the people had a venue for their voice. At first, the population was small enough that all freemen (even the landless) were called to the Assembly, gaining valuable experience in the administration of local affairs. Gradually some men, such as James Baldridge, carpenter Francis Gray, cooper Thomas Sturman, and Nathaniel Pope, who came to Maryland as free but poor men, went as delegates for others to St. Mary's, and although they perhaps did not carry much weight in decision making at first, they learned by observation the work of the legislature. After Lord Baltimore vetoed early Assembly statutes, discussions about the jurisdiction of English law and the limits of Baltimore's authority demystified, little by little, the machinations of power. As the historian of Maryland's government describes, "Gentlemen and recent freedmen, the well-educated and the illiterate voted side by side and sat together in the assembly." Thomas and James Baldridge served as sergeant and sheriff, respectively. These freemen, occupying a middling place in the social hierarchy, often aligned with servants rather than gentlemen. Francis Gray intervened on behalf of some servants who felt that their Catholic master was preventing their religious practice, because the servants "had no knowledge what to doe in it, nor could so well goe to the Governor for redresse as the freemen could."[5]

Arriving in 1638, Thomas Gerard was considered gentleman enough that soon Baltimore awarded him one of the manors, St. Clement's Hundred. As one of the younger sons of a gentry family in Lancashire, Gerard could not inherit land in England, but his relatives helped him get started in life with a lump sum to invest. While many men in his position joined the military or the Church, Gerard took another popular route—seeking his fortune in the colonies. In return for the generous land grant, Baltimore demanded he protect the game from poachers and prevent any of his tenants or servants from trading with the Indians, "Specially Such as Shall give or Sell to any Indian any arms or ammunition." Gerard was also obligated to provide arms for the defense of the English on his property. He would serve as the local justice for St. Clement's and eventually as councilor to the governor.[6]

Governor Calvert chose only Catholics for his inner circle, a fact that drew the suspicions of the majority-Protestant residents of the colony. But Gerard stood out. His wife, Susannah, née Snow, the sister of Justinian and Marmaduke Snow, wealthy merchants in 1630s Maryland and well connected to the Calverts, was a Protestant. She raised their ten children in that faith without any apparent conflict with her husband. Susannah Gerard, very sadly, left no voice, for her influence over events in Maryland can only be described as profound, given her husband's and daughters' roles over the next few decades. All evidence suggests that she was a mediatrix, as Julie Crawford defines the term for seventeenth-century women: "politically and culturally powerful, but with an edge of oppositionism; at once a patron to be honored and a force to be reckoned with." Crawford describes the lives of several women like Gerard in England, women whose papers have been saved and archived, as Gerard's were not. They were not "mere support staff . . . [but rather] the leaders and spokespeople." These were upper-class women, of course, as was Susannah Gerard. That no one recorded any of Susannah's words means that she never earned a reputation as a "brabbling" woman, one who faced court proceedings for unruly and inappropriate public speech. On the contrary; in the seventeenth century, the gendered restrictions on political discourse had not fully developed as they would later.[7]

This family situation helps explain Thomas Gerard's actions throughout his life in the colonies. A man of toleration in an intolerant era, his philosophy could not easily be predicted from his external group identities, such as class or religion. In addition to the influence of his wife, he perhaps took his relative Gilbert Gerard as his role model. Gilbert played a prominent role in the administration of Elizabeth I and managed to protect his Catholic relatives from persecution, despite their long history of conspiracies to reinstate a Catholic monarch. Another relative of Thomas, Father John Gerard, had to escape to France after the Gunpowder Plot, because of his close association with many of the main players in that attempt to blow up the king and the House of Lords. Like Gilbert, described as "a Protestant in London, a papist in Lancashire," Thomas Gerard in Maryland was a pragmatist devoted more to family and to having a say in government than to any theology.

Younger sons of elite families, fed by stories of Hernando Cortés and of the sugar barons of the West Indies, often dreamed of accumulating great riches in the colonies. But these dreams did not materialize in Maryland as quickly as many hoped. About half of the gentlemen returned to England. Plus, the terrible death rate of the early decades paid little respect to social rank. Most died before their mid-forties.[8] Those who survived and stayed would form factions and quarrel among themselves in their quest for power. Gerard stayed out of this internecine squabbling, forming friendships and alliances with his neighbors in St. Clement's instead.

The initial settlers in St. Clement's, as with the rest of Maryland's manors, were primarily young men, some free, but mostly indentured servants. Although they mostly volunteered, some had been outright kidnapped, or "spirited," as contemporaries referred to the practice. Few had any input into their destination once they left England. Over the seventeenth century, the Chesapeake's reputation as a torture chamber or deathtrap would grow, for the protections of an indentured servant were minimal. A ballad described the dehumanizing practices at the dockside up on arrival: "Some view'd our Limbs, tur[n]ing us round, Examining, like Horses. . . . Some felt our Hands, others our Legs and Feet. . . . Some view'd our Teeth." The trade in servants made them feel like commodities. In 1644, Gerard gave up on a run-away servant considered valuable for his brickmaking skills and would "Sell Bargaine and make over . . . [his] Right, Interest and Title in the Said Servant for the full Terme of years belonging unto [him] by Indenture" to a Virginian. The brickmaker had been promised 200 acres with a furnished house and some livestock in return for three years' labor, but three months working for Gerard was apparently enough. Other court cases reflect the commodification: Sarah Hall pleaded to be released from a cruel master. She got her wish, but the court ordered that appraisers decide her value for another "buyer."[9]

From the beginning the servants mixed primarily with others in their local area. St. Clement's lies twenty-five miles to the northeast of St. Mary's City, on the banks of the Wicomico tributary of the Potomac. The outer coastal plain sees tidal salt water come up the river, creating wide creeks like the Wicomico and much marsh and wetland. Unfamiliarity with the region and presumably a lack of boats restricted travel around the colony. Lorena Walsh, the expert on Maryland's colonial social history, studied the interactions of residents of St. Clement's Manor closely, explaining that "all the repeated and ordinary contacts of male residents involved other households lying within an approximate five-mile radius of the home." Within this geographically limited world, neighborly social engagements included fun activities like drinking and gambling, but also political debate. Far from the tight censorship of England's Star Chamber courts, the only policing could come from Gerard himself. Walsh's research disclosed that St. Clement's men showed no signs of the social deference enforced in the home country, freely "expressing resentment about the social pretensions of the emerging ruling class. Talk about the sexual irregularities or incapacities of county officials or of the alleged promiscuity of their wives served to bring those in power down to the level of the politically powerless."[10]

The material culture supported this refusal to acknowledge social rank. Carving out small homes in the wilderness, the elite of seventeenth-century Maryland rarely went to the trouble and expense of transporting across the Atlantic the fancy trappings used to distinguish social class in England.[11] In addition to the lack of status symbols, the opportunity for many of humble background to own land blurred the lines of class distinction always at the forefront back home. Population density in England made the ownership of land the predominant marker between the haves and the have-nots. In the British colonies in the Americas, as disease decimated the native population, land seemed plentiful. So elites had to find workers to produce tobacco through the backbreaking labor of clearing forests and then cultivation. In the seventeenth and eighteenth centuries, control of the labor of others gradually emerged as the definition of status. By the turn of the eighteenth century, the racialized nature of labor made race itself the carrier of status in the southern colonies.

But in the early 1640s, before the African slave trade made much impact on Maryland's economy or society, transplanted Englishmen fought among themselves for the chance at profit from land and trade. Serious tension between an individual based in Virginia named William Claiborne and the Calvert family over ownership of Kent Island had already come to blows. Claiborne, having built a close and lucrative partnership with the Susquehannocks, constructed an elaborate trading post on Kent before the Maryland Charter granted the island to the Calverts. Claiborne and his trading partners and employees fought off attempts by the new Maryland regime to claim the island and the business in the mid-1630s. They believed that the fur trade would be threatened by settlers, whose desire for land would damage the peaceful and profitable relationships between the Susquehannocks and Claiborne. But by 1638, as Thomas Gerard arrived, Calvert had finally taken the island, and Claiborne had been charged with sedition.[12] He had not surrendered, however, and would continue to plead his case.

Both Claiborne and the Calverts had high connections in London, where the final word on jurisdictional issues sat. Until 1640, the most powerful of all these connections was of course the Calverts' friend, the king. But as the tensions between Crown and Parliament came to a boil, Claiborne's allies John Pym and John Hampden, leaders in Parliament's opposition to Charles I, emerged at the forefront of the struggle to limit monarchical absolutism. The colonies thousands of miles away were not so removed from the enormous upheaval of the next two decades as we might expect. Roger Williams, founder of Rhode Island, while attending his patron Edward Coke, witnessed the king's arrest of Pym and Hampden and met Oliver Cromwell before setting off for the colonies. Hugh Peters of Massachusetts headed back to join his Puritan friends in their fight and became a leader of the regicides, those who would bring about the execution of the king and the establishment of a short-lived republic in England. But the future of no mainland colony more than Maryland would become enmeshed with the English Revolution. William Claiborne probably intended only to exploit the situation to secure his business interests, but war and revolution unleashed a freedom of thought and action that authorities would spend the rest of the seventeenth century trying to curtail.[13]

It is surprising that Americans find their ideological precedent in the work of the philosopher of the Glorious Revolution, John Locke, when that "revolution" replaced one king with another. The republican origins of the United States truly belong in the earlier revolution, traditionally referred to as the English Civil War, and now often called the War of Three Kingdoms. As the most brilliant new history of the era explains, this error is due to deliberate obfuscation by historians since the seventeenth century. For several hundred years, the English establishment did not want its people to consider the dismantling of monarchy and aristocratic privilege as a positive, and so painted a picture of Cromwell as a fun-destroying tyrant and Charles II as the fun-loving natural ruler of England. After all, Charles II reopened the London theaters, where England's most revered icon, William Shakespeare, had produced the genius body of work posited so often to help justify English supremacist action around the globe for centuries.[14]

So why did the English revolt? Throughout the 1630s, Charles I introduced his religious reforms without consultation with Parliament. Just as Cardinal Richelieu helped Louis XIII seek absolute power in France in this same period, Archbishop Laud and Charles's marriage to a Catholic princess seemed to be linked to his desire to subvert the unwritten English constitution by ignoring elected officials. Thus many of those who fled to the new colonies blended the separate political and religious concepts of despotism and Catholicism into one enemy in their minds. Most clearly seen in the Plymouth and Massachusetts Bay colonies, the democratic tendencies of Puritan populations were seldom disentangled from their religious purposes. In the City on a Hill, there would be neither aristocracy nor the primogeniture system of inheritance that supported power in the hands of an exclusive few. In Maryland, however, the fusion of the religious and the political made for an explosive cocktail, for wealth and power within the colony lay in Catholic hands.[15]

In 1636, Charles called for the courts to approve "ship-money," a tax traditionally levied on port towns to help defray the costs of war. But this was peacetime, and everyone clearly understood that the king sought a way around the English laws demanding Parliament's approval of taxation. Claiborne's friend Hampden led the protest against the tax, refusing to pay and arguing that the king could not raise taxation without the consent of the people through their elected representatives in Parliament. He lost the trial, but his arguments provoked the king's attorney general to comment, "What would be the consequences . . . but the introducing of democratical government?" Despite his victory in court, the king found no way to enforce the payment of ship-tax among a population well educated by the popular broadsides on the principles at stake. Further trials in the Star Chamber in 1637 brought horrific public punishments to those who dared challenge Laud. Puritan ministers had their ears cut off and faces branded in public, while another opponent was marched through the streets of London, enduring the sting of the whip the entire route. Pamphlets describing the scenes circulated widely, feeding the growing disquiet.[16]

Meanwhile in all-Presbyterian Scotland, the signing of the 1638 National Covenant marked the coalescence of a major movement against Laud's attempts to bring back a liturgy and prayer book perceived as popish. "We agree and resolve all the days of our life constantly to adhere unto and to defend the aforesaid true religion, and forbearing the practice of all novations already introduced in the matters of the worship of God," they would "labour by all means lawful to recover the purity and liberty of the Gospel." The innovations of Laud "do sensibly tend to the re-establishing of the popish religion and tyranny, and to the subversion and ruin of the true reformed religion," the Scots proclaimed. They added "and of our liberties, laws and estates," thus interweaving religious protest with a political statement that magnified the issue for those less committed to one liturgy over another. "Liberties, laws and estates" indicated that Charles's heavy-handedness over a prayer book meant he might be heavy-handed about the personal freedoms and properties of any individual. While the Covenant also included a statement of loyalty to the king, the intent to disobey that king could not have been articulated more clearly. Loyalty to God trumped loyalty to monarch. What blow did such words deliver to a theory of divine right? Suddenly all the grounds for royal authority were called into question. At this moment in the proceedings, Thomas Gerard sailed for Maryland.[17]

With the ship-money revenues sharply declining, Charles needed tax money to lead his army against these rebellious Scottish Presbyterians. He briefly called Parliament (the Short Parliament), but his minister received such rough treatment at the hands of the now highly charged Parliamentarians that the king quickly dissolved the meeting. But when the Scots then repelled his invasion, Charles was forced to recall Parliament in 1641. This time, the House of Commons immediately passed a law that prevented the king from dissolving them, a huge, revolutionary step away from divine or absolute monarchy and a move that again called into question the legitimacy of all or any source of power. In their next order of business they impeached the king's chief minister and executed him for treason, prompting massive celebrations in the streets of London, another indication of the level of public political consciousness in this moment. And if everyday people were politically knowledgeable before, now Parliament, led by Pym and Hampden, abolished the Court of Star Chamber, the system by which the king had censored the press. The outpouring of publication, from serious discussions by lawyers of needed reforms of the justice system to bawdy broadsides satirizing the high-born, begat an unprecedented constitutional education of the English Atlantic world that would continue for two decades.[18]

News of a rebellion in Ireland told how Catholics killed English Protestants and a largely Catholic army declared its allegiance to Charles. The House of Commons reacted by passing a Grand Remonstrance in late 1641, condemning the actions of Charles's ministers and the failure of many in the House of Lords to counteract those ministers over the course of his reign. Charles rode into Parliament at the head of a troop of soldiers, demanding the arrest of Pym, Hampden, and others. His military attack on the representatives of the people showed once and for all that he intended to rule with absolutism. There could be no further attempt at compromise. England went to war.[19]

During the spring and summer of 1642, both court and Parliament prepared for military engagement. The Cavaliers and the Roundheads first met in battle that fall at Edgehill, and for the next two years, the Parliamentarians suffered defeats at the hands of the king's soldiers. Determining that some of their problems lay with the officer corps, who tended to be in charge because of their lineage rather than their ability and to be more sympathetic with the king because of the close ties between the king and the peerage, the Parliamentary leadership made a momentous decision. They would build a new fighting force.[20]

Oliver Cromwell and Thomas Fairfax created the New Model Army, a national army rather than a conglomeration of local militias serving under local leadership. The crucial element of the success that immediately followed, however, was the principle under which they would choose officers: ability meant more than family tree. Promotions based on merit, rather than social status, would mean that the most competent would lead, not those whose only qualification was an illustrious ancient ancestor. More than a century later, America would come to embody this notion of a level playing field and, through it, become a dominant world power. Napoleon, too, organized his military forces under the catchphrase "la carrière ouverte aux talents" (a career open to talent) and conquered Europe. But Cromwell came first.[21]

If we can grasp that this commonsense concept—that any organization or entire society will succeed if the most talented are allowed to flourish in their respective endeavors—was revolutionary in 1645, we can truly understand the seventeenth-century history of the Western world. For a millennium, Europeans had been building societies under the concept of *inherited* value, using Christianity as a bulwark when the assumption that breeding equaled merit showed its inherent structural weaknesses, such as rule by incompetent sons. Extraordinarily disproportionate amounts of wealth and power funneled into the hands of the few at the top of the feudal pyramid, while those at the bottom eked out survival. The Church, run by demi-royal families like the Borgias and the Medici, found Bible verses indicating that God intended everyone to stay in the place they were born. Apparently He endorsed the status quo. Those who suffered on earth would get rewards after death, so they should tolerate vast inequities now. Mystique creation by means of incense, costumes, chantings, and ritual both in churches and in royal courts grew to absurd proportions. The system self-sustained. Only the rich had access to education, so they appeared more informed and articulate or "smarter"; their wealth purchased finery, and they developed elaborate etiquette for every social situation to seem more sophisticated. But when Martin Luther nailed his Ninety-Five Theses to the church door in 1517, he initiated a process of fundamental change that would slowly erode the pyramid.

Luther's declaration of the "priesthood of all believers" did not merely undermine the papacy and church hierarchy; the concept inherently assumed that everyone had the ability to make even the most important decisions. Its concomitant assertion of the need for everyone to know how to read their Bible would eventually undermine political hierarchies around the globe. However, we must think of a painstaking pace of change as we consider the 500 years since, for those with power used (and continue to use) every weapon in their always considerable arsenals to fight the erosion of their wealth and influence.[22] But this very gradual change was punctuated by moments of fast, intense questioning of entire structures of power. These episodes we call revolutions. Cromwell's decision to build an army on ground aside from the standard of inherited social status deserves the title "revolutionary."

News of the massive political upheavals spread across the Atlantic, and equally revolutionary steps were taken in St. Mary's City. Every freeman, without any property qualification, had a vote. While back in London Pym roiled the political atmosphere, Gerard and Gray were elected to the Assembly in February 1639. The following month, the Maryland Assembly passed "An Act for the liberties of the people." By the summer of 1642, the burgesses, led by Gerard's former attorney, Robert Vaughan, demanded that the Assembly become bicameral and that, like London's Parliament, they could not be adjourned but by themselves. Vaughan and Pope took leadership roles, including an investigation of the actual costs of government and assigning a levy to equitably spread the costs. This put them at odds with Giles Brent, deputy governor while Calvert was temporarily back in England to get married.[23]

As the war continued, a normal strategy in this period was the seizing of enemy ships. Ships setting out from London were identified as Parliamentary, while those that left from Bristol carried royal papers of authorization. This meant that the colonies could be pulled into the war if they chose to do business with traders from one port or the other, even when they might be behind on news of the fluctuations of the war. Claiming an enemy ship as a prize could be very lucrative; a ship and its cargo might be worth several thousand pounds. Governor Calvert negotiated with Charles for the commission to take any Parliamentary ships that might arrive in Maryland.[24] In January 1644, an Englishman sailed into St. Mary's City in a ship named the *Reformation*, signaling the captain's allegiance to the Roundheads. Richard Ingle's trade had brought him back and forth from England to Maryland and Virginia on multiple visits over the previous five years, and he had business with both Thomas Gerard and William Claiborne; Gerard had traveled with him.[25] But this time Deputy Governor Brent immediately arrested Ingle and charged him with high treason, while authorizing the seizure of his boat and crew. Ingle escaped, and with the help of his crew and presumably some friendly locals retrieved the *Reformation*. They hurriedly departed St. Mary's City, but managed to conduct some business around Maryland—they needed the tobacco to avoid a total loss on their season—and headed to Virginia.[26]

A grand jury called to investigate Ingle proceeded without his presence, but with Thomas Gerard as a witness. The jury, which included Vaughan and Thomas Baldridge, found insufficient evidence to try Ingle for either treason or escape. Brent continued to impanel juries (including Pope, Gray, Thomas Sturman, Vaughan, and Baldridge) to no avail. These dismissals, especially on the latter charge, of which Ingle was undeniably guilty, are the first insights we have into the attitudes of the general population of Maryland settlers. In England until the nineteenth century, ordinary people had no vote, so the only access they had to their government came through the jury system. By dismissing or acquitting an obviously guilty party, which happened frequently, ordinary people sent a message that they disapproved of laws or that they found the standard sentences much too harsh to fit the crimes. Thus the right of an Englishman to a trial by a jury of his peers would be considered perhaps the most crucial of all liberties. Through this mechanism, the community could protect an individual from the tyranny of the elite, long before they achieved the right to cast a ballot for their representative. The acquittal of Ingle shows that the colonial population of St. Mary's City, including Gerard, thought it ridiculous to prosecute a man for his loyalty to Parliament.[27]

By April 1644, ships from London and Bristol were firing at each other on the James River in Virginia. That summer, as debates on English politics raised the sophistication of many Marylanders on constitutional matters, Governor Calvert returned to Maryland with a commission (in the form of letters of marque) from the king to seize not merely London ships, but even any goods or cash owed those London traders. In other words, anyone in the whole Chesapeake region indebted to Ingle as a result of their business now must hand over that money or tobacco to Calvert. Calvert would send that revenue to the king, after keeping a share for himself. He would have trouble extracting funds from the Virginians, however. Whatever their political loyalties, they did not appreciate any interference in or disruption to their tobacco transactions, and they were dependent on experienced Atlantic traders such as Ingle.[28]

Over the summer and fall of 1644, as Cromwell secured his reputation as a formidable military commander at the battle of Marston Moor, Ingle prepared for his annual trip to the Chesapeake. Like Calvert he would bring official letters of marque, but his were issued from Parliament, granting him permission to confiscate the goods of anyone still professing loyalty to the king. Ingle and his crew would assume that this included most of the Catholic manor lords in Maryland. He dropped anchor in Virginia in December.[29]

William Claiborne immediately contacted him to warn him of Calvert's commission to claim Parliamentary ships, but their discussions went further than that. Claiborne wanted to exploit the situation to cement his hold on Kent Island. Ingle should drum up support in Virginia to take Maryland for Parliament, which would rid the region of Catholic lords. Ingle would take charge in St. Mary's, while Claiborne led a force to claim Kent Island. Claiborne's partnership with Pym and Hampden may have been a factor, but certainly his political leanings nicely dovetailed with his economic goals. In any case, Claiborne's part of the plan buckled: Calvert got wind of it and sent militia to hold Kent, while the residents could not be convinced that Claiborne really had the backing of Parliament and would not fight for him at this stage.[30] Nonetheless, Ingle, in a quick scouting trip to St. Mary's from his base in Chicacoan Virginia, on the southern bank of the Potomac, sent messages out to leading Protestant residents that the time had come to free themselves of the "papists." By early 1645, Virginia had declared itself a free-trade zone. Ingle moved around safely in the Chicacoan area, on the bank of Nomini Bay, where both Claiborne and another trader, John Mottram, had established posts. He recruited at least a dozen men to aid in the plan, mostly ex-Marylanders who had crossed the Potomac because of their disgruntlement with Calvert. Launching an attack was a risky venture, whatever their political principles, but the promise of plunder from the manorial estates helped ease their fears of punishment for sedition.[31]

The *Reformation* sailed back to St. Mary's on February 14, 1645, and approached a Dutch ship in the harbor. The Dutch captain and crew, well aware of the rumors that Ingle had letters of marque, had prepared their guns, but stood down as they saw a white flag atop Ingle's mast. He boarded and seized the ship, capturing Giles Brent below. The following day, his crew seized Cross House, "the richest prize in Maryland," to serve as their land base for a full attempt on the government of Maryland. Cross House belonged to Thomas Cornwalyes, whose wealth far exceeded that of even his manorial peers. Cornwalyes happened to be in London and was amazed to learn of Ingle's decisions, as they had been close business associates. Some of the servants joined the rebellion, helping to divide up the estate's silver and giving the "Plundering Time" its name, but that designation has been applied to discredit the protagonists and disguise the politics of the era. Sharing out the goods of a political or military enemy was standard procedure for both sides in the English Civil War. The next year's actions would clearly demonstrate that political goals drove Ingle's Rebellion.[32]

Ingle ordered the capture of Calvert and most of his councilors, while Calvert called up his militia to defend the colony. Running to Margaret Brent's property, he and his supporters quickly fashioned a fort. But the Protestant militiamen supported Ingle, and they, too, improvised a fort on Calvert's own land. For the next few months, Calvert held out, while the other Catholic gentry and the Jesuit missions fell to the rebels. Undoubtedly valuables were seized and shared, but many of the reparation claims made by the gentry and priests in the aftermath were marked by obvious fraud. In any case, Ingle took what he needed: tobacco for trade (rather than the Jesuit diamonds he would later be accused of plundering) and several of Maryland's leading Catholics as prisoners for Parliament. Of all the manorial gentlemen, only Thomas Gerard retained his freedom. We must assume he made abundantly clear to Ingle that his loyalty toward representative government surpassed his loyalty to Catholicism. With his crew commanding the Dutch vessel, Ingle stopped briefly in Virginia before setting off for London.[33]

Calvert escaped in the early summer and found safe exile in Virginia, and for the next eighteen months the rebels held Maryland and established a functioning government. Many people deserted the colony in these certainly unsettling times. The surviving records are scant. Court cases in London centering around Ingle, who was sued by both Cornwalyes and the owners of the Dutch ship, reveal the details of Ingle's time in the colony, but little of what happened in the interim between his departure in March 1645 and Calvert's return to power in December 1646 can be reconstructed. However, some were charged with plundering in Maryland's courts in the years to follow, and those cases reveal the leadership of Maryland during Ingle's Rebellion.

The rebels created one document that articulated their goals. This "Petition of Diverse Inhabitants of Maryland," carried to London by James Baldridge in support of Ingle, made a special plea to the Committee of Foreign Plantations that Maryland should have a Protestant government. This should not be interpreted as pure religious bigotry. In this time and place, a request for Protestant government equaled a request for representative government. The committee responded with strong support and brought an "Ordinance for Maryland" before Parliament. The Lords and Commons, in an unambiguous declaration backing the rebels, declared that Calvert "hath wickedly broken the trust reposed in him," revoked the charter, and ordered the removal of Brent "and all other Officers of the said Calverts appointment."[34]

While Ingle's arrival enabled the overthrow of the Calvert family, the smallholders and craftsmen of Maryland took advantage of him, rather than the other way around. Despite the epithet "Plundering Time," conjuring up images of anarchic mayhem, once the colony rid itself of the Catholic gentry, order ensued. The servants of the Catholic masters claimed freedom; they had most to gain from supporting Ingle. While opportunities existed for land ownership after indenture and thus control over their own fate, the servants had already witnessed that their early death was a more likely scenario. Less than 30 percent of those who had come to Maryland by 1645 would ever own land. Men like Thomas Sturman, a cooper, Thomas Baldridge, "Capt & Comder of those Rebells," Robert Vaughan, one of those who "pretended to have authority at that time, to be Rebells," Nathaniel Pope, and others assumed the mantle of a very devolved government; Francis Gray apparently served in the role of Speaker of the House. Many of these men had experience in governmental office in the first decade of the Maryland colony, and had seen the limits set on their Assembly by Governor Calvert and his Catholic Council. Making the analogy with the king and his ministers did not require a huge leap. And their experiences and those of Marylanders who stayed through the year of their administration helped shape a corps of activists dedicated to the notion of government for the people, by the people. That life ran along as smoothly under the direction of a tradesman as it did under a gentleman must have been a revelation to those who had never had the opportunity to observe a meritocracy.[35]

In the summer of 1646, after a year of government by the locals, a Virginian by the name of Captain Edward Hill arrived in St. Mary's City with a "commission" signed by Calvert. Hill claimed he should be governor and, given the official paperwork, the rebels ceded authority. Hill called for elections and the meeting of a new Assembly in the fall. But Hill had mixed with the radicals over in Nomini Bay, and the anti-aristocratic feeling of the revolutionary era persuaded him to work with those currently in power. In fact, afterward, Hill would claim that his authority emanated not from Calvert, but from the "Council of Maryland." (Only one councilor remained in Maryland—Thomas Gerard.) A later and more conservative legislature described the Assembly under Hill thus: "The whole House of Commons (two or three only excepted) consisted of that Rebelled Party." And Lord Baltimore himself later would decry that "Captain Hill had never any Lawful Authority to Act anything there as our Lieutenant or chief Governor of that Province nor for acting anything else Concerning that Government . . . we are inform'd that some of those Laws so enacted as aforesaid are very prejudicial to our rights and Royal Jurisdictions."[36]

Thomas Gerard stayed in Maryland through the rebel government's time in office. His name is mentioned in court records only in indirect association with the rebellion, and he did not assume a major leadership role. Nonetheless, that someone of his social standing cooperated with the rebels speaks volumes. We know he was not treated by others in the same manner as the rest of his social class. A wealthy Catholic, he might have expected to meet the same fate as Brent and the other gentry taken prisoner. He did observe much of the normal class relations in his daily interactions with servants and, later, with enslaved people. What saved him?

His wife raised their children in the Church of England, which helped earn the trust of his neighbors. During Maryland's Interregnum, he seized much of the property of William Lewis, a Catholic loyal to the Calverts. But there was more than that. His daughters married the rebel leadership. For nearly forty years, men who married one of the Gerard sisters assumed leadership roles in the fight for representative government in Maryland and Virginia.[37] The action emanating from St. Clement's Manor and the Nomini Bay community of Virginia over the next few decades paints a picture of the family's political position. Increasingly the Gerard clan would prove to be the source of opposition not merely to the proprietary family, but to the whole idea of hereditary privilege in terms of political power. Gerard's observation of government by a tradesman must have had as significant an impact upon him as those in England experienced observing the New Model Army. In the summer of 1645, a cooper conducted the administration of a British colony. Few records tell much of the story of daily life under the rebel government, but nothing indicates that anarchy ensued. And across the ocean, Englishmen high and low watched as Cromwell's army based on a career open to talent smashed the army that structured its ranks by breeding. It seemed the English Civil War was over. In reality, the Revolution was just getting under way.[38]

Theoretical understanding of a political principle can be a very shallow way to come to a position. Once tested in the centrifuge of a real-world experience, theorists often change their position. And at the same time, those who have never considered themselves "political" find that living through a moment of huge shift marks them forever. The lived experience of being politically educated, feeling the blinkers fall off about large, often previously invisible sources of power within one's society; the experience of helping effect change for the good; even the observation by nonparticipants of a new social structure: this creates a more permanent shift in perspective than the study of political philosophy.[39] For many people who lived in the English Atlantic in the 1640s and 1650s, the Civil War became a social and political revolution as they saw regular folk demonstrate their competencies in war and in government. And the change was most pronounced in those who actually led others. During Oliver's Days, a cadre of men and even some women witnessed for themselves their own ability to play a real role in the organization of their society, not to passively allow others to take charge of matters that affected their everyday lives. This was as true in Maryland during the Plundering Time as it would be in England. Fewer people would be involved, certainly, but the lessons bore more significance, for the colonies on the wilderness coast of North America lacked the infrastructure to contain dangerous democratic ideas. In Rhode Island too, the freemen gathered in 1647 to declare that their government would be "democratical."[40] Despite their best effort, elites could never appoint quite enough sheriffs, hold enough courts, or build enough jails to squelch the fruits of freedom.

Perhaps Calvert had considered Hill a strong man who might prepare the ground toward his own return to power. But that backfired. Instead Calvert had to organize a military force among whatever Catholics he could find in Virginia and a few Protestants who had enjoyed a successful business relationship with the Jesuit missions. Mustering only twenty-eight men, he needed to employ a little stealth. Arriving by surprise around the Christmas holidays, his force captured the individuals he believed were the ringleaders.[41]

Calvert moved quickly to reestablish his authority. On December 29, 1646, he recognized the recently elected assemblymen as legitimate representatives and read a mass pardon at his first meeting with them. The men who had accompanied him from Virginia testified that Calvert had instructed them that "if he found the Inhabitants of St. Maies had accepted his pardon for their former rebellion and weare in obedience to his Lordship, the Souldiers weare to expect no pillage there," demonstrating that soldiers of every side of this affair would normally expect to plunder.[42]

On January 2, Calvert's troop rounded up many others suspected of leading or collaborating with the rebel government and insisted on an oath of loyalty. Many of the rebels appeared to capitulate. While the ringleaders were imprisoned, he cut deals with Hill and Pope. But two weeks later, Calvert was forced to issue an embargo on movement and communication with anyone outside St. Mary's, "that noe Intelligence may be communicated or practice entertain with fforraigners." Sturman, Gray, and others had escaped and made their way to the home of John Mottram in Nomini Bay, also called Chicacoan, where a witness claimed that they "hatched & Complotted divers Machinations and Conspiraces agt the person of Leonard Calvert Esq now Govr." (Breaking out of prison will feature frequently in these pages; "there are in effect noe prisons but what are soe easily broken," commented one Virginia governor even thirty years later. The fragility of colonial infrastructure meant that efforts at repression were very ineffectual, allowing radicals to spread their egalitarian message in a way impossible in Europe.) They sent out messages to the remaining rebels in Maryland that Claiborne and a Captain Wyatt were on their way with commissions from Parliament legitimizing their authority. But when Sturman, Gray, and the rest came back to St. Mary's, they were caught and swore under bond not to escape. Calvert's troop under the leadership of Captain John Price effectively policed most of the colony, and the governor was prepared to pardon any who recognized his position.[43] Kent Island remained independent of St. Mary's City authority, however. Over the course of the spring of 1647, both sides would muster small armed bands to try to hold the island, but by April Calvert had brokered a peace with the holdouts there, granting them control over the local court.[44]

Back across the Atlantic, as Parliament weighed the competing claims, early decisions went the way of the rebels. The Ordinance for Maryland demanded a Protestant, representative government for the colony. But the inexperienced delegate James Baldridge could not compete with Lord Baltimore himself, well acquainted with both powerful individuals and parliamentary procedure. In late 1646, as his brother orchestrated things on the ground from Virginia, Baltimore pleaded for his right to testify and then sought successive delays to allow the Ordinance to lose all momentum and quietly die from attrition.[45] In the intensity of the English revolution, Maryland's affairs seemed far away and of little consequence.

In the months following the surrender of the rebels, the courts dealt with the claims of Calvert's friends hoping to recoup their plundered goods. The death of Leonard Calvert in June 1647, shortly after he had regained power, almost instigated the renewal of the rebellion. An unpopular Catholic named Thomas Greene was appointed governor by Calvert on his deathbed. Those with democratic tendencies restarted the campaign for control of the colony. From Chicacoan, Captain Hill asserted his authority, claiming that "throngs" were "dayly clamarious" for his return. At Gerard's house, ex-rebel Walter Broadhurst proclaimed that "there was now noe Governor in Mary-land. Ffor Capt Hill was Governor & him only." James Johnson was fined and subjected to thirty lashes for his mutinous talk. Johnson had publicly declared that the soldier troop that had placed Calvert back in power were "Rogues: ffor tht they had undon a brave Country: ffor had it not bene for them, to witt the soldiers, they might have enjoyed this Country to themselves." Johnson too longed for self-government and the return of Hill; if Captain Price tried to impress anyone to resist Hill's return, Johnson "would shott him (meaning Capt Price)." In the January 1648 Assembly, John Hatch, burgess for St. Clement's and attorney for Gerard, opposed raising taxes to pay wages to the soldiers who had returned Calvert to power. Vaughan led a unanimous protest against any laws passed at St. Inego's Fort during the first few days of Calvert's return. They issued a Remonstrance the next month, a statement of protest modeled on the Long Parliament's 1640 Grand Remonstrance against the tyranny of the king. Governor Greene would not enjoy a long stay in power.[46]

Most of the rebel leadership left Maryland for good, searching for a spot where they could control their own destiny, to "enjoy this Country to themselves." Two Gerard sisters, Frances and Temperance, would find husbands among the leadership and make Northumberland County, later to become Westmoreland County, a haven for Maryland rebels for decades. Clustering around Nomini Bay, the land patents of Francis Gray, Thomas Speke, John Sturman, William Hardige, and the Baldridge brothers show how they settled down permanently beside Nathaniel Pope and started anew to build their own society. Their political philosophy, incorporating the right of men to govern themselves, would be handed down through generations of Virginians. Ten years later Pope, leader of Maryland's rebels, would see his daughter marry a new arrival named John Washington. Nathaniel Pope, antimonarchical leader of Ingle's Rebellion, was the great-grandfather of George Washington, and when his daughter Ann, grandmother of the first president, died, her son—George's grandfather, Lawrence—would be raised by John Washington's third wife, Frances Gerard Speke. Over the eighteenth century, Virginia planters would strip their philosophy of self-governance of its more radical egalitarian component. Nonetheless, we can see the origins of the United States in Ingle's Rebellion.[47]

This struggle to control their own fate, politically and economically, echoed the struggle on the other side of the Atlantic. Since the end of censorship in 1642, thousands of political pamphlets had flooded England, many espousing ever more radical ideas about how government should be formulated in the aftermath of the war. Estimates put the literacy rate among London's men at 80 percent; some of these pamphlets reached huge audiences. Soldiers in Cromwell's army had become Agitators in the years that followed their victories over Charles. Witnessing their own success against the nobility proved that lineage guaranteed nothing in terms of competency. In the months that followed, they would demand massive alterations in the framework of English society and government. While Cromwell and other officers were still willing to sanction the return of the king and the House of Lords, John Lilburne, a radical leader, helped draft a document, the Agreement of the People. These soldiers had not risked their lives just so that only the top 4 percent could have a voice in Parliament. They demanded a vote for every free man, with elections every other year and an end to the "rotten boroughs," the absurdly unrepresentative constituencies purchased by the gentry. The lower house, the voice of the people, should have the ultimate say in legislation, not the king or the lords. Their written-in-English constitution should include a Bill of Rights protecting equality before the law, in addition to religious and other freedoms. [48]

Before Spinoza, before Locke, and long before Paine and Jefferson, the Agitators of "Oliver's Army" called into question the legitimacy of power inherited by accident of birth, or proclaimed to be ordained by God. They met Cromwell and his fellow commanders at Putney, London, in October 1647 to thrash out the political goals of the campaign. While the top brass certainly believed in limits on royal authority, they could not escape their class-bound ideas of social ranking. In their eyes, only those who owned land should have input into government decisions. But poor soldiers who had sacrificed and who had clearly seen that wealth was no indicator of ability argued forcefully that every man born in England should have access to the ballot. As Thomas Rainsborough put it, " I think that the poorest hee that is in England hath a life to live, as the greatest hee; and therefore truly, Sr, I think itt clear, that every Man that is to live under a Government ought first by his own Consent to put himself under that Government; and I do think that the poorest man in England is not at all bound in a strict sense to that Government that he hath not had a voice to put Himself under." [49]

From the Putney debates grew the Leveler movement, a term at first used derisively but adopted by the participants. We incorporate the term now into the concept of the level playing field, whereby everyone should compete on the same ground to ensure equality of opportunity. It is the place where political principle and economic desire meet. To be egalitarian is to believe that everyone should have equal justice before an impartial law and that everyone should have equal opportunity to prosper. To protect that playing field, we need equal access to the ballot box, lest the powerful try to build structures that will privilege their children at the cost of others. But for the Leveler spokesmen to speak such principles aloud in the seventeenth century, calling into question all authority in Europe, threatened not merely the king, but even the gentry and noble families to which the likes of Cromwell were related. Throughout 1648 and 1649, the movement built and spread its message, reaching across the ocean in the ships carrying tobacco and lumber and into the taverns in St. Mary's City and Jamestown.

Levelers, like most seventeenth-century Europeans, tended to be devoted Christians. This crucial component of the development of democratic thought cannot be overstated. The New Model Army had been recruited among the most Puritan of regions, attracting particularly devout Bible-readers into the ranks. Harvard's first graduates had sailed back to fight for Cromwell. They now rejected the Catholic and Anglican interpretations of the Bible, which had emphasized obedience to hierarchies both earthly and divine. Reading the Bible for themselves allowed them to reach very different conclusions about God's message: that Christ did not revere the rich and that the lowly on earth would be exalted in heaven. The divine right of kings was thus absurd. In this way, politics and religion grew more entangled on both sides of the Atlantic, as one's theology affected how one felt God would want government to be run. Economics were also deeply enmeshed in the Levelers' worldview. Poor harvests and the disruption of civil war led to hunger in England in the late 1640s and heightened concerns over arrears in soldiers' pay. Christ's love for the poor brought a moral dimension to the situation. It seemed that He would want a parliamentary system that would protect those at the bottom, "the poorest hee," from those born to great riches who had traditionally oppressed the rest of society.[50]

Cromwell was a devout Puritan too, but this pushed further than he could comfortably go, and he also knew he could not broker a deal with Charles and the royalists under the terms of the Agreement. He called for a unifying prayer meeting, but the army representatives still voted for the franchise extension and wanted a general rendezvous of the entire force as a show of strength. Cromwell's response was to suppress. Despite Charles's attempt to escape and intercepted letters that proved he would never honor any deal he cut with Parliament, Cromwell still believed he must bargain with the traditional political nation: the 4 percent. So at the scheduled Army Council at Corkbush Field a few weeks later, he turned on the Agitators with their Agreement of the People texts pinned to their hats and purged them from the army.[51]

He could not wipe out the ideas immediately; an updated draft of the Agreement gathered the signatures of a third of London. Charles's actions against his own people and his Parliament also fostered the growth of republicanism over the next two years. His 1647 alliance with the Scots and launching of the second stage of the Civil War proved the soldiers right; God had not ordained this king. And when 8,000 Roundheads defeated a royalist force three times their size at Preston in August 1648, God's message apparently came into focus. This leveling army must represent His will. A new *Remonstrance of the Army*, this pamphlet supported by Cromwell, called for the king to be put on trial for the blood of Englishmen. More conservative members of Parliament did not agree and continued to try to negotiate with the king. On December 5, Colonel Thomas Pride led a detachment to arrest the offending MPs. The army now ran the country. While Cromwell and his fellow commanders Fairfax and Henry Ireton harbored no leveling instincts, their soldiers had experienced for themselves how a meritocracy surpassed aristocracy.[52]

The trial of the English king began in January 1649. There could be no jury of "peers" for the man at the top of the feudal triangle, so his fate would be decided by a panel of commissioners from all over England. Eighty judges traveled to Westminster voluntarily, including John Blakiston from Newcastle. Blakiston, an ardent Puritan in the Long Parliament and a supporter of the settlement in New England, had expressed republican ideas even before the war. "Blakiston . . . was later styled one of the 'Levelling sort,' who apparently supported the Levellers' 'large petition' of September 1648." Now he would attend every sitting of this High Court of Justice as the king faced charges of high treason. Charles snubbed the court's jurisdiction, and his refusal to enter a plea was taken as an admission of guilt. The High Court called all the witnesses, however, in order to determine a sentence. Charles might have been demoted to a constitutionally limited monarch, or perhaps forced to abdicate in favor of his son. But Blakiston became the twelfth regicide, signing the death warrant of the king of England on January 26, 1649.[53]

Four days later, no divine intervention stopped the beheading of a man who claimed that his position had been ordained by God. His last words on the scaffold denied the right of any Englishman but himself to have a say in their own destiny, "For the people . . . having a share in government, Sirs: that is nothing pertaining to them." Contrary to popular myth, there was no great public groan as the king's head rolled. Although that was claimed decades later by a courtier of Charles II, nothing corroborates it in the many accounts of the execution. Before the first day of spring, Parliament officially abolished the monarchy and the House of Lords. England was a republic, a "Commonwealth," as they called it. The act declared, "It . . . has been found by experience, that the office of a king in this nation and Ireland, and to have the power thereof in any single person, is unnecessary, burdensome, and dangerous to the liberty, safety, and public interest of the people." In this revolutionary era, there was no public protest, no attempt to save Charles, no effort by anyone to proclaim his son as king.[54]

Royalists, however, launched a propaganda campaign based on a fake autobiography of Charles, *Eikon Basilike*, portraying the king as a sainted martyr executed by low-born craftsmen. Playing on the tradition that breeding determined value, royalist pamphlets for the next decade, and indeed for centuries afterward, appealed to the class snobbery so deeply enmeshed in English culture. The rationality of republicanism, so recent a philosophy, could not wipe out a millennium of cultural practice for an entire society instantaneously. Seven-year-old Isaac Newton had not yet defined scientific method. Before the Commonwealth could develop roots, England would crown another king and regress to its system of horrendous inequalities of power, justice, wealth, and opportunity.[55]

Snobbery meant that even some of the leading republicans balked at the Levelers' agenda. Lopping off the tip of the feudal triangle proved enough for Cromwell; he did not need the entire world turned upside down. At Salisbury and Banbury, he crushed Leveler troop mutinies that spring. Captured soldiers were executed, like Charles, sending a clear signal that the Revolution served only the "people" as Cromwell would define that term: the better sort.[56]

The funerals of Leveler soldiers brought thousands of citizens to the streets, and while Cromwell's intimidation brought success in disrupting the Leveler movement, not all thinkers would regress. In the years to follow, a new religious movement took shape. The Society of Friends transformed a political philosophy into a theology, creating a hierarchy-free church. No pulpit would literally or symbolically raise one above another. Language signaling rank became anathema, as brethren addressed each other only as thee and thou, brother and sister. Throughout the 1650s, the Quakers spread their message of a lowly Christ, the man who on his hands and knees washed the feet of others.[57]

Regicide Blakiston did not live much longer. But his attitude to power had been nurtured in his children. Eleven years later, when Charles II brought his wrath to bear on those who had sentenced his father to death, Blakiston's son Nehemiah would escape to the hospitable locale of St. Clement's Manor in Maryland, bringing his father's ideas about the power of the people with him and then, of course, marrying a Gerard sister.

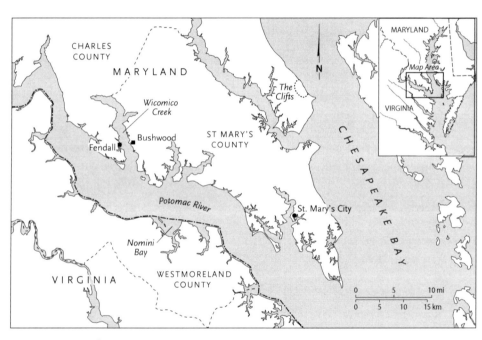

Potomac settlements, 1630–1670

CHAPTER TWO

Fendall's Rebellion, 1650s

> It is not the unfrocking of a priest, the unmitering of a bishop . . .
> that will make us a happy nation; no, if other things as great in
> the Church, and in the rule of life both economical and political,
> be not looked into and reformed, we have looked so long upon
> the blaze that Zwinglius and Calvin have beaconed up to us, that
> we are stark blind.
>
> —MILTON, 1644

Revolutionary eras are always marked by a rich and widespread public discourse on power, with a full spectrum of philosophies on offer. Even elites can get involved in questioning authority; after all, the Roundhead leaders were gentry. Poet John Milton learned that censorship hurt that discourse, so important for improving the country. As he said in 1644, Puritans who had invested great personal energy into reform of the Church should now investigate political and economic matters, for corruption was counter to "a happy nation." Milton became a republican. Just so in Maryland, where in the 1640s and 1650s all manner of people with every mix of concern over money, power, and religion voiced their feelings and took up political stances as each new constitutional crisis unfolded. The 1650s saw the arrival of more of Oliver's New Model Army, reinforcing the strength of those who had rebelled in 1645. The arguments got convoluted sometimes, and some individuals behaved cynically, using constitutional niceties to defend their wealth. But as the debate raged, so did the political education of all. And gradually the fog lifted to reveal that, if one wanted to protect one's economic opportunities, one's property, or one's freedom to worship, one had to have access to the political process. Thomas Gerard's egalitarian neighbors saw the distinct possibility of a commonwealth in Maryland. Josias Fendall and Gerard brought together many Marylanders in search of a republican meritocracy in what has become known as Fendall's Rebellion.[1]

THOMAS GREENE HAD assumed the role of governor upon the death of Baltimore's brother Leonard Calvert, while Margaret Brent was charged with settling his estate. Greene called his first Assembly in January 1648. Calvert had not fully paid the soldiers who had come from Virginia to reinstate proprietary authority, and because most people had acquiesced, they had not been rewarded with the standard plunder. Fearing that the soldiers would violently protest, "to the utter subversion and ruine" of the colony, the administration attempted to raise a tax to pay them in the first business of the Assembly. The act went further than that, however. Clearly, some opposed to Calvert had refused to sell corn to him, and the governor would be empowered to "veiw and measure every mans Corne" and force him to sell anything above that essential for his household. Gerard was not present, but another representative, his attorney John Hatch, voted against the act. Others more frightened of the soldiers assented. But as the delegates spent time together each evening, they grew more assured of their right to oppose aristocratic authority. They would not agree to a full restoration. They refused to confirm Baltimore's patent the next day, and two days later, they unanimously protested that the laws passed by Calvert's hastily rounded up Assembly at St. Inego's Fort in January 1647 had no legal standing, for there had been no proper summons to the inhabitants. Greene "absolutely" protested against such "undue proceeding," but the struggle continued. The assemblymen drew up a Remonstrance in February, and with clauses that voided the laws of St. Inego's Fort and protested the power of Greene, passed it on March 3. Greene promptly vetoed the act. Clearly, Ingle's Rebellion had not been fully quieted.[2]

The Assembly also demanded that the Calverts assume all costs associated with their return to power and brought soldiers as witnesses who testified that Calvert had told them that "the charge should be payd out of his owne estate & his Lordship's estate," rather than taxing the general population. Margaret Brent, whose job it was to settle this dispute and ensure that the soldiers were paid, had demanded a seat in the Assembly, but the governor refused to allow a woman a voice.[3] Later, the Assembly would defend her, claiming that "it was better for the Collony's safety at that time in her hands then in any mans else in the whole province." So the unrest simmered through 1648.

Baltimore, with one eye on the arrest of Charles I and another on Maryland, realized that the wisest route to securing his wealth was by removing the Catholic Greene and appointing a Protestant, William Stone from Virginia, to serve as governor that summer. Baltimore hoped to demonstrate that he was on board with the Commonwealth. He encouraged Stone to offer free land in Maryland to Virginian Puritans. In 1648, the governor of Virginia, loyal Cavalier William Berkeley, had persecuted Virginia's Congregational parish, and Stone brought many of them north. Again, this would prove to Cromwell that, despite his Catholicism, Lord Baltimore had no loyalty to the ex-king on trial. Baltimore also thought it would ease the concerns of his rebellious Protestant tenants in Maryland. Instead, it led to a decade of hostilities between Marylanders who wanted equal representation for all and the intolerant Puritans who imagined a new Jerusalem.[4]

A new Assembly met in April 1649, this time composed of many inexperienced men. They composed a strange, long letter to Baltimore, on one hand describing themselves as the most loyal of "Friends" opposed to the "Heinous Rebellion" of "that Pirate Ingle," but on the other hand unequivocally declaring that the soldiers must be paid from the Calvert purse and that they would not assent to any "perpetual Laws" that the proprietor might ever demand: "Send us no more such Bodies of Laws which serve to little other end then to fill our heads with suspitious Jealousies."[5] Such a declaration, however wrapped in obsequious language, reveals how far the upheavals in England and the colony had dissolved deference. Even those who had not aligned with the 1645 rebels had subsumed the notion that they need not acquiesce to hereditary power. Almost no one paid their rents.[6]

The 1649 Assembly did consent to passing Baltimore's Act concerning Religion. This famous early toleration law allowed Baltimore to believe matters might proceed smoothly when he invited Puritans into a Catholic colony. All Christians were accepted, and were not to be "any waies troubled, Molested or discountenanced for or in respect of his or her religion nor in the free exercise thereof." The law condemned hate speech; any resident or trader who used pejorative terms against another Christian, such as "heritick, Scismatik, Idolater, puritan, Independant, Prespiterian popish prest, Jesuite, Jesuited papist, Lutheran, Calvenist, Anabaptist, Brownist, Antinomian, Barrowist, Roundhead, Sepatist," would suffer fines.[7] That the toleration did not embrace non-Christians should not color our reading of the act; this represented a revolutionary leap forward. Accompanying it was a law forbidding hate speech against Baltimore, too; mutinous talk unaccompanied by threat of violence might lose the rebel his ear or earn him a branding "with a redd hot Iron"; if the speaker brandished a weapon, he might lose his life.[8] That the House passed this law, but sent it back to England with a letter demanding Baltimore pay his own soldiers and quit sending more laws, must be seen as a temporary compromise in the negotiations between the operators of power in the immediate aftermath of the execution of a monarch.

Baltimore's response would not be read for a year, but when it came, it showed the limits of the lord's willingness to compromise. He cared little for religion and was most concerned with his power and his wealth. He issued a general pardon for all but Ingle and a few others for the plundering during Ingle's Rebellion, thus ending the trials. But in his letter, he called out those who had protested his laws. Those who said that oaths of fidelity to him meant "slavery" were ridiculous; such talk amounted to the "Deceiptfull Suggestions of Subtile Matchiavilians pretending Religion, and an extraordinary care of the Peoples liberty." The Remonstrance was seditious, and the idea of paying soldiers out of his personal estate was a step beyond the pale. "It was never yet heard of, in any other Christian Countrey, but there, that upon any occasion of forreigne or domestick war a People should [be] Soe unreasonable as to expect that the Prince State should bear the charge thereof out of their owne privat and p'ticular fortunes . . . the Preservation of their Estates and persons ought to be in the first place provided for, and the last that should suffer any prejudice." Baltimore might compromise on religion, but he drew a constitutional line when it came to his property. He would not even part with a few cattle to pay the men who had restored his authority.[9]

Meanwhile, in the volatile Atlantic world of the English Revolution, Stone had helmed a short-lived truce in a colony with a Catholic elite and a Puritan community for a year. But when he stupidly deputized Thomas Greene to act as governor while he returned to Virginia on business, the uneasy peace dissolved. In the fall of 1649, Greene declared Charles II "the undoubted rightfull heire. . . . Long Live King Charles the second."[10] He issued a general pardon in celebration of Charles II's ascendancy, but if Greene hoped the pardon would win the support of Marylanders for monarchy, he was roughly awakened. The worst fears of the newly settled Puritans had come to pass, and these were people on a mission from their God. Berkeley had called Charles II king also.

Stone tried to calm the situation down, hurrying back to remove Greene and to clarify that he was a commonwealth man, but as the new group made their settlement on the Severn River, in the north of the colony, their hackles remained up. And now William Claiborne had an opening to reclaim Kent Island and all that he had lost to the Calverts. Claiborne hated how Baltimore had treated him. Now he seized upon the opportunity presented by Greene's attachment to the Stuarts to rid the Chesapeake of the Calverts forever. His motivation, like that of his nemesis, Lord Baltimore, may have been his personal fortune, but Claiborne would use constitutional arguments to muster support for his efforts to oust the proprietors. In doing so, he helped maintain the momentum of the debate about hereditary power versus careers open to talent, just as fresh arrivals from England's new republic were taking up lands in Maryland. By the spring of 1650, he had declared publicly that he would reclaim Kent. Baltimore recognized that Claiborne was a problem and had the Assembly pass an act forbidding all Marylanders from aiding Claiborne in any way. But even as they agreed to pass that bill, they showed they were not in lockstep with Baltimore. The Assembly declared a bicameral legislature, removing the governor and the Council from the Lower House's debates over legislation.[11]

Claiborne did not need help from Maryland residents for the next step in his scheme to overthrow the Calverts. Help came in the form of a Parliamentary commissioner sent by the Lord Protector in 1651, to bring Virginia to obedience to the new Commonwealth regime. William Berkeley retired quietly to his Green Springs home. Stone had already declared Maryland for the Commonwealth, but Claiborne grabbed the moment. Presenting himself as a willing assistant to the commissioner, he read the language "Bay of Chesapeake" in the document in its widest sense. One of the Severn River Puritans, Richard Bennett, joined forces with Claiborne, and they arrived in St. Mary's in March 1652 and removed the incumbents from office. In the ensuing political maneuverings, Stone again swore his oath to the Commonwealth and promised to not vest any authority in Baltimore. Bennett and Claiborne took papers back to England's Committee of the Navy to try to get a ruling that would revoke Baltimore's charter completely, arguing that "the said Patent constitutes an hereditary Monarchy in Maryland."[12]

But in England, Claiborne could not match the power and experience of Baltimore, a canny politician. That summer, the latter convinced the State office that he should maintain his charter, for, unlike the Virginians, he had immediately declared his loyalty to the Commonwealth. Given the strength of support Berkeley and perhaps the other Virginia planters had shown the Cavaliers, Maryland could be used as an "Instrument (as occasion shall require) to keep the other in their due obedience to this Commonwealth." The Committee of the Navy upheld that decision in December. Claiborne was thwarted for now, and William Stone continued to be in charge of Maryland. But Claiborne awaited his chance.[13]

That moment presented itself two years later. In 1654, the Puritans petitioned Bennett and Claiborne that Stone was enforcing oaths of loyalty to Baltimore, which in their eyes meant an oath to defend the "Roman Popish Religion." The papers in question were various court documents and writs, issued under Baltimore's name rather than under the Commonwealth, and certainly not containing any mention of Catholicism. But such was the atmosphere in the seventeenth century that Puritans felt that any association with a Catholic meant condoning the pope, or, as another Severn River Puritan described it, to "uphold Antichrist."[14] They might have ignored many of these documents, but they could not get their land deeds without taking the oaths. Stone saw the hand of Claiborne at work and charged Claiborne and Bennett with sedition, "Wolves in Sheeps clothing" who exploited the religious fears of the Puritan settlers to further their private ends. "Opprobrious & uncivill Language" was exchanged in the ensuing months, and Claiborne would later claim that Stone mustered up a military force. But in the end, in July 1654, with Thomas Gerard by his side, Stone submitted his resignation to Claiborne to prevent "the effusion of blood." He sent word to Baltimore in England.[15]

Claiborne and Bennett appointed ten commissioners as the new executive for Maryland, all ten from the new Puritan settlements. They called elections for a new Assembly in the fall, but, ignoring the recent Act of Religion, Catholics were disenfranchised. The proceedings did not go without resistance; two Protestant burgesses from St. Mary's County refused to acknowledge the legitimacy of the Assembly. Recognizing Baltimore as proprietor and rightful authority did not presume any approval of Catholicism, they felt. They refused to take their seats on principle. The Puritan-dominated Assembly went even further in October, declaring that Catholics were not protected by the rights of Englishmen, changing the name of Anne Arundel County to Providence County and introducing strong prohibitive legislation against any fun on Sundays.[16]

However, although they controlled the Assembly, the Puritans all lived along the Severn and Patuxent Rivers in Anne Arundel County to the north of the main settlements and had to trust the everyday court matters to locals in each area. Gerard had of course been the ranking individual in St. Clement's, but as he was a Catholic, his son-in-law Robert Slye and attorney John Hatch assumed those roles.[17] Slye had married Gerard's oldest daughter, named Susannah like her mother, in 1652, and her father had gifted them several thousand acres along the bank of Wicomico Creek, where they built a home named Bushwood Manor. Gerard's marriage to a Protestant and his children's choice of spouses with his blessing clearly demonstrates that he affixed no importance to distinguishing between Christian sects. Stone and the Gerard clan saw that the threat to a free, tolerant, meritocratic Maryland came as much from dogmatic, inflexible Puritans as it did from Jesuits. They understood that Catholicism was not the only religion that threatened political liberty.[18]

As soon as Baltimore was apprised of the Puritan takeover, he sent a letter accusing Stone of cowardice in not vigorously defending the proprietorship across the Atlantic in the hands of Dr. Luke Barber. Also testifying to Cromwell's regime's support of Baltimore was a letter of recommendation for Barber signed by Oliver himself. William Eltonhead, a Council member and another son-in-law of the Gerards who had made a trip to England, also confirmed Cromwell's approval of the Catholic proprietorship and encouraged Stone to retake the reins of power. The documents arrived in January 1655.[19] Stone now seriously began to muster a force of men strong enough to seize the official seals of government. Joining him was Josias Fendall, who had a new land grant from Baltimore.

Stone tried to explain to the Puritans that he had no more desire to cause bloodshed than he did to impose Catholicism, but wished only to restore government to St. Mary's and toleration for all. In late February, he sent a small force including Eltonhead and Fendall to Patuxent, where they took some government records and seized guns and ammunition.[20] At this point, the narrative of events prior to the outbreak of violence diverges widely, with each side claiming that they peacefully asked for clarity and compromise, only to be brusquely dismissed by aggressive language and behaviors from the other. Whatever the reality, in the third week of March, at least eighty men, and probably twice that many, including Stone and Gerard, set off in small boats to mass for the attack on Providence and the Puritan commissioners. As the Puritans described it, "Capt. Stone with a party of Roman Catholics, malignant and disaffected persons who had called to their assistance a great number of heathen were in arms . . . to destroy men, women and children that should not submit to their wicked design."[21] "Heathen" referred to Indians; the positive French relationships with northern Indian groups led to decades of associating Catholics with Indians in the minds of Protestant settlers in the colonies. No Native Americans were actually involved.[22]

The brief and unnecessary Battle of the Severn on March 25, 1655, was the first fight between groups of British colonial settlers. Two groups of Protestants, few of whom had any allegiance to monarchy or Catholicism, skirmished, and about thirty died. Manipulated by Claiborne, the Puritans of Providence believed they were fighting for an important religious and political principle. For Claiborne, however, as the longer-standing residents of Maryland understood, "it was not religion . . . it was that sweete that rich, that large Country."[23]

The action began on the evening of March 24, as the Puritan commissioners, with William Fuller serving as commander of the military operations, ordered Captain Heamans of the *Golden Lion* to defend Providence against the oncoming forces of Stone. At dusk, Captain Heamans saw the sloops approach. He fired warning shots hoping to frighten them, but as they moved forward, he ordered his gunner to aim a shot right at them. Stone's force, yelling, "Rogues and dogs" at the Puritans, quickly altered their course, turning into Acton Creek, out of range. Fuller ordered an armed boat to block them in.

At dawn on the following morning, Stone's force massed for the attack. Fuller sent to Heamans's ship for the Commonwealth flag, and then prepared his smaller force to make a stand. Stone was trapped, with his retreat blocked by Heamans's ship. A witness sympathetic to the Puritan force described the charge, portraying one side as on a mission from God. Fuller's men apparently called out, "In the name of God fall on, God is our strength," while Stone's troops charged to the cry of "Hey for St. Mary—hey for two wives," insinuating that Stone's men would rape the Puritan women after the battle. Despite their fewer numbers, the Puritans were the superior soldiers. Pushed back, Stone surrendered in half an hour, having rapidly lost seventeen dead and over thirty more wounded, while the Puritans suffered only four casualties. Most of the rest were captured. The Battle of the Severn was a complete rout of Stone and the men of southern Maryland.[24]

Their surrender did not end matters. They were held captive while the Puritans debated how to savor their victory. In the religious and constitutional context of the English Civil War, the actions of Stone and his Council appeared to be treacherous. Charged with treason, ten faced a death sentence. Eltonhead and three others were hanged. But cooler heads then prevailed. Apparently the women of Providence had seen enough bloodshed and pleaded for some mercy on behalf of the remaining prisoners. Stone, after all, had been the man to offer them a refuge from Berkeley's persecutions. The executions halted, but the members of the Council remained prisoners for at least several weeks. Witnesses for both sides were on their way to England to sell their versions of events, for once it became clear to the Puritans that Cromwell had given his blessing to Baltimore and Stone's administration, they had to defend their actions and portray the men of St. Mary's as violent Papists. They were not ready to acknowledge Stone as the legitimate ruler.[25]

Stone went back to Virginia, presumably banished, and that fall the Puritan commissioners seized his estate "to Satisfie the Publick Damage," awarding thousands of pounds of Stone's tobacco to those who had been captured by him or lost arms or provisions to his force. The trials of the rebels, as the Puritans called them, were held in October. Some who admitted to being Catholics lost their entire estates, in lieu of fines for rebellion. Protestants who had helped Stone were fined, as were any who signed "Rebellious Petitions," which were still apparently in circulation months after the battle. Captain Josias Fendall had kept the fight going, "assuming a pretended power" from Stone, and rebellious enough that he would make no plea in response to the charges, "rather disowning the power of the court," and was imprisoned. Less assured soldiers who claimed they had been forced to fight still faced fines, albeit lighter ones.[26]

Fendall made a deal for his release the following summer, when he promised the court he would accept their government until official word came from England.[27] Although Cromwell had indeed endorsed Baltimore in 1654, once the news of the Battle of the Severn had reached London, Cromwell's administration investigated and, in a report dated May 1656, again concluded that Baltimore and Stone were the legitimate leaders of Maryland. Baltimore, confident that matters would be decided in his favor, had already made the decision to install Fendall as his new governor, as Stone had become such a divisive figure. Stone and Gerard would serve in his Council. But it took a year of negotiations to ensure that the passage of power went peacefully, although signs that diplomatic negotiations bore fruit are seen in the General Assembly of September 1657, when Gerard's son-in-law Slye took a seat representing St. Mary's and began building relationships with Fuller and the others of Anne Arundel. Both Fendall and the Puritans' representative went back to England during the year, until finally, in November 1657, an agreement was reached, assuring the Severn River community that there would be no vengeful retribution. Everyone regained their estate, the widows of the executed men were provided for, and Fendall was granted an extra 2,000 acres. The settlement stipulated that Puritans must take the oath of fidelity to Baltimore and promise to abide by the Act of Toleration.[28]

Baltimore had also dispatched another younger brother, Philip, to Maryland early in 1657, but only to serve as secretary of the colony, again carefully not putting a Catholic, even a member of his family, in the governor's seat. On March 22, 1658, Fuller and the Severn River Puritan commissioners rode south, surrendering the seal of government back to Fendall at St. Leonard's Creek two days later. This time there would be no trials. Everyone seemed to be on the same side: that of the Lord Protector. But the Puritans had highlighted the inconsistency in the constitutional situation of 1650s

Maryland. If hereditary power had no place in a commonwealth, how did Lord Baltimore continue to be the authority? The violent struggle wrapped up in the language of Christ and Antichrist had only masked the central problem: an issue of political power, not a religious matter. All the residents of Maryland would engage in that debate now that the factions were settled and religious toleration took God and the afterlife out of the discussion.

THE POPULATION OF the colony had soared over the previous decade, as a boom in tobacco prices had attracted both freeholders and indentured servants, who were promised an opportunity for land. While approximately 2,500 white settlers had come in the 1630s and 1640s, almost twice that number immigrated in the 1650s. These thousands of young men, who had come of age in revolutionary times, settled in Maryland to find that the constitutional debate raged on both shores of the Atlantic. If any group had a vested interest in a career open to talent, it was these new colonists, so many of them bound laborers, the bottom of the Chesapeake strata in those days before African slavery was widespread. While we recognize today the vast difference between servitude and slavery, with the latter encompassing complete ownership of the body of another, perpetual bondage, and inheritable status, the *perception* of indentured servants in these decades was often that masters enslaved them, too, for they had no pay and little hope for relief from cruel treatment. Some came straight from England, but others ran from Virginia whenever they could, to escape the horrors of the relentless labors on the tobacco plantations where they saw their shipmates die. The risk was high; Virginia planters might brand them upon recapture. Hoping for land in Maryland and the autonomy it would bring, those who served their full time in Virginia also came north, for the big planters had claimed all the good arable land in their colony. Throughout the second half of the century, fugitive and freed servants sought a place of their own along the Chesapeake's waterways.[29]

As the newcomers stretched out north, east, and west of the original settlement around St. Mary's, new counties were named in the 1650s. Calvert County was separated from Anne Arundel in 1654, and in 1658 the area west and north of St. Mary's County was designated Charles County. There Josias Fendall laid out the large land grant Baltimore awarded him as governor.[30] He chose a tract in the south of the county, on the bank right across Wicomico Creek from Bushwood Manor. Travel between Fendall's and Slye's homes took minutes across the Potomac. Removed from the rest of the settlers, the men and women of Wicomico began to discuss how to forge a new

Maryland out of the ashes of the Battle of the Severn. Fendall shared Gerard's interest in Parliamentary politics. Neither of them had been philosophically far from William Fuller and many of the Puritan commissioners; they had merely not shared their religious sentiments. And now also removed from any manipulations of Claiborne, they could begin to build a coalition on the grounds of the republican doctrine. This was not always a smooth process. They had seen friends executed; Eltonhead had married one of Gerard's daughters too, and Gerard had trouble forgiving the Puritan commissioners. When Fendall decided to offer another Anne Arundel leader, Richard Preston, a seat on the Council, Gerard feared that Fendall placed too much faith in his own abilities to control such men. Drunk one spring night in 1658, Gerard started talking loudly and dismissively about the Council's discussions to a crowd of locals gathered at Bushwood, and Governor Fendall charged him in October 1658 with breaking an oath of secrecy.[31]

In England during the 1650s, with the king's censorship apparatus gone, a wild array of political philosophies emerged, usually melded with religious theology, as each group found in the Gospels a way to remake their material world as well as their spiritual one. Fifth Monarchists, Ranters, Seekers—these and other groups of dissenters interpreted the Bible in ways that challenged civil and religious authorities. Cromwell had crushed the Leveler movement in England for their dangerously egalitarian brand of politics, but a new religious sect arose from the midst of the soldiery. Quaker theology and practice emphasized the humility of Christ and that all were level in the sight of God, demonstrated by their pulpitless meetinghouses and in their denunciation of class-ranking manners and speech. All were brothers and sisters, addressed as thee or thou, no matter one's societal background.[32] An early leader explained his faith this way: "There is a spirit. . . . Its crown is meekness, its life is everlasting love unfeigned; it takes its kingdom with entreaty and not with contention, and keeps it by lowliness of mind."[33] While the meekness might not evoke threat now, in a time and place of such class stratification as seventeenth-century Europe, Quakers called into question all inherited status. And as the Battle of the Severn illustrated, church denominations marked one's political stance. Joining a Quaker meeting meant a thoroughgoing rejection of all the traditional rules and customs. Both Anglicans in Virginia and Congregationalists in Massachusetts would persecute the Quakers in the early 1660s, trying to drive out those who would turn the theological world upside down.

The first Quaker missionary in Maryland, a woman named Elizabeth Harris, found quick success in Anne Arundel County among that Puritan community, including leaders like Fuller and Preston, revealing the underlying political philosophy of the residents. While they had resided in Virginia, the Puritan Church had seemed the furthest from Catholicism, so they had formed a congregation. But when offered an even more radical break from the Church of England, with an interpretation of the Gospel that invoked their radical egalitarian tendencies, the Anne Arundel group embraced it. Perhaps this helped convince Gerard that he could sit at the table with the men he had fought in 1655.[34]

Also around Susannah Gerard Slye's table some nights sat John Hatch and a recent arrival, John Jenkins.[35] Jenkins and his wife Ann arrived in Maryland in the mid-1650s. She was listed as a "transport," an indentured servant, although he was not. Perhaps they met shortly after she arrived. She served for about four years, and the couple claimed a tract near Fendall in Charles County. Jenkins's background in England is unknown, but he was assigned the title "Captain" from the beginning, suggesting he had served time in Oliver's Army and been exposed to Agitator politics. Jenkins immediately served as county commissioner in local courts for Charles County, alongside Hatch and Fendall. He probably drilled a local militia, for some young men were subpoenaed to answer to charges of calling him "Captain Grindingstone." He quickly became a part of Fendall's circle. Neighbors Thomas Jarvis and William Crawford joined the group, talking politics while they cooperated in the building and maintaining of their new farms and in the evenings over dice and card games. Jenkins's wife Ann died just as her time in service ended, and John married Johanna in 1658. Johanna Jenkins, like the women of the Gerard family, was no shrinking violet.[36]

So as 1659 passed, Fendall and Gerard pulled together the radicals of Maryland, with men like Jenkins in Charles County and Fuller from Anne Arundel, planning a way they might end the reign of an aristocratic overlord without encroaching on the religious practices of each other. As Cavalier William Berkeley stepped back into power in Virginia, and news of the death of Cromwell reached the Chesapeake, the stakes grew higher for those who had taken on board any of the new ideas about the allocation of power. Not everyone would subscribe to the Levelers' philosophy; old, ingrained notions of rank and value could not be washed away so easily. Personal ambition and economic competition might trump the Quaker appeal to lowliness. By now, the largest landowners and officeholders in Virginia had committed to slavery, an essential element in the colonial stage of primitive accumulation. That was not yet the case in the Potomac region, however; the obscene profits produced by hereditary enslavement had not quite yet poisoned political philosophy.[37]

But many had at least grasped the basic assumptions from the turmoil in England: that an elected Parliament protected the rights of Englishmen better than a hereditary monarch and that one's birth should not entirely exclude one from representation in that legislature. These conversations, less about religion than representation, could take place safely in Susannah Gerard Slye's Bushwood home, distant from the usual seat of power in St. Mary's City, where too many—whether schooled in deference, cowed by fear of retaliation, pulled by divided loyalties, complacent with the current system, or cynically ambitious enough to sell any principle—might report to Baltimore's brother Philip the dreams and schemes of the rebels. The recent history of Ingle in Maryland and of Cromwell and James Naylor the Quaker in England gave them pause. The successes and setbacks had to be dissected for lessons on how to proceed. How far could they go down the road of radical change and maintain unity? How could they forecast and plan for the countermeasures Baltimore would surely take? Building a consensus demanded many tough discussions, learning to listen and forge compromises. Preparing to declare a revolution meant bolstering each other for the risk of reprisal. Men and women of different faiths and different social classes—planters, artisans, smallholders who had fulfilled their indentures—determined they wanted a commonwealth in Maryland. Servants still under indenture and perhaps some enslaved workers fetched and carried food for the free; they, too, were exposed to the arguments.[38]

Like her mother of the same name, almost nothing is recorded about Susannah Gerard Slye, but if we can surmise anything about her from her choice of husbands, it is that she was an ardent revolutionary. Each of her spouses would in turn lead efforts to rid Maryland of the Stuarts, and it was in her home, Bushwood Manor, that the plans were made. The younger Susannah is heard from only once, thirty years after her first marriage, when she "did Hector my Lord [Baltimore] at a rate I never heard from a Woman before." The writer, a relation of Baltimore, painted her as on the edge of insanity, but we can see that this was a woman who showed no deference or fear even to the highest authority.[39]

That women rarely filled public roles in seventeenth-century Atlantic societies should not lead us to believe they did not play significant roles in private. Bushwood was a domestic sphere—or a base of operations. Previous studies of political thought have failed to account for the importance of domestic spaces in facilitating, congregating, and communicating radical ideologies. With no words from the Gerard women, some historians might feel that we cannot make big claims about their part in keeping Maryland mutinous for decades. Yet it cannot be a coincidence that the daughters and not the sons of Thomas and Susannah Gerard were at the heart of the rebel movement. Had the father been the driver of egalitarian thought, surely his sons would have emerged as the next generation of leaders. But it was the women of the family who are at the center of this story. It was their mother who was the Protestant, not their father. Daughters are taught by mothers. And the maintenance of a network such as the one we will read about in these pages was women's work. Recent groundbreaking work in England on an underground group of Protestants in England under the persecuting rule of Queen Mary used quantitative techniques on a trove of letters. Their work revealed the crucial role played by the women who wrote these letters, showing how "the robustness of a network relies on figures who encourage high levels of interconnectivity." The letter-writing, the hosting of secret meetings, the prison visits, so that the men who were more likely to be arrested stayed in the loop—this is what sustained the people, the ideology, and the mobilization efforts.[40]

On January 12, 1660, Fendall issued the call for elections to an Assembly that would meet six weeks later, for the first time, at "Mr Thomas Gerrards," in St. Clement's. As secretary of the colony, Philip Calvert would of course be in attendance. Slye represented St. Mary's County, Hatch and Jenkins took their places in the Charles County delegation, and Fuller brought the men from Anne Arundel. They assembled at Gerard's home on Tuesday, February 28.[41]

Now the rebel leadership sold their idea to a wider audience: the collection of representatives from around the six counties. While the Council stayed at Gerard's, the Lower House moved to Slye's place at Bushwood, and for three days the delegates adjourned the official proceedings as they talked behind Calvert's back about the Maryland they wanted—one where hereditary titles had no place, but men of low birth might climb a ladder to success if they had talent or dedication. This was a place where those discussions found fertile ground, for Maryland had no property qualifications for voting or holding office. Ex-servants, who had toiled unpaid for years, shared meals of fresh beef, venison, and oysters with those who had come to Maryland as free men, as the seminar on governance continued into the evenings. Those who had been around a dozen years had witnessed the colony managed well by a cooper and described it to the others. Those who had come more recently from England related the stories of Oliver's Army defeating the royalists, and their officers-by-birth. British class distinctions—so sharply demarcated back at home—blurred in the Slye home, a primitive, poorly furnished home for someone with such acreage, yet a place where even poor men might eat fresh venison, the stuff of nobility. The normal status symbols differentiating people according to their birth, reminding some to be humble, to listen to their betters: these had not yet appeared along the Wicomico. Given the events that followed, all manner of conversations must have taken place on those days, and men may have decided to go along for reasons other than the idea of a "career open to talent." Undoubtedly some were still driven by anti-Catholic leanings. Some perhaps tired of ill-fitting rules sent by a distant ruler. There were questions about taxes and customs. But the answer to all the problems pointed to self-government with representation for all the free men, without an English nobleman operating a veto.[42]

On Saturday, March 3, the Lower House asked the Council for papers about taxation and to issue a call for a new election for St. Mary's County, for there had been irregularities. As the conversation turned more toward the revolutionary, they needed to ensure that no procedural errors could be used against them. The Council sent over what they had to Bushwood on Monday, but the House had a new request: that the governor requisition a boat and hands for a special mission, this time to fetch (presumably from St. Mary's City) "the Statutes of England." They continued to adjourn, for a full week more. The debate continued until the consensus forged.[43]

They selected their words carefully, according to their study of the statutes. And on March 12, the clerk was sent to the Upper House with their Declaration: "That this Assembly of Burgesses, judging themselves to be a lawfull Assembly without dependence on any other Power in the Province now in being, is the highest court of Judicature." In January and February 1649, in a series of acts surrounding the execution of the king, the House of Commons had declared itself the supreme authority. They had abolished the House of Lords, until then the court of last resort, and now, in Maryland's Declaration, the claim that the Assembly formed the highest court was also an abolition of the Upper House. There was no fancy preamble, no justification, no long list of grievances. The crisp statement "without dependence on any other Power in the Province now in being" wiped out the power of Lord Baltimore's governor and Council and made the elected representatives of Maryland's free settlers subject only to the Commonwealth Parliament of England. But they left open a way to include Fendall and Gerard, while ridding themselves of Philip Calvert. "If any Objection can be made to the Contrary, Wee desire to heare it."[44]

Baltimore's brother must have been astonished. Fendall quickly responded to the burgesses with a request for clarity about the inclusiveness of this new claim. Were the members of the Council as an Upper House, "Members summoned by special writ," rightful members of the Assembly too? Slye, Gerard's son-in-law, Speaker of the House, came to the Council for the negotiations. What happened that evening we cannot know. But the next morning, Fendall and Gerard declared that they agreed with the burgesses that, as long as the laws passed by the Maryland Assembly did not run counter to the laws of England, they were binding. Speaker Slye then returned that they would not allow an Upper House, for this was to be a unicameral legislature with no check on the voice of the people. Fendall, Gerard, and the others could, however, sit in the Lower House and use their vote to represent Lord Baltimore's wishes if they chose. Calvert was willing to consider this if the governor took over the Speaker's role, setting the agenda and holding the power to adjourn the body at any moment, a type of veto power. But the burgesses would not allow this; Governor Fendall might be granted an honorary title of president, but the Speaker would be chosen from among the elected burgesses. Fendall agreed, and won for himself the right to any tiebreaking vote.[45]

Was this a piece of theater by Fendall and Gerard to pretend to Philip Calvert they had not been a part of planning this revolt? Perhaps, but they were not particularly good actors, for Calvert would soon assure his brother that Fendall and Gerard indeed formed the leadership. In any case, Calvert understood that he had borne witness to a "manifest breach of his Lordship's Right Royall Jurisdiction and Seigniory." With one loyal councilor he formally requested permission to leave from Fendall, who breezily replied, "You may if you please, wee shall not force you to goe or stay." And with that, the Commonwealth of Maryland began its first legislative session.[46]

The Lower House's Declaration was not a claim of independence from Britain, but it was a statement about the equality of all free men. The combination of the franchise without property qualification and the refusal to acknowledge the peerage meant that for a few short months of 1660, Maryland stood out as the most egalitarian society in the Western world. Men like John Jenkins sat alongside those of greater wealth and higher social standing such as Gerard, and their vote carried equal weight in decisions that affected the society and the economy. Fendall held meetings and courts all year, and again the Chesapeake bore witness to government by the people and for the people without the oversight or approval of those born to status. Many had not been in the colony in 1646 to witness a tradesman govern. This was their first taste of a meritocracy, of something close to a political democracy—a heady experience for yeomen and those who had just finished years of indenture, and perhaps scarcely believable.[47]

TIME DID NOT ALLOW for the sense of equality to entrench itself. The death of Oliver Cromwell left a power vacuum in England, for his son had none of the political skills of his father. While factions and generals fomented coups, George Monck sat quietly at the head of the army in Scotland, gauging the direction of the wind. He had served time as a royalist officer in the mid-1640s, but Cromwell's high opinions of his military talents led to his release upon his willingness to pledge allegiance to the republican regime. This he swore, and fought alongside Cromwell, who considered him a great asset. But Monck harbored no loyalty to republican ideas when he set off to restore order in London in late 1659. Many owners of manorial estates who might have been Roundheads in 1640 had developed an appreciation for monarchy in the ensuing revolutionary years. Quakers and their leveling philosophy seemed to be growing in popularity, and the logical conclusion of recognizing one's equality before God leaned toward a redistribution of any wealth that had been ruthlessly extorted from the powerless rather than earned. They might roll back the enclosures; the radical Diggers had seized back common lands for cultivation. "Rioting" that involved the destruction of many enclosures in the western part of England stemmed from the loss of the usual social control apparatus. Bringing back the son of Charles I could restore not just a monarchy, but also the peerage, the state church, and censorship, all the mechanisms of control that had preserved the comfortable privilege their families had enjoyed for so long. None wanted a return to a Catholic tyrant, but the Stuarts might be willing to negotiate now.[48]

Edward Hyde, Earl of Clarendon, negotiated with Monck through intermediaries, and together they developed a plan that would allow Charles II to sit on his father's throne while guaranteeing the safety of any among them who had flirted with republicanism. Clarendon set sail for Holland, Monck marched his army on to London, and less than a month after Fendall had contrived the overthrow of Maryland's aristocrat, Charles II signed his Declaration at Breda, agreeing to grant a pardon to all Roundheads, bar those who had actually signed the death warrant of his father. By the end of May he sat again in a palace in London and initiated the planning of his ceremonial coronation.[49]

Just like that, it was over. The first attempt at abolishing rule by inheritance failed, and the English elite set about washing away all signs of their recent unpleasantness, quashing religious dissidents and hauling Cromwell's body out of his grave to be properly hanged as a traitor. The lords and ladies heaved an enormous sign of relief as they stocked away in their memory banks the lessons learned. Next time a Stuart king behaved not to their liking, they should arrange his removal without resorting to the abolition of the institutions designed to keep the commoners in their places. Some commoners celebrated, not because of their attachment to monarchy, but because the Puritan culture the devout had tried to impose had been so restrictive. They had not yet had an opportunity to vote, nor to appreciate fully what a meritocracy would mean for their children and grandchildren. There had been no redistribution of wealth; the system might slowly have evolved to the breaking up of those manorial grounds and game parks, or at least the destruction of the enclosures, but now all those egalitarian developments must await the rise of a labor movement in the nineteenth century and anticolonial movements in the twentieth. In the meantime, they would toil downstairs, forced to bow and scrape to a few who, only by accident of birth, would command extraordinary luxury.

When the news of the Restoration reached St. Mary's, Fendall, Gerard, Slye, and others huddled at Bushwood. Forced to accept the return to monarchical rule, they would not concede that they must accept Baltimore. If they claimed allegiance to Charles II, perhaps that would keep them in a constitutionally defensible place. On September 15, they published a pronouncement that Marylanders should "owne no authority but what came imediatly from his Majesty or the Grand Assembly of this Province." A faraway monarch with several kingdoms to bring back under control could scarcely be expected to concern himself with the doings of some poor farmers scattered around a few remote creeks feeding off the Potomac.[50]

However, Lord Baltimore, another like Monck who had cleverly navigated his way through the various regimes of the Interregnum, quickly declared his allegiance to the king and moved to regain his personal empire. His brother Philip had returned to England immediately upon Fendall's Rebellion. The Calverts assessed the realpolitik of the British Atlantic. One Cavalier operated the reins of power close to their holdings. William Berkeley had already retaken the governorship of Virginia. To Berkeley they turned now.

Charles signed the order in July that Virginia and any British ships in the vicinity would help Baltimore "settle his Jurisdiction there." Philip Calvert brought that declaration to Maryland and on November 19 had it posted and read in every county courthouse, accompanied by a general pardon to all but Fendall and Gerard. As he wrote a few weeks later to Berkeley, "the person of greatest merit and honor that ever governed in Virginiea," the Commonwealth needed little more than the threat of force from Virginia to collapse. "Imediately on sight of the enclosed from his Sacred Majesty directed to yourselfe and Councill of Virginea. Of whose readines to Comply with his Majesties pleasure both the Mutiners and my Selfe did so little doubt that they chose rather to submit to mercy then to obliedge me by a resistance to Crave ayde from you."[51] Berkeley had already started persecuting Quakers; Maryland residents knew that threats from him were not idle. The Calverts were back in control.[52]

Fendall refused to adopt a deferential attitude, however, making clear to all in Maryland that he surrendered only to the physical force of the state, rather than in awe of some title. He sent a "menacing" note to Calvert on November 20, demanding that the general pardon also apply to him. A week later, as he met Calvert and the Council in St. Mary's to turn over the seals, he again threatened, claiming that his neighbors in Charles County "were in Armes to rescue him" should Calvert attempt to imprison him.[53] Captain John Jenkins did not want to sacrifice a career open to talent without a fight.[54]

The Council considered this an empty threat and debated the future of the dangerous Fendall. Baltimore had directed specifically that ringleaders Fendall and William Fuller not be pardoned, and while he allowed for the discretion of those in Maryland to make the best call, he sanctioned the use of capital punishment. Gerard and Hatch might be pardoned, but if so, must suffer the loss of their entire estates. The sheriff was ordered to detain Fendall in custody indefinitely, but he and Hatch were released over the next week under a bond to appear in court in early February.[55]

That winter, tension rose as Calvert sought to reimpose his authority, forming a militia, seizing the estates of the rebels, and finding a jury willing to convict. Rumors flew that many would be hanged for supporting the rebellion. As the trials of the rebel leadership approached, Fendall rode around the Wicomico drumming up support, and Calvert stepped in, trying to curtail the activists. Fuller of Anne Arundel had avoided capture, and the Quaker would steadfastly refuse to acknowledge the authority of Baltimore, so Calvert issued an order to search and apprehend him or any who might abet his escape. Fendall and Hatch were arrested, and Calvert appointed a new captain to replace Jenkins's command of the Charles County militia. Jenkins responded by calling up his men, including Jarvis and Crawford, to ride to Fendall's rescue, just as Fendall had forecast in November.[56]

Three dozen armed men massed at Fendall's house on February 8 under Jenkins's command. They called on Thomas Lomax to draw up a petition articulating their desires, lest they later be accused of being an undisciplined mob. They declared themselves subject to the king of England alone (bypassing the authority of the Baltimores) and stated that should their actions be considered "not fit" they should be tried only under the laws of England, rather than any acts passed under Baltimore's jurisdiction. They had had to surrender the dream of a republic. Yet, political theory mattered less than political practice. Rid themselves of the Calverts and they could still be masters of their own destiny in a society without inherited status.[57]

The next morning, Captain Jenkins organized his men on a military footing, drawing them into two files, ready to march to spring Fendall and Hatch from their prison. Servants brought out powder and bullets from Fendall's supply. Other organizers set off on a boat across the Wicomico to Slye's home and up to Port Tobacco, a little further north in Charles County.[58]

Their attack was frustrated, however, and the trial of the leaders of Fendall's Rebellion began on February 19. Fendall, Gerard, and others faced charges that they "mutinously . . . hath plotted contrived and by force attempted" to remove Baltimore from any power over Maryland. The list of charges included their September reaction to the Restoration, "colourably sheltering his Rebellion under a pretence of his Majesties Sacred Name." Eleven days later the verdict and sentence came in: guilty and banished, their estates confiscated.[59] Yet the very next day, Gerard and Fendall had those sentences converted into fines by Calvert and the Council. They had to abase themselves, of course, humbly pleading that they would be unable to support their families, and begging the "Gratious Consideracon" of Calvert. The sentences were commuted with the added punishment/restriction that they could never hold public office in Maryland again.[60]

Calvert was canny enough to see that the local community had an attachment to the Wicomico Creek leadership and that too heavy a hand of punishment might provoke yet another round of unrest. So Fendall's public admission of his subject status and his removal and that of Gerard from any place in government served the governor's needs. Any autonomous spirit raised by the actions of the rebel leadership should be deflated by their deferential behavior before the Baltimore family. For example, Gerard had to face court in October, to be judged whether an argument with his neighbor constituted a breaking of his bond for good behavior. Calvert and the magistrates let him go, but there was no doubt he was under scrutiny.[61]

One last manifestation of that autonomous spirit remained to be squelched. Thirteen of Jenkins's Charles County band of mutineers were charged with sedition in the provincial court in April. Jenkins and several others escaped, never to face their charges. As for the others, a jury of their peers acquitted them, despite damning testimony. The community sent another message about where their sympathies lay. Enraged, Governor Philip Calvert immediately went to the Assembly, "concerning the persons indicted for Mutiny and Sedicon in Charles County that they were contrary to the lawe by the Jury accquitted and desired them to provide for the future against such mischeife by some Lawe."[62]

They could not catch Jenkins or William Fuller. They were charged several times that fall, but never appeared in court. And then shortly after the new year turned, the Calvert administration went on high alert. Jenkins, "whoe raysed the mutiny in Charles County in February last," was back on the Wicomico and visiting Fendall. Warrants were issued to the sheriff to arrest him, as was another to put Fendall under house arrest, and many of the acquitted mutineers were subpoenaed to testify against him. Again he slipped away.[63]

CHARLES CALVERT, son and heir to the Baltimore title, came to Maryland in late 1661 to assume the role of governor from his uncle Philip. With those warrants and subpoenas, he delivered a strong signal that he understood that Wicomico Creek was a hotbed of political dissent and that he would not tolerate it. Any who wanted to fulfill the quest for a free and equal society would have to look for a new spot, another place hidden away in the Chesapeake region's creeks and rivers, where the lords of empire could not encroach. They scattered out, always keeping in communication with their brethren of the glory days of 1660. Maybe they could make it happen: a world without those aristocratic land barons sneering down their noses at the people born without land.

Some would stay and continue the struggle in Maryland. A young man traveled to Bushwood in February 1661 and learned of the sentiments there. John Blakiston was the nephew of the John Blakiston who had signed the death warrant of Charles I. The uncle had died before the Restoration, but as Charles II pursued the regicides, he seized the estates of the Blakiston family, leaving in his wake some well-educated, politically engaged republicans. Young John Blakiston identified a safe place along Wicomico Creek for some of the next generation of the family.[64]

On the other hand, Charles Calvert, like the Quakers and Levelers migrating to the colonies in these decades, also witnessed the revolutionary era. This governor revealed that he staunchly believed that the restoration of monarchy and House of Lords had indicated that proper order had been put back in place. Calvert was the highest-ranked man in the colonies—heir to a baronetcy—and he demanded the appropriate level of deference. Launching a policy to improve oversight of his colony and to encourage obedience, he began the construction of symbolic manifestations of power through impressive architecture. Calvert identified Wicomico Creek as a dangerously secluded area. Over the next decade, he patronized a merchant, Thomas Notley, who lived in the area, appointing him to offices so that he could keep a watchful eye for skulking radicals.[65]

Fendall stayed on, but Thomas Gerard had had enough. Just a slightly further boat ride away was Westmoreland County, Virginia, and Nomini Bay, where old Ingle's Rebellion leaders Nathaniel Pope, James and Thomas Baldridge, Francis Gray, and others had secured themselves in Indian country. In the peace treaty to end the 1644–46 Anglo-Powhatan War, Virginia had promised not to occupy the Northern Neck. So the rebel government of the 1640s had found a place they thought safe from any English government bar one they could make for themselves. But the Virginia government broke their treaty just a couple of years later and annexed the region, naming it Northumberland County in 1648. It was further subdivided in 1653, and the cluster of Ingle rebels in what was now Westmoreland County took over the local administration.[66] It was to this community that Gerard would relocate after his beloved Susannah died in 1666.

Jenkins and his friends Thomas Jarvis and William Crawford took the Restoration of both a king and the Calverts as a tough blow. Not yet defeated, they considered what they had learned along the banks of Wicomico Creek. Geography mattered. Jenkins had purchased land in the mid-1650s alongside Speke in Nomini Bay (he later sold it to Temperance Gerard's husband), but he remained unconvinced that the distance from Jamestown and St. Mary's could protect them from the long reach of imperious governors. Nathaniel Batts, a Chesapeake merchant's interpreter familiar with remote locations, told Jenkins and another Nomini Bay rebel named George Durant about a beautiful spot outside the British Empire where Batts had established a trading base and a friendly relationship with local Indians. South of Virginia, barricaded by an almost impassable swamp to the north and a string of islands and shifting sands to the east, they could try one more time to rid themselves of the scourge of aristocratic bias and privilege.[67]

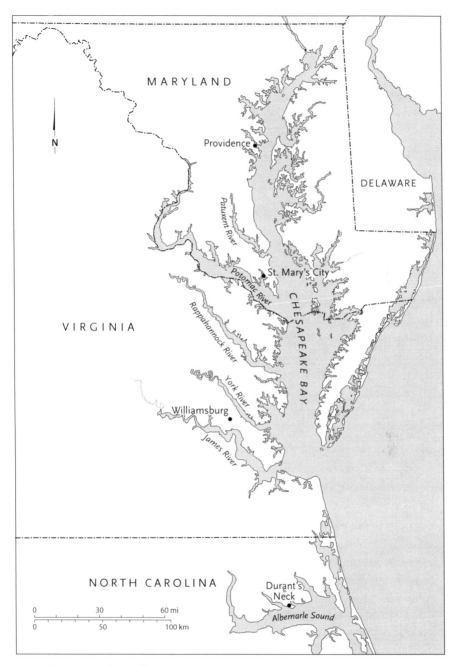

Maryland to North Carolina, 1650–1690

CHAPTER THREE

Albemarle and Other Fringes, 1661–1674

> If we return to kingship, and soon repent (as undoubtedly we shall,
> when we begin to find the old encroachments coming on by little
> and little upon our consciences, which must necessarily proceed
> from king and bishop united inseparably in one interest) we may
> be forced perhaps to fight over again all that we have fought.
>
> —MILTON, 1660

By 1663, Captain John Jenkins had been on the run two years since his ill-fated attempt to rescue Josias Fendall from a Calvert prison. He refused to come on bended knee before the Baltimore family and repent of misguided decisions, as others would do, pressured to surrender to save the farms they had worked so hard for. For Jenkins and his wife Johanna, the principle of a commonwealth, a society where one's lineage did not determine one's rights, was more important. Few can hold such principles in the face of economic destitution, yet Jenkins was not alone. Johanna had had nothing before, living as an indentured servant. Friends like Thomas Jarvis and William Crawford also held the faith. With confidence in their abilities to survive and hearts full of righteous leveling passion, they set out south, leaving the British Empire behind them to build a new community.

They were not isolated in their dream of a freer, more egalitarian world. As the shiploads of poor laborers destined for tobacco fields arrived ever more frequently in the Chesapeake Bay, men like Jenkins who had served in Oliver's Army and women like Johanna who had heard the messages of the sects poured into Virginia. Most would be kept too hungry and exhausted to focus on anything but sustaining life. The worst of the Starving Times had passed, but life expectancy remained horribly short for servants. That any could resist the powerful men who held them in bondage so far from home is remarkable. But resist they did. By the mid-1670s, small groups of radicals scattered themselves around the Chesapeake, protected by rivers, woods, and swamps, and set about living their lives with as much autonomy as possible. Their careers could not be fully open to all their talents, but they did not have to suffer through the indignities of bowing and scraping to fools born in high places, and with a little luck they might avoid sending any of their very hard earned money to keep such men in their palaces and regalia.

The Revolution had wiped out deference among these settlers, leaving them immune to the enchantments of pomp and title.

EVEN BEFORE THE JENKINS FAMILY wound their way south and through the Great Dismal Swamp, others in Virginia filled with revolutionary ardor made their feelings known. York County, close by Williamsburg, housed all kinds of rebellious people, not yet so crushed by the Restoration of Charles II and William Berkeley that they would not speak out. Of course, Berkeley and the rest of the planter elite used their control of the local courts to squelch mutinous talk as ferociously as possible. In June 1661, Thomas Cheney spoke out against the new king and refused to take the oaths of allegiance and supremacy acknowledging the rightfulness of His Majesty, "the onely Supreame Governour of this Realme . . . in all Spirituall or Ecclesiasticall things or causes, as Temporall." Cheney's punishment was to be thirty lashes, "well layd on till the blood come," the court specified. He played mad, and his sentence was suspended, for, in the magistrates' eyes, he served to send another message to the community: only a lunatic would not accept the new reality that the republic was over.[1]

Some were crazy enough to keep resisting. Mrs. Mary Chisman continued to attend Quaker meetings after Berkeley prohibited them, given their "schismaticall and hereticall Doctrines." The Quakers' leveling philosophy threatened the whole social order, attracting as it did "especially the Women," but Chisman went a further step, bringing "Two or Three negroes belonging to hir husband" with her to the meeting that August. Given that none of these Quakers could be witnesses in court, all the magistrates could do was admonish Mr. Chisman, and bid him "restreyne his said negroes & whole family."[2]

In 1662, the Virginia House of Burgesses enacted a further statute to control women who might threaten social order. "Women causing scandalous suites [lawsuits] to be ducked," it stipulated, reinforcing male power by allowing husbands to choose whether to pay any damages that they incurred from their wives' behaviors or to subject those wives to become a humiliating spectacle. Tied to a chair on a long beam, the woman was dipped and immersed in the river, for as often or as long as prescribed. That the lawmakers felt such a law was necessary tells us how the era of the English Revolution and Quaker missionaries had inspired women to find their voices. Many would not be silenced; fifteen years later, as we shall see, Mary Chisman's daughter-in-law would admit to Berkeley that she had been the rebellious voice in her household, not her husband.[3]

The day after the Chisman case was heard, the York County court heard how another Quaker, Thomas Bushrod, openly defied Virginia's gentry, challenging them before their servants to disturb the meeting he would be attending with his wife the following Sunday. According to the gentry's reading of the situation, "church & State [were] at once strooke at." Bushrod's willingness not merely to be a practicing Quaker, but to upbraid the gentry in public, marked him as "very dangerous."[4]

Other freemen and servants alike demanded rights in a "mutinous" manner. After a suicide by one of magistrate Thomas Beale's servants, others in the neighborhood began to speak out about ill-treatment. William Clutton, a freeman, would not stand by and see servants ill fed. Isaac Friend overheard Clutton make the claim to Beale that there was a law requiring masters to give servants meat at least three times a week, a ration the laborers on Major James Goodwin's plantation did not receive. Recalling the glory days of the New Model Army, "captaine gen." Friend declared to the rest of the servants that they should rise as a group, "forty of them together, & get Armes & he would be the first & have them cry as they went along, 'who would be for Liberty, and free from bondage' . . . either be free or dye for it." Friend swore later that it had been idle bragging and that he had no intentions of acting upon it. Clutton, seen as ringleader, was bound over for good behavior.[5]

Berkeley and the other planters of the Assembly had passed a law in 1658 exiling all Quakers and, two years later, another Act for Suppressing the Quakers. The governor continued to issue more general commands to his sheriffs about heeding the danger of that "most pestilent sect" over the next few years. York County was not the only nest of such radicals; Northampton, Nansemond, and Lower Norfolk County also sheltered communities resistant to the persecutions. When arrested, they were brought to the jurisdiction of William Drummond, James City County sheriff.[6]

Drummond had been an indentured servant in Virginia and part of a "most dangerous conspiracy" of servants hoping to escape the brutality of their masters and find freedom outside of the colony in 1640. For his organizing efforts, he endured a public whipping and then served an extra year. After his indenture, he became a tenant farmer on Berkeley's estate, and his education and eloquence allowed him to represent others in court. He was a walking example of the fact that talent, intelligence, and leadership qualities resided in every social strata. When his daughter married up into the gentry class, Berkeley assigned Drummond as a James City County magistrate and sheriff. Thus Drummond received a political education, for these positions brought him into close proximity to power. It also brought him a close proximity to the Quakers Berkeley had ordered him to persecute. Married to a self-assured, politically conscious woman, as we shall see, Drummond had no problem with a sect that contentedly followed female leadership. He would gradually move from prosecutor to ally.[7]

Other veterans of the New Model Army, still fixed on a career open to talent, did not take easily to the restoration of Cavaliers and the vicious ways they reintroduced hierarchy. Harvest time often meant the tension between a planter and his labor force reached its height. Planters wanted to extract extra labor, but workers would try to leverage planter dependence upon them. Workers usually lost, given planter control of court and whip.[8] For a Roundhead, the disrespect was too much. In early September 1663, a group met secretly at a hut in the woods and laid out a plan to overthrow the planter elite and reclaim their status as free men. They had overthrown a king and an aristocracy in England; surely they could do it in the wilderness of Virginia. Each soldier should recruit others and bring as many munitions as possible. En masse, they would attack the home of Councilor Willis at Poplar Springs, where they knew a colonial arsenal lay in store. His marching drum would be seized too, for they intended to "Drumme their freedom," trooping from plantation to plantation to attract an army of servants. If Berkeley would not grant that freedom immediately, they would leave Virginia for somewhere more welcoming of Oliver's veterans.[9]

This Gloucester County bid was thwarted by an informer and the ringleaders were speedily caught, tried, and hanged for treason. Berkeley and his fellow planters understood the magnitude of what they had averted. Experienced military men might undermine their oligarchy; the English Revolution was a very fresh memory. The snitch was richly rewarded as "an encouragement to others," and the Assembly marked September 13, "the day this villainous plot should have been putt into execution . . . in perpetual commemoration" as an annual day to give thanks to God for their salvation. How the rest of the servant class felt was not recorded, although another councilor noted a few years later that the planters remained under threat "att our backs with the Indians [and] in our bowels with our servants." The appearance of deference was maintained only through rigorous lashing of a revolutionary generation.[10]

The trouble with Quakers was their doggedness in the face of harassment. The same week, in the southernmost reaches of the colony, the sheriff reported that the county had chosen a Quaker, John Porter, to represent them in the Assembly. Porter tried to hold onto his seat, claiming there was no evidence he had attended Quaker meetings, but when he refused to take the oaths, he outed himself and was dismissed from the legislature. Another Cromwellian soldier-Quaker who found himself in Drummond's jail, George Wilson, described the "cruell Sufferings" his co-religionists were subjected to in Virginia.[11] Such stories fueled Quaker missionaries as *Fox's Book of Martyrs* had encouraged early Protestants to persevere against Catholic rulers. Those less brave found shelter in nearby sanctuaries, such as Somerset County, Maryland, and the Albemarle.[12]

The Albemarle, the most northeast section of current-day North Carolina, had only recently opened up as a possibility. While various land claims had been made and expeditions sent, the imperviousness of the Great Dismal Swamp, combined with tales of the Spanish and, of course, Roanoke Colony's mysterious disappearance, discouraged most from trying to settle a farm. In the 1650s, however, a young Chesapeake man named Nathaniel Batts served as interpreter of Indian languages for merchant-planter Francis Yeardley of Lynnhaven, then in Lower Norfolk County. His work brought him into Maryland and occasionally deep into Indian country, sourcing beaver furs and deerskins.[13] In September 1653, he made his way to Roanoke Island, scene of the infamous Lost Colony, but Batts, unlike those first settlers, had learned local languages and customs and easily formed a positive bond with Indians he met hunting, who were interested in doing business with him. While the Yeopim and other smaller groups occupied the lands bordering on the swamp, the Tuscarora were the predominant tribe of the region. If Batts wanted to create a positive business relationship, he would need to honor their power.

"After some days spent to and fro in the country, the young man the interpreter prevailed with the great man, and his war-captains, and a great man of another province, and some other Indians, to come in and make their peace with the English, which they willingly condescended unto." Yeardley claimed that he sent Batts and others with two hundred pounds to purchase

> what land they should like, the which in little time they effected, and
> purchased, and paid for three great rivers, and also all such others as
> they should like of southerly; and in solemn manner took possession
> of the country, in the name, and on the behalf, of the commonwealth
> of England; and actual possession was solemnly given them by the
> great commander, and all the great men of the rest of the provinces,
> in delivering them a turf of the earth with an arrow shot into it; and so

the Indians totally left the lands and rivers to us, retiring to a new habitation.[14]

Yeardley's claim amounted to self-aggrandizement. There was no condescension on the part of the Indians and no understanding by anyone that the Albemarle belonged to England. Nathaniel Batts made a peaceful negotiation to allow himself access to some land in Albemarle and to the deerskin trade. His language skills and experience help explain the lack of tension between English settlers and local Indians there for a generation. He would guide future settlers to make purchases from the Yeopim and others, for Yeardley had not "purchased" rivers, but merely begun a process of reciprocity. As an interpreter for Yeardley, Batts had learned enough to approach more powerful chieftains with an envoy to testify to his character. "The great emperor of Rhoanoke, he undertook with some of his Indians, to bring some of our men to the emperor of the Tuskarorawes, and to that purpose sent embassadors before, and with two of our company set forth and travelled within two days journey of the place, where at a hunting quarter the Tuskarorawes emperor, with 250 of his men, met our company, and received them courteously." An elaborate ritual of diplomacy preceded Batts's encounter with the Tuscarora to acknowledge their legitimacy and supremacy, rather than that of Charles II. A powerful group, the Tuscarora still numbered 8,000, fifty years after contact, when other groups such as the Meherrin and Chowan had lost many to disease. That the English side of the interactions was led by Batts, a man conversant in the local dialect and customs, made for a long-lasting relationship. Almost twenty years after these early encounters, a Quaker missionary reported that Batts still met with "the emperor and his thirty kings under him of the Tusrowres" to maintain the peace.[15]

Batts was interacting with Thomas Gerard and Robert Slye in Maryland the following spring and perhaps told many of his adventures, for Jenkins and Jarvis would shortly become his neighbors.[16] Yeardley died in 1655, and his scheme to claim Carolina for England dissolved, but Batts seized the opportunity to carve out a life for himself. He had found an idyllic spot just a little outside the British Empire. Hidden away from easy detection by tax collectors of any kind, by 1657 Batts and his Indian wife took over the Albemarle home and frontier trading post that Yeardley had paid a carpenter to build for the Indian chief, and there he brought English goods from Virginia and traded for deerskins and beaver furs. The Virginia authorities granted him special "privilege" for his explorations that year, perhaps a monopoly.[17]

George Durant's father, William Durand, had been a Puritan commissioner with William Fuller (like Jenkins, a rebel fugitive) on the Severn River during the troubles of the mid-1650s, and converted to Quakerism, if not devoutly. So the young man had presumably also been on the side of Fendall, Fuller, and Jenkins. Durant married his wife, Ann, in Nomini Bay, the stronghold of Ingle's rebels in Virginia in early 1659. He immediately sought a place even further away from Cavaliers and headed south with Jenkins and the few who were willing to carve out a spot for themselves along Albemarle Sound. He witnessed a deed for land on the Pasquotank River that Batts purchased from the Yeopim in 1660 and acquired a tract for himself on the Perquimans River the following year. Jenkins witnessed another legal paper for Durant in early 1663.[18]

Batts, Durant, and Jenkins and a few others moved into Indian country, and with Batts's leadership, they agreed to land deals with the local populations and settled into a life of their own making. But English aristocrats would find them and claim both ownership of their land and the right to make laws restricting them without their representation or consent. William Berkeley voyaged back to England in 1661. There he found his brother and other Cavaliers who had stayed true to Charles II combining with men a little less true, but instrumental in his Restoration nonetheless, to exploit Charles II's debt to them. Traditionally, a king rewarded fidelity with land, so valuable for both wealth and status in tiny England. Batts's and various other expeditions to the south of Virginia revealed that the Spanish were not actively contesting for much of the region north of Florida. Here was free land for the taking. Charles would grant his Restorers a charter for untold acreage, and settlers would take all the risks, do all the labor, and send back to London rents and mineral profits. With Baron John Berkeley's younger brother William nearby to oversee it, Carolina represented a perfect opportunity to amplify their wealth. The charter had not been signed as Berkeley departed, and conflicting claims drew out the legal process, but by the spring of 1663, the Carolinas, north and south, supposedly belonged not to the Yeopim and the Tuscarora, nor Batts and Durant, but to eight Englishmen. George Monck, head of the army that put Charles II back on the throne, had earned the title Duke of Albemarle. His name would now be attached to the great sound and by extension to the whole region.[19] Having endured the Interregnum's religious tensions, these Lords Proprietors of Carolina declared to all prospective settlers that they would enjoy full "liberty of conscience in all religious or spiritual things." Quakers could meet in peace.[20]

In the interim, a mix of people were making their claims to the lands between the Great Dismal and the sound. Berkeley signed more land grants in September 1663, including 700 acres to "capt John Jenkins . . . on the North with pyquomons River on the East wth ye mouth of pyquomons &c Carolina, & on the West with A great swamp wch parted this Land from Thomas Jarvis his Land."[21] From Berkeley's perspective, why not be generous to anyone ready to venture into this new territory? His fellow proprietors wanted him to encourage settlement. Supposedly Jenkins brought fourteen people; he and Johanna had not been married long, and although they had several children, he could hardly have amassed many servants as a fugitive. His headrights claims were probably exaggerated, or perhaps he initiated the tradition of claiming new headrights each time one crossed over the colonial boundary, as many would in the future. Berkeley had no idea Jenkins was a wanted man in Maryland; his grant was issued along with several to Virginia planters. But only a few were willing to endure the hardship of starting from scratch. If one had a thriving plantation in Virginia, real estate on the other side of the swamp was only for speculative purposes. For Jenkins, Jarvis, Durant, and others, it was a refuge. Fendall's supporters had landed in a safe place, their backs up against the Great Dismal, just as Batts had described. And gradually they would be joined by an "abundance of people that are weary of Sir Williams Government," including William Drummond and many Quakers and their leveling sympathizers, imbued with the ideas of their generation about overthrowing government by lineage.[22]

These settlers were free people, but they had little. Historian of Virginia Peter Thompson identifies this moment as when "poorer householders began to develop a class consciousness." The gulf between rich planters and everyone else in Virginia widened as the bigger planters along the York and James Rivers switched to an enslaved workforce. Smallholders and laborers, their numbers swollen each year as increasing numbers of servants outlived their indentures after 1650, could clearly see how intermarriage among the elite closed off opportunities, material and political, to those beneath them. And the primary marker of that large section of the population, free but poor whites, was their use of the English Revolution term "commonalty," described by Thompson as "a group defined by injustice and oppression . . . bound together by an organic conception of social relations encapsulated in the notion of the commonweal." It was a particularly seventeenth-century concept; a couple of generations later, use of the term "commonalty" had died out. It resonated especially well with Quakers and Puritans, but religion alone cannot explain it. Thompson cites Milton's 1660 pamphlet *The Readie and Easie Way to Establish a Free Commonwealth* as commonalty equaling the "self-governing polity or commonwealth." Although Milton explained that at the local government level, a commonalty might exist within a monarchical nation, "the needs of the commonwealth however, were more likely to be protected and advanced within a republic." Thompson sets his discussion as an explanation of the forces at work in Bacon's Rebellion, at the fullest manifestation of the desires of the revolutionary generation, but they are visible earlier. We have seen them in Maryland. Jenkins carried Fendall's model to North Carolina. They did not need to read Milton; Cromwell's soldiers and the women testifying at Quaker meeting were already the embodiment of his vision. The hope of moving the Commonwealth to America was alive and well after the Restoration.[23]

William Drummond knew before Berkeley that Quakers from Lower Norfolk County would seek shelter in the region opened up by Batts. He would do business with Thomas Bushrod, the defiant Quaker who challenged the gentry in York County.[24] While Drummond served as sheriff, he kept his views to himself, but gradually as Berkeley and his cronies began their systematic fleecing of those they deemed lower than themselves, Drummond's roots as a rebellious servant emerged. Unaware of that, Berkeley chose him as Albemarle's first governor in 1663, although Drummond's official appointment awaited confirmation from the proprietors in England, and so he did not move across the line until 1665. By that time, Jenkins and Durant had established themselves as the leading men. Batts had stepped aside as a political leader by then. Although Batts played little role in the democratic development of North Carolina, his legacy, marked out in the places bearing his name around the Albemarle, is well deserved. As a type of secretary of state, keeping goodwill with small and large groups of neighboring Indians, he allowed Jenkins and Durant to build a polity without the threat of war, a condition that so frequently sacrifices democracy to strengthen the hand of a military commander.

Free, then, from the twin threats of Indian hostility and Berkeley's oppression, the first white freemen claimed land: one hundred acres for each head of household and extra acreage for every servant they might bring. The collection of quitrents of a halfpenny per acre would be suspended for several years, officially, and as they looked back at the swamp, it must have struck those commoners as unlikely that any proprietor's minion would ever fight his way through to assess rents.[25] The scary landscape of roaming wolves, insect-thick groves of cypress trees growing out of the malarial swamp, and poisonous snakes lurking at every water-logged step protected the commonalty from debt and tax collectors. The boat journey around the Great Dismal, via the Chowan River, was cumbersome too, while trying to get to the Perquimans River via the Atlantic involved navigating the shifting sands of the Outer Banks, then the intracoastal waterway, and then an overland journey without roads. Enough boats wrecked that the region became frightening to sailors; only shallow draft vessels could navigate coastal North Carolina's shoals or the sound.[26] In any case, rent payment was years away. This land was really free. It carried, too, the promise of political liberty: representation in decision making over the rules of this new society. The men who had recently fled the Restoration in Maryland would make sure of that.

As they had in Maryland and Virginia, these people sought good bottomland along the rivers and creeks and began the tough work of building shelter and establishing their farms. They framed their homes by driving posts in the ground, and the small structures with their dirt floors would be continually rotting and susceptible to the wild Atlantic storms of hurricane season each year. Only a few who would bring servants or slaves from Virginia could develop the plantation complex of outbuildings for laborers and kitchen and tobacco drying. The rest gathered their families into twelve-by-fourteen-foot homes, perhaps with a loft, and devoted most of their energies to the work of tobacco farming.[27]

Tobacco required neither capital nor even a large labor force to earn enough to sustain a family. Gradually the trees were cut from a few acres, and, hoeing around the stumps, the farmer created little tobacco mounds as the first Chesapeake settlers had learned from Indians. Planting seeds in the early months of the year, the family tended the plants through spring and summer, then harvested and prepared the leaves for market in the fall. All of this they had learned during their indenture. Now, with corn and hogs for consumption, supplemented by all the venison and wild fowl and fish they could shoot, catch, or barter friendly locals for, they could eke out a life of security and stability.[28] While settlers in Virginia and Maryland would use tobacco as currency until the end of the century, North Carolinians' money reflected their gradually diversified farming. They could use pork, deerskin, whale oil, or corn in their transactions. No rents or taxes were due to a king or a governor unless they approved them in their own Assembly.[29]

Drummond arrived with the title of governor, and legend has it that he held the first Assembly in 1665 under a tree in Pasquotank, with a vote for every man. The only decision this Assembly made was to request even better terms of land ownership: the proprietors needed to grant more acreage per person and cut the nominal rent in half. As royalist Thomas Woodward, the newly appointed surveyor, explained to the proprietors, "To thenke that any men will remove from Virginia upon harder Conditione then they can live there will prove (I feare) a vaine Imagination, It bein Land only that they come for." He noted that the planters, "Rich men (which Albemarle stands in much need of)," were not making their way south.[30] The Assembly also demanded that the proprietors remove a ridiculous requirement that one had to own servants to get land. Few who commanded servants had settled, and everyone who had claimed free land satisfied the era's standard property qualification for the franchise.

The proprietors, William Berkeley excepted, held important offices in England and had to run extensive estates there and in the Caribbean. Unlike the Calvert family, to whom Maryland mattered, the Carolina lords placed their American lands low on their priority list. They did issue some booster propaganda to encourage immigration to the new colony, advertising religious toleration and free land. Understanding how the revolutionary years had raised political dreams, they promised that governors would serve only three-year terms, while only the Assembly could raise taxes.[31] They dispatched a couple of young relatives named Peter and Philip Carteret to serve as their eyes on the ground in the colonies. Philip headed to New Jersey, recently seized from the Dutch and awarded to some of the same group. Peter was instructed to serve as assistant governor to Drummond and also to fill the roles of secretary and chief registrar. He was also supposed to check that the lands granted personally to Sir John Colleton, one of the proprietors, were being run properly. Colleton had a Barbados estate, where he had spent the Interregnum, and he had planned to use his lands in Carolina to let livestock run wild and produce pork to sell in the Caribbean for slaves. But by the spring of 1665, shortly after his arrival in Albemarle, young Carteret reported back that the settlers complained that their land grants depended on ownership of servants. Colleton regarded their complaint as ridiculous. "I would fayne know what there land signifies without people," he replied, but admitted that he and the other proprietors would address the issue when they could finally gather in one place. Colleton understood that the Americas reversed Europe's concepts of wealth. In Europe, people were plentiful and land was rare. Ownership of land commanded wealth and status. In the Americas, as the native population collapsed, land was plentiful but laborers few. Ownership of people's labor commanded wealth and status. The Albemarle Assembly's wish for land tenure to be independent of their command of labor made no sense to a Barbados planter like Colleton. But to men like Jenkins who prized equality, the request made sense. The Albemarle would be occupied for the next half century by those who could "live by their own hands of their own produce." The wish for land grants without servants would eventually be granted in 1668, delayed by years of plague and more important commitments.[32]

Carteret also reported that the horses, cattle, and hogs Colleton had paid for to stock his personal Albemarle estate were not to be found. The culprit was none other than Jenkins's ally from Maryland, William Crawford, who cared little for protecting the assets of any of England's great lords. Colleton wrote again in March 1666, demanding Carteret recover the livestock, emphasizing their value to sugar planters: "You know what a Comodity hoggs flesh is at Barbados & beefe Likewayse." He instructed Carteret to move quickly in establishing vineyards and to "send a small Caske of wine of the grape of the Country assoone as possible."[33] This absurdity reflected the proprietor's lack of knowledge of Albemarle. This was not an extension of Barbados, which after a generation of settlement and sugar production had a population of 50,000, half of whom were enslaved. Despite Carteret having brought several servants, he could not establish a successful tobacco plantation, let alone a profitable wine-making venture. His diary of the 1660s reads like a tragedy of sickness among man and beast, while annual Atlantic storms destroyed harvests and buildings. He tried to produce whale oil, too, "butt could nott get fright [freight] for it that yeare soe that their was great Lakages [leakages]." Twenty pounds a year salary was just not enough.[34]

As the population of the Chesapeake continued to soar with new immigrants, all of whose labor would be dedicated to tobacco, the supply led to a glut and therefore a drop in price and profit. The big planters of Virginia had already demanded that Berkeley take action, and the only course seemed to be a collective cessation of growing for a season, so that the consequent shortage would allow the price to recover. This would hurt for a year, but the planters' hope was that the long-term benefits would more than make up for the short-term pain. Of course, the greatest pain would have fallen on smallholders who lived hand to mouth and could not rely on the credit lines offered the larger landowners. However, it necessitated cross-colonial cooperation, for if Maryland's tobacco farmers continued to produce, Virginia's pain would be for nought. Berkeley had frequently proposed a stint since 1663; smaller planters in Virginia had little input in such decisions. But the tradition of a representative democracy in Maryland led to strong opposition in the Lower House of the Maryland Assembly, and without their cooperation, Berkeley could not get his way.[35] He tried again in 1666; while

Calvert was very receptive to the idea, the small tobacco farmers' representatives jealously guarded their prerogatives against elite power. They specified that such a deal would encourage more to migrate south and, in that warm climate, produce extra crops of tobacco each year, and that it would discourage merchant traders from coming to the Chesapeake, cutting them off from all kinds of trade goods. So Drummond and the men of Albemarle must be included, or the deal was dead.[36] Members of Virginia's House also had reservations, but Berkeley managed an approval.[37]

A conference held in July 1666 brought to Jamestown a collection of Chesapeake leadership from across the political spectrum, including Berkeley, Drummond, and Robert Slye, the latter representing Maryland. A treaty was signed, but in the end, no deal could be finalized; both the smallholders of Maryland and Albemarle and Baltimore himself refused to suffer to help out the Virginia grandees.[38] After the upheavals of Ingle and Fendall, Baltimore understood the political ground he stood on in Maryland. Anything that would "compel the poorer planters to enter into new servitudes to the more rich to gain subsistence . . . would very probably endanger the peace of the Province and provoake the people to sedition." Thus the benefits of Maryland's radicals' seditious behavior lasted long after their insurrections had been repressed, as a chilling effect on the Calvert family. Jenkins would have told Drummond about Slye and Fendall and the radical meetings at Bushwood; republicans met again in Jamestown, fostering new bonds across colonial boundaries.

These discussions coincided with discussions on the other side of the Atlantic, also concerning the imperial trade in commodities. From 1660 to 1673, Charles II and his ministers pushed mercantilist legislation through Parliament, designed to bolster both English merchants and the royal treasury. Known as the Navigation Acts, the new rules ordered that certain commodities of the colonial trade, including tobacco, must be sold only to English merchants, cutting off the Dutch. Should colonists seek to sell their tobacco to anyone else, they must pay duties. This might benefit the colonies in that the English market could not buy Dutch tobacco, but the initial reaction in the Chesapeake was very negative, as the Dutch ships were the most reliable and frequent traders. Berkeley's mission to England in 1661 was to try to push for at least an exemption for Virginia, if not the repeal of the acts, but it had been unsuccessful, for the tobacco revenues directly lined Charles's pockets.[39] In fact, the 1673 act only made for better enforcement.

While Carteret suffered, Drummond, Jenkins, and Durant built a coalition of like-minded people. Berkeley felt Drummond had mismanaged the tobacco cessation, allowing it to fail. When the Virginia governor appointed one of his cronies, a more typical Virginia planter named Samuel Stephens, to replace Drummond in 1667, the republicans refused to accept his authority. Stephens arrived with detailed instructions from the proprietors and a political philosophy from Berkeley. We have only Berkeley's words, but they are vivid. "I often heard that there were great factions fomented against [Stephens]," he complained just three years later, "and by such alsoe as should have rather studied the peace of the Collony and the upholding the authority of the Governor." The biggest landowners, Berkeley felt, should support the structure of government. Those men were Durant and Jenkins. "But . . . I have heard that some were soe Insolent as to draw their Swords against him." We know Captain John Jenkins had no fear of violent conflict. Berkeley warned that this crime would have met with capital punishment "in any Collony of America but that, where this mild gent presided." Already Virginia's governor recognized that the society forming to the south was heading down a different path. Without naming the culprit, he made it clear that he should not be named the next leader.

So in 1670 a Council made up of Jenkins and other early settlers chose Carteret as their official governor and continued to go about their business. Meanwhile the Earl of Shaftesbury and other proprietors in England began to focus on the southern portion of their grant, making plans to encourage Barbadian planters to settle along the Ashley and Cooper Rivers. They employed John Locke to help as they wrote the Fundamental Constitutions, which arrived in the Albemarle at the end of 1669. Shaftesbury admitted in the accompanying instructions that this feudal constitution with its invention of a provincial hierarchy to "avoid a numerous democracy" would scarcely apply to Albemarle, for they did not have enough great landowners among them to establish the various ranks of authority. But the Council was to put it into effect as best they could.[40]

The Fundamental Constitutions remind us how some of the most powerful men at the time saw good government, and how one young philosopher, who would be influential for centuries, remained clouded in his understanding of the world changing around him. The Revolution's upheaval had taught Shaftesbury and Locke that there should be some form of representative government and that toleration of all branches of Christianity would create better odds of civil peace. Yet they had not grappled with attempts to change English class structure, in terms of access to power. They knew of no examples of a stable society without a class pyramid; the Levelers were madmen if they would trust the landless with a vote. Locke began drafting his *Two Treatises* at least a decade later, after witnessing Charles II's gradual slide toward absolutism. But in 1669, he placed his emphasis on stability, and the prerequisite was hereditary power.[41]

The Council ignored the Constitution at first, but when an update arrived in the fall of 1670, it seemed wise to counter anything that really affected their everyday lives. They wrote a response, reaffirming they felt bound only by the tenure agreement of 1668's Great Deed of Grant, not the Constitution, which increased rents. And the Council emphasized that the voice of the people in the Assembly must remain the source of legislation rather than Carteret or his Council. "Restraininge persones chosen by the people from a freedom of propossall will bee deemed in the people a Compelled Unnessarie Charge," they protested. They received no reply, so after seven years of misery, Carteret accepted the task of returning to England to report to the proprietors in the spring of 1672, never to return. He appointed his second-in-command, John Jenkins, the fugitive from Fendall's Rebellion and republican of Oliver's Army, now bearing the rank "Leftenant Collonell," the governor of North Carolina.[42]

When Quaker missionary William Edmundson made a trip to Albemarle, he entered a welcoming world, where no sheriffs pursued and no governor fumed at the threat his theology posed. His first stay was at the home of Hannah and Henry Phelps, who had endured fines and lashings from the Puritans of Massachusetts, only to be finally driven out when the authorities seized their entire estate. They joined the community in Albemarle. George Fox, head of the Quaker church, came a few months later, toward the end of 1672. Both Batts and the Jenkins family came to meet him; the Jenkinses offered him their home and escorted him around. Several officeholders of the colony would help him organize meetings.[43]

Edmundson and Fox described a watery world of hard-scrabble farmers, rough around the edges. The men smoked at religious services, and the women hitched up their skirts to pull boats out of the river, shocking behaviors in the Englishmen's eyes. Although the two missionaries were often bewildered and lost in the swampy woods, struggling with their leaky boats and wet through to the skin, their experiences stood in sharp contrast to those of Quaker missionaries in Virginia who had been whipped and deported. Here, so close to Virginia's Lower Norfolk and Nansemond Counties, where planters and sheriffs persecuted the Society of Friends, the Quaker leader received the warmest hospitality Albemarle could offer. Clearly, a friendly rapport with local Indians had been established, with some mixed gatherings and no signs of hostility. Batts was not the only multilingual inhabitant; Fox found others to translate for him in an Indian village near the English settlements.[44]

Jenkins governed for several years without interference from proprietors, a welcome change from the Calverts of Maryland. Not all who joined him in Albemarle shared his egalitarianism; certainly a few, such as Valentine Bird, had aspirations of grandeur, accumulating land and slaves. Yet that the leading church of the region was the Quaker meeting, while the Church of England would not have a parish or building for a generation, indicates the dominant philosophy of Albemarle in the 1660s and 1670s. And some planters would join cause against the common enemy of customs duties paid to a king. Even slave owners might protest that.[45]

AS DURANT, JENKINS, and the commonalty began to establish their republican commonwealth in Albemarle, Maryland, too, continued to attract radical thinkers. By early 1662, some Virginia Quakers were escaping persecution by moving into the area soon to be known as Somerset County, together with others hostile to the Cavalier old regime. A cooper named Stephen Horsey had been at the forefront of a movement on the Eastern Shore of Virginia back in 1652, when the locals had not merely declared their allegiance to the Commonwealth, but gone on to challenge the colonial government in Williamsburg. They would not pay taxes unless their small settlement was accorded representation: "That Llawe wch requireth & inioyneth Taxacons from us to bee Arbitrarye & illegall; fforasmuch as wee had neither summons for Ellecon of Burgesses nor voice in their Assemblye." The protest was known as the Northampton Oath of 1652, and the situation was settled by Bennett, who secured an act a few years later awarding Northampton with a great deal of local autonomy.[46] A few years later, Horsey referred to Virginian officeholders as "Asses and Villanes" in public hearings, "Endevoringe (as much as in him laye) to cause an Insurrection and Mutiney Against the Magistrates," and he quickly emerged as a leader in the new Somerset community.[47]

The region was claimed by both Virginia and Maryland at first; a local royalist grandee named Edmund Scarborough had designs on the lands and had some initial support from Berkeley. In the fall of 1663, he rode in with a Virginia militia to wrest power from Horsey and the Quakers, but met with a strong rebuff. "The quakers scoft and dispised" Scarborough's reading of a declaration of Virginia's authority, infuriating him. His scathing descriptions of the leaders in his report reminds us that the English Revolution had not been entirely squelched. Horsey, according to Scarborough, "a man

Repugnant to all Govmt," joined with associates such as George Johnson, "father of his Negro wenches bastards . . . hee now professeth quaking"; Thomas Price, a leather dresser, who "saith nothing else but that he would not obey Govmt"; Ambrose Dixon, a caulker, "a receiver of many quakers, his house the place of their Resort . . . averse to Govmt, for which he stands arrested . . . but bids defiance until severer course reforme him"; and Henry Boston, "a Rebell to Govment & disobedient to authority." Resistant not to all government, despite Scarborough's assertions, but only to one that favored lineage, they would prove successful in their defiance. Calvert intervened with Berkeley to protect his lands, and Scarborough was ordered to back off. Another safe spot for Quakers and Levelers had been secured.[48]

Horsey and Johnson secured the endorsement of Calvert for their positions as court officers, for the latter wanted the land held from Virginia's encroachments. George Fox spent time among them in 1672 before he arrived in Albemarle, preaching at meetings in the homes of Dixon and Johnson. By then, Dixon was also a justice in the local court, for he and the others were quite prepared to participate in a government of their own making.[49] Quakers and Levelers had grasped that they could create their own communities if they went to the liminal spaces at the edges of settlements, places that made travel awkward for authorities. A few even crossed into Delaware Bay, joining a Dutch Mennonite settlement. That area, the Whorekill district, would be claimed by the Dutch and later contested between Lord Baltimore and William Penn.[50] They might not overthrow the Stuarts or the House of Lords, but they could live as if those people had no power.

THE GERARD FAMILY certainly never surrendered their opposition to monarchical regimes. After the death of Susannah in 1666, Thomas Gerard had joined the rest of the Ingle's Rebellion settlers in Westmoreland County, Virginia, marrying Thomas Sturman's daughter Rose.[51] His daughter Temperance married Daniel Hutt, a ship captain with the decidedly anti-Stuart vessel *Mayflower*, who had conspired to bring about Fendall's republic.[52] Other daughters had married Ingle's rebels Broadhurst and Speke. In 1669, Elizabeth Gerard married Nehemiah Blakiston, son of the regicide John Blakiston, who fled to the Chesapeake when the Restoration government seized all the property of those who had sentenced Charles I.[53] When Robert Slye died in 1671, his widow, Gerard's oldest daughter, Susannah, remarried quickly, in the custom of the country. Her second husband was John Coode.[54] Mary wed Kenelm Cheseldyne. These three sons-in-law of

Susannah and Thomas Gerard would pick up the baton of republicanism and lead the struggle in Maryland through another generation.

Thomas Gerard died at his home in Virginia in 1673, but at his request, his body was taken to Maryland and interred beside Susannah. During his time in Westmoreland County, he made a new friend, Reverend John Waugh. Stafford County had been formed from the western portion of Westmoreland County in the early 1660s, just across the Potomac from Fendall's stomping grounds. Waugh, a Scottish nonconformist clergyman, became the minister shortly after. When he met the Gerard clan, he found a group who shared a common outlook. Waugh performed the marriage ceremony for Gerard's daughter Temperance and witnessed Thomas's 1672 will.[55] In the ensuing decades, Waugh would come to know the Maryland branches of the family and work with them to rid America of monarchical rule.

The Bushwood group and outliers in Somerset County Quaker meetings, in Virginia's Westmoreland and Stafford counties, and in North Carolina, were not the sole carriers of revolutionary desire. In Surry County, Virginia, a gathering of Lawnes Creek parishioners in late 1673 included a call to collectively resist paying taxes. Charles II had declared the third Anglo-Dutch War the previous year, rendering the Virginia tobacco fleet vulnerable to attack from the many Dutch vessels always in circulation around the Caribbean. Although Berkeley had collected fort taxes from the settlers, funds designated for the public defense, he had used those revenues for other purposes and allowed the defenses and munitions to deteriorate. Two British frigates fended off an attack by some Dutch men-o'-war in July 1673, but the incident highlighted Virginia's susceptibility, and Berkeley knew that the brutalities of the plantation system would not induce indentured servants to fight for their master or the Crown in the event of a more successful Dutch invasion. "Wee may reasonably expect upon any Small advantage the Enemy may gaine upon us, [our servants] wold revolt to them in hopes of bettering their Condition," he reported to England, begging desperately for military materiel. While Charles considered his request, Berkeley imposed a big increase in taxes on the settlers to fortify the colony.[56]

Infuriated by this latest demand for their money in tandem with gross corruption of previous payments, restlessness abounded in Virginia (so much so that the Council saw the need to write a letter to London defending Berkeley's performance in leadership). By December, a group of fourteen smallholders met to plan a tax strike, proclaiming that if necessary "we will burne all before one shall suffer." They were quickly hauled into court, where they "demeaned themselves of great stubbornness and contempt." Berkeley did not want to stoke any further discontent, however. All but the ringleaders were forgiven, and even the fines against those were later remitted.[57]

And down in Charles Town, South Carolina, where the proprietors sponsored Barbadian planters to establish a new colony on the Caribbean model, some with leveling tendencies did not take kindly to hierarchical order. Of all the colonies on the Eastern Seaboard, South Carolina would quickly become the most tiered of all, lorded over by an immensely powerful, wealthy, and brutal oligarchy. John Culpeper, a bright and literate young surveyor, had hired on to the experiment. When food shortages brought pain, he started to organize, "laying the designe & indeavouring to sett the poore people to plunder the rich," as authorities would tell the story. His plan stymied, and finding himself "in danger of hanging," Culpeper ran for cover in the summer of 1673 and found sanctuary among people of like mind in Albemarle.[58]

The hidden places also attracted those who did not have an explicit political agenda, but who deviated from social and cultural norms. Race and racism still fluctuated in meaning and practice in the seventeenth century, although the English had the most stringent demarcations of the European colonizers. For the lower orders to sleep with non-Europeans officially set them outside the pale, the civilized zone. For those who mixed with Indians, the price was exile, and many moved to Indian communities, lost to our records. But the areas on the periphery did not police such relationships. Batts, like many traders, had an Indian wife, and the Albemarle settlement's long tradition of peaceful coexistence may be due as much to that unnamed woman as to him. A 1700 report described the area as "peopled with English, intermixt with the native Indians to a great extent." Dr. Bray, the author of this report, never visited northern Carolina, but he did spend time in Maryland, and evidently this was Albemarle's reputation at the time.[59]

It was in this era that the royalist planters in Berkeley's House of Burgesses made the "Terrible Transformation": a commitment to a slave society. They reversed centuries of law and tradition when they designated that children would be "held bond or free only according to the condition of the mother," instead of inheriting their father's status.[60] As the Chesapeake planters committed to a racist slave society, the children of encounters between blacks and whites posed an enormous problem of categorization. Note how Scarborough accused George Johnson of Somerset County of fathering black children, perhaps indicating that Johnson did not hide or enslave his children. Anthony Johnson, the free black man whose story has been told often, moved into Somerset County in 1665, too, from Virginia's Eastern Shore and rented a large tract from Horsey, on a second Maryland river coincidentally called the Wicomico. This new community sheltered the last best hope for those who refused to conform to planter rules on religion, politics, or race.[61] Fox and Edmundson, so influential on these outlier settlements, discouraged the enslavement of others, and while Quakers around the colonies in decades to come would make their peace with slavery, most of the individuals who met Fox in 1672 resisted the economic incentive to twist their conscience.[62]

A slave society demanded a patriarchal society, just as Quaker women pushed gender boundaries in the opposite direction. Berkeley had been particularly concerned about Quaker women.[63] Status derived from one's mother led to severe controls on the bodies of servant white women so that they might not birth free black children and muddy the waters of racial slavery. But ignoring the rules applied to gender, too. Up the creeks and through the swamps at the frontier of colonial America, social behaviors considered scandalous in Boston and Williamsburg were intrinsic to everyday life. On Wicomico Creek, Susannah Gerard Slye Coode would demand a say. In her groundbreaking work on gender in eighteenth-century North Carolina, Kirsten Fischer argues that among the poorer settlers in that region existed "considerable tolerance for interracial socializing," including illicit sex. "Among both Indians and Quakers . . . women . . . had socially sanctioned channels of influence that appeared aberrant to people accustomed to English familial norms of subordinate wives and daughters."[64] Until 1715 (when North Carolina's new Anglican planter-dominated Assembly banned Quakers so that they could pass a rigid race code that severely penalized any white woman bearing a child of color), no rules prevented free men and women from sleeping with whom they pleased. Hannah Phelps no longer feared the whipping post when she led prayer meetings. Both Ann Durant and Johanna Jenkins took part in political and legal proceedings. The secretary's wife hitched up her skirts and pulled George Fox to the creek bank.

But those still in Berkeley's snare, however, continued to be confronted with a Cavalier regime that behaved as if the Commonwealth had never existed. They were close to the breaking point.

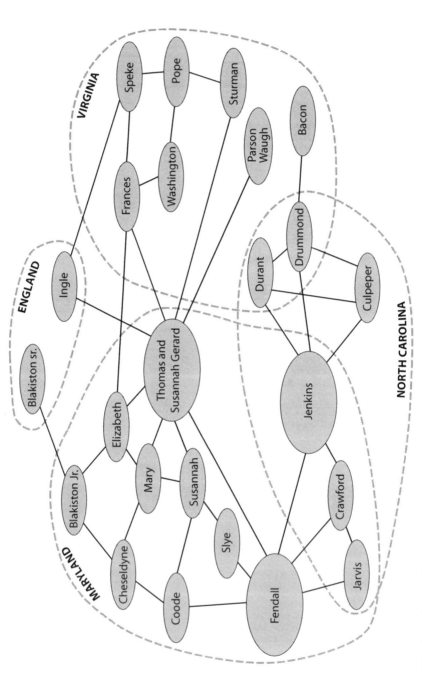

The Gerard network

CHAPTER FOUR

Revolution in the Chesapeake, 1675–1679

> We are accounted poor citizens, the patricians good. What
> authority surfeits on would relieve us: if they would yield us but
> the superfluity, while it were wholesome, we might guess they
> relieved us humanely; but they think we are too dear: the leanness
> that afflicts us, the object of our misery, is as an inventory to
> particularise their abundance; our sufferance is a gain to them. Let
> us revenge this with our pikes, ere we become rakes: for the gods
> know I speak this in hunger for bread, not in thirst for revenge.
>
> —SHAKESPEARE, *Coriolanus*

The poor citizens of Rome, as portrayed in Shakespeare's *Coriolanus*, describe
a circumstance common through many regions and many eras. The rich (the
patricians) present themselves as rewarded for excellence; they are a higher-
quality people. Their surfeit or superfluity would be more than enough to
relieve the suffering of those who lack, but instead of closing the gap by paying their workers more, they enjoy the gulf between themselves and others.
That status brings as much satisfaction as the material luxuries. But sometimes the people who do the hard work for little recompense say "Enough!"
Let us revenge this with our pikes, ere we become rakes. In the Chesapeake, this
moment came in the mid-1670s.

While radicals sought out safe spaces through the 1660s, Cavaliers cemented their control of the political machinery and the economy of Maryland and Virginia. Virginia's Berkeley and his cronies attempted to re-create
Restoration England in the Americas, a land where the oligarchy absorbed
all the spoils, piling layer after layer of taxes and fees upon the poorer settlers. With their tight control of the General Assembly and the county court
system, there seemed no avenue for redress. Only when a crack appeared
within the ruling group could the colonists grab the moment to seize their
colony and make their commonwealth. They came very close. But Virginia
was a royal colony, and the king needed those tobacco revenues; he could
not tolerate a republican democracy in a place so vital to his personal wealth
and power. His ship captains in Chesapeake Bay remained loyal and saved
the day for the Cavaliers. They could not control North Carolina, however,

and Generalissimo Jenkins and his mutinous band would fight more success-fully for their independence.

IN 1670, Charles Calvert, Lord Baltimore's son and heir, currently serving as Maryland's governor, added property qualifications to the franchise. Cal-vert was responding to the 1669 "Public Grievances," arguments put forward by the Lower House that a levy was collected "without the consent of the Free-men" and that "Privileged Attornys," sheriffs, and other colonial officials il-legally took excessive fees and seized property for debt. Calvert dismissed such complaints, arguing that he needed to raise money for defense expen-ditures and that this was another attempt to undermine the proprietor's rights. "Whatsoever he lawfully doth by power of his Pattent must not be Styled a Grievance unless You mean to quarrel with the King who granted it," he explained, as he and his Council refused to make any changes to the fee structure. The following year, the poorest men were disenfranchised.[1]

This suddenly shut out landless men from the political system just as the numbers of such men were growing fast. The previous two decades had seen a big rise in the numbers of immigrants, and now they were surviving their term of indenture and asking for their freedom dues. If they had been prom-ised land, they would get none of the prime acreage along the rivers of the settled areas, for that had all been claimed by the councilors. They would be forced to work as laborers, and lose their vote—as at least one-third of all the freemen would over the next generation—or venture onto the frontier to face hostile Indians and fend for themselves.[2]

The Quakers of Maryland began to organize. After the visits of Fox and Edmundson, the Friends felt it imperative that they follow the rule forbid-ding the swearing of oaths, which shut them out from a variety of legal pro-cedures, such as serving as guardians and executing wills. They made appeals to Baltimore, explaining their theological position and requesting an exemp-tion whereby they could subscribe their loyalty by signature, but to no avail. So they organized themselves, carefully selecting candidates who would champion their interests in the Assembly, which did not normally require an oath. Quakers throughout the Chesapeake thus became influential be-yond their numbers over the next decades, for they were literate and politi-cally shrewd. Although the Quakers of future generations might become conservative, this first generation remained radical for the most part, refus-ing to acknowledge the hierarchy of birth.[3]

This occurred just as the Calverts attempted to tighten control on some of the outliers. In 1673, Baltimore ordered a troop to take out the settlements of the Whorekill, in present-day Delaware, for they did not hold warrants issued by Maryland. The cruelty visited upon both Dutch and English was recalled later, as something not yet seen by settlers.

> Baltimore sent a Company of horsemen in number about fortye under the Command of Cap Thomas Howell whoe came into the Whoorekill Towne with swords drawn; And threatened & Terrified the Inhabitents whoe being frighted thereby submitted to them. After that they kild many of the Inhabitents Cattle; and when they had bene here about forteene days Cap Howell went to the Lord Baltimore as he pretended to Aquaint him that the Inhabitents of this place was poor and not able to maintaine soe many souldgers . . . when the Inhabitents ware Come together the said Cap Howell Told them that he must tell them with Greife that his orders from the Lord Baltimore was that he must burne all their houses and that he must not Leave one stick standing; . . . And that he was to give but one quarter of an hour warning before he did it. Soe Immediately the houses ware by them sett on fire and Burnt downe to the Ground; . . . sume women very big with Child and others made their Addrass to Cap Howell and Intreated him to spare one hous for their Releife in distrasse; the said Cap Howell Answered that he must obsarve his orders and that he could spare non.[4]

FROM THE BEGINNING OF representative government in Virginia, the die had been cast that power would stay in the hands of the richest few. The largest planters created a class-conscious legal system and then presided over the courts: the lower the social rank of the perpetrator, the more degrading and physical the punishment. The planters exercised another layer of control through lay parish vestries. Over the decades, intermarried families constructed a Virginian gentry, and gradually considered themselves entitled to act as nobility, commanding the deference of all beneath. They carved up the best lands and established their plantations, ruling a thinly fed labor force of servants and enslaved workers as feudal lords might have done.[5]

In the desire for a competency, many in Virginia felt that the best bad option was to move as far away from Jamestown as possible. Some headed into the Dismal Swamp, and further south into Albemarle. For those who ventured to the north and west of Jamestown, that meant dealing with the Susquehannocks, the Piscataways, and the Doegs, who occupied or hunted in those lands. Officials of both Maryland and Virginia had signed treaties of peace and trade with certain groups, but settlers who moved onto frontier lands did not necessarily honor such agreements and alliances. Pushed out by the big planters, competition for land led many to see all Indians as enemies. Still, their biggest problems were not the native warriors, but the men of English origin who governed them.

The same pattern that Maryland's 1669 Public Grievances described was magnified in Virginia, where the firmly entrenched oligarchy had welcomed back Berkeley and run rampant through the 1660s and early 1670s in their enrichment on the backs of the taxpayer. As the Virginian political system evolved out of the Starving Times, office-holding at the local level "was a badge of success that symbolized arrival at the head of Virginia society." From councilors to burgesses, sheriffs to justices of the peace, "a mazy patchwork of kin . . . enveloped Virginia's political establishment," and the holding of multiple offices simultaneously was not uncommon.[6]

The corruption of this oligarchy after the Restoration was unchecked, in terms of land acquisition, treatment of servants, and taxation through an array of levies and fees due officeholders. Burgesses and officials at the county level had an exemption to such taxes; instead they enjoyed the money for expenses and in fees for the multiple offices they held. Nepotism abounded. "Wee are much Greeved that the major pt of the Commissioners of our County Court are men of a Consanguinity," complained the poor men of Henrico County, as they sought a voice in the assessment of local taxes. They demanded that "at least six of the Comonalty"—specifically representatives of their class—play a role in decisions of levies. A particular anger was directed at the poll tax, which demanded the same payment of every man, whether rich or poor. Rappahanock County called for a land tax, "according to the Estate of the Inhabitants," but given the power of the establishment, this would remain a dream. "Oppressive in amount, misappropriated in practice, the tax burden was doubled by the Berkeleyan method of assessment," explains historian Stephen Webb; the justices reckoned a low value on the tobacco poor men brought in and then sold it for twice the price they had judged it to be worth.[7]

Surely not coincidentally, Berkeley's Assembly made exactly the same move as Maryland's Calvert to remove the propertyless from the electoral rolls in 1670. In Virginia, the percentage of men who lost their right to vote was even greater. And once even more were disenfranchised, the taxation ran amok. Levies to pay for fort construction made no sense in the first place, given the mobility of the Susquehannocks, Piscataways, or Seneca, but to add insult to injury, the forts were poorly built; the money was totally wasted. A new poll tax of sixty pounds of tobacco, most of which went straight into Berkeley's pocket, "a Pressure that occasioned the first discontents among the people," threatened to break them. The purpose of this new levy was not explained. The king had granted ownership of the Northern Neck to some favorites in England to Berkeley's dismay, and he felt that the most efficient way to deal with this headache was to tax the poor and buy out these new proprietors. But he considered it "treason" for the people of Virginia to dare "enquire what use [the levy] was for."[8]

IN THE SUMMER OF 1675, Metacomet of the Wampanoags brought a pan-Algonquian alliance to war with the New England colonies. During the conflict, better known as King Philip's War, the Indians wreaked havoc on the outlying towns of Massachusetts Bay and Plymouth colonies all summer long. As reports reached the South, rumors fed on fears, and the threat of an organized attack by Indians against all European settlers seemed very real. A small tit-for-tat set of attacks between Thomas Mathew and some Doeg Indians escalated when a militia troop rushed to seek revenge and killed over twenty Susquehannocks, allies of Virginia, instead of Doegs.[9]

The frontier was on edge. Susquehannock response was relatively muted; pressure on them from the Seneca and their Iroquois brethren meant that the Virginia alliance had to be maintained to guarantee arms and ammunition. The revenge killing necessary to their honor was limited to only half a dozen Potomac-area settlers that summer, but given the news from New England, many felt that a full-scale war was imminent, and some took it upon themselves to launch a preemptive strike. In September, a combined force of Maryland and Virginia militia rendezvoused at the Susquehannock fort between the Potomac and Piscataway Creek. Despite the Susquehannock leadership producing evidence of their commitment to a peaceful outcome, the militia commanders killed the chiefs under a white flag and laid siege to their fort.[10]

They would not succeed in defeating the Susquehannocks, who moved seemingly invisibly in and out of the fort, attacking their besiegers and then escaping en masse one night, shifting their home that winter to the Piedmont of northern Carolina. From there, they would seek satisfaction upon the English who lived at the westernmost points of settlement and then ask Berkeley to renew "the ancient League of amety" in February 1676. Meanwhile, Berkeley struggled to keep a general war from breaking out, as his subjects in other exposed parts of the colony requested authority and ammunition to attack Indians in their localities.[11]

One of these subjects was a recently arrived young man named Nathaniel Bacon, a well-to-do Englishman with kinship to Lady Berkeley. Another of

Bacon's kin, however, had served Cromwell through the Revolution, so while Berkeley had spent the 1650s safely ensconced on his Virginia tobacco plantation, Bacon had been exposed to radical ideas and rhetoric through his childhood. He was not exactly an egalitarian, but he could see that birth alone did not determine ability and that here in the New World, a man could perhaps make his own destiny. He opted to begin his new life in Henrico County, and while the Susquehannocks were under siege, Bacon stirred up discord with the Appomattox to his governor's great chagrin, "it beeing donne at this time when all the Country was all Armed by a feare and Jelouise that all the Indians were conspired against us." Bacon sensed that his neighbors appreciated his bold action, and while he apologized that fall to Berkeley, when the Susquehannocks began their January campaign against the poor planters in the outer reaches of settlement, he stood ready to organize a frontier militia with or without approval.[12]

Berkeley called the assemblymen to Jamestown in March to announce his defense policy, which included the construction of forts and limited militia officers' powers to matters of defense, without granting them any initiative. To the overtaxed, and not merely those living on the frontier, this sounded like another fort tax to line the pockets of Berkeley's cronies, "a great Grievance, Juggle and cheat, and of noe more use or service to them," exploiting instead of protecting. For many, it was the final straw. The smallholders and those who labored on their farms decided to organize their own forces. Bacon was recruited as commander by disgruntled neighbors who brought him to Jordan's Point to meet up with the volunteer troop, composed of men from Charles City and Henrico Counties.[13] But elsewhere, men were mutinying against the government for reasons other than the Indian threat. In Nansemond County, the "Commonalty" refused to cooperate with their gentry commanders who were ordering them to build houses on the gentry land, "intitul'd Forts." As both commanders and the militiamen knew well, the Susquehannocks could only be "destroy'd by a moving force," so when the local officials flagrantly directed the fort tax to be spent on buildings on their own lands, poorer men had had enough.[14]

Bacon raised men in the surrounding region, and they marched off "against the Indians," provoking the fury of Berkeley. Whatever Berkeley's corruption, he was right to be angry at Bacon for taking it upon himself to lead such a campaign. Bacon led his force south into the Carolina piedmont and met up with friendly Occaneechees who agreed to attack the Susquehannock post nearby. Their success in that enterprise did not bring them Bacon's gratitude; instead, the Virginians also slaughtered the Occaneechees.

Afraid of a general war, and aghast at Bacon's personal flouting of his authority, Berkeley marched out from Jamestown to try to arrest him and prevent further escalation. But the expedition did not find Bacon; instead, during his travels around the colony, Berkeley finally became aware of the level of unrest directed at his government. "In every part the Rabble so threatened the better sort of people that they durst not sterr out of their houses," he told a friend.[15]

He acknowledged the "too great complaints" about the fact that he had not held fresh elections since 1660, and dissolved the House of Burgesses, calling for an election in late May, even offering to resign should the new Assembly think it wise. The 1670 disenfranchisement of the poor would not be enforced everywhere, it turned out; even the Council advised Berkeley that "al the freemen should have Votes." And in the counties bordering on Albemarle, "every free borne mans voat was hear'd in Election." Although Berkeley's proclamation of Bacon as a rebel was read at the polling place, the Henrico electorate declared him as their representative.[16]

Bacon had other officeholders in his camp, men like James Crewes, William Byrd, and Richard Lawrence. William Drummond, the original governor of Albemarle, who had also served as one of the dreaded sheriffs, declared his allegiance. Their motivations are murky; perhaps some hoped to ride the popular wave of protest into high office. Others were true believers, like Drummond and his wife. Lawrence had already shown himself to be a man willing to scoff at social rules. Some carried letters from Bacon to Berkeley in the weeks between the election and the Assembly's first meeting, in which Bacon pleaded that he had nothing but loyalty to Berkeley, but that action had been desperately needed against the Indians and was therefore "just." Those who lived further from Jamestown had some sense of the mutinous atmosphere building around the colony in the 1670s and thought it wise to join the side with the most men. Factions within the planter elite also accounted for part of the trouble. The alliance between the poor and most of these men, however, would hold until their deaths.[17]

The Assembly met in Jamestown in June, and with the burgesses came the grievances of the colony's settlers. From Nansemond County, the cry was for justice, not for Indian war. "The great oppression . . . is the Unequall way of taxing them by the poles for that a poor man that hath nothing to maintain himself wife & child pays as much for his levie as he that hath 2000 acres of Land." Meanwhile, as the burgesses and county sheriffs billed them for their official expenses, they pointed out that the people of Virginia had been pushed to breaking point, and "began to Mutinie in the year 1674." This may be a reference to Lawnes Creek, but Berkeley had also mentioned that he had "appeas'd two mutinies" in 1675.[18]

The gathering of the Assembly in the first week of June also brought the showdown between Berkeley and Bacon. The latter approached Jamestown with a troop of fifty men, but was captured and forced to beg forgiveness on his knees. Both men thought that might be an end to the matter, but they had not reckoned with the anger of the poorer sort. "An incredible Number of the meanest of the People were every where Armed to assist him and his cause," the governor discovered when some of that number converged on Jamestown to plead with Bacon to join their rebellion. He left town under cover of darkness to amass his force and prepare strategy.[19]

Frightened now, Berkeley and his councilors understood that the burgesses in the Assembly must address the grievances they had heard at election time. They passed immediate reform of local government, stripping away many of the privileges of sheriffs and magistrates, cutting fees, and insisting officials pay their share. The commonalty had to be included in decisions about county levies. But they also praised Berkeley's leadership and revoked none of his power to punish rebels, including the hundreds currently mustering with Bacon.[20]

Bacon and his "file of Fusilleers" marched up to the statehouse, where he publicly demanded a military commission. Berkeley stormed out with his councilors, baring his chest and daring Bacon to shoot him, then marching past him to his home. Bacon and some went after him; others threatened the burgesses of the Lower House to grant the commission. By the weekend, both burgesses and mutineers had departed, the latter group now with a commander in chief, "Generall Bacon."[21]

July 1676 saw both sides attempt to build their armed forces, Bacon with more success than the old governor. News of the Assembly's reforms failed to spread thoroughly, or perhaps a fear that Berkeley might veto them meant that hundreds joined Bacon, while Berkeley pondered how tough it was to govern a place "where six parts of seaven at least are Poore Endebted Discontented and Armed," unlike old England, where the absence of the last of those qualities allowed the one-seventh to exploit the rest.[22] He might have added that some were enslaved and some were female, for as the rebellion developed, those with the most to gain became the most fervent supporters. One historian claims, "Women led both the Berkeleyan and Baconian camps." Sarah Weeks of Charles City County drew the hate of those whose authority she dared question in very gendered ways: "an Idle infamous slutt," they called her, while the organizing work of Sarah Grendon, "the first great incourager and setter on of the Ignorant Vulger," had Berkeley wanting to hang her. Drummond's wife, too, would play a part in riling up the rebels. "The child that is unborn shall have cause to rejoice for the good that will come by the rising of the country," she told those who feared the risk of rebellion. Mary Chisman's daughter-in-law Lydia confessed later that she had been the instigator of her husband's actions with Bacon. The enslaved joined such women. In the 1670s the differences between servants and slaves were not yet fully legislated, but Berkeley's most loyal men, those rewarded with lucrative public offices, had converted to enslaving their workforce. Captives left the plantations of the Gloucester County elite and joined Bacon's forces.[23]

Berkeley rode to Gloucester County to summon the militia, but found them unwilling to follow orders. And upon hearing of Berkeley's attempt, Bacon led his men back from the frontier to Middle Plantation, where the goal of his operation switched from reducing Indians to reducing the governor. This required a statement capable of winning over both Virginia's farmers and the king, who otherwise might demand Bacon's head. So on July 30, "sincerely to aime at his Majesty's Honour and the Publick good," the rebels drew up a manifesto and list of grievances, foreshadowing the Preamble and Declaration of another Virginian a century later. Filled with protestations of loyalty to the king, the manifesto argued that Berkeley was the traitor in his protection of the Indians, who should be regarded as "enemies to the King and Country, Robbers and Theeves and Invaders of his Majesty's Right and our Interest and Estates." And to his fellow Virginians who might as yet be undecided as to who to support, "Wee appeale to the Country itselfe what and of what nature their Oppressions have bin or by what Caball and mistery the designes of many of those whom wee call great men." Nothing was held back in this class warfare. "See what spounges have suckt up the publique Treasure," the rebels proclaimed, "and wither it hath not bin privately contrived away by unworthy Favourites and juggling Parasites."

They enumerated the specifics of the charges. "For haveing upon specious pretences of publiqe works raised greate unjust Taxes upon the Comonality for the advancement of private Favorits," began the Declaration of the People, the justification for the overthrow of the government of Virginia. Echoing the county grievances, "for haveing abused and rendred contemptable the Magistrates of Justice, by advanceing to places of Judicature, scandalous and Ignorant favorites," read the second grievance, again pointing out the administration's corruption, this time at the local level. The Declaration turned to the matter of the Indians, charging Berkeley for sacrificing the welfare of frontier settlers to his "Monopoly of the Beaver trade," enriching himself in a manner that emboldened Indians to attack settlers. And now, although the Assembly had granted Bacon his commission, the governor had refused to accept it and instead had come to Gloucester County to summon forces, "even against the consent of the people, for the raiseing and effecting civill warr and distruction," so Bacon had had to bring his army back, leaving the "most weake Exposed Places" open to Indian attack, to confront him. "Of this and the aforesaid Articles we accuse Sir William Berkeley as guilty of each and every one of the same, and as one who hath traiterously attempted, violated and Injured his Majesties interest here, by a loss of a greate part of this his Colony and many of his exposed to the Incursions and murther of the heathen."[24]

The Crown would have to make sense of these arguments, to consider that in fact royal governor Berkeley and his cronies, "his wicked and pernicious councellours Confederates, aiders, and assisters against the Comonality in these our Civill comotions," were the rebels against His Majesty's government and interests. How likely was that to be considered credible in London, once the smoke cleared? More likely if the rebels won and could control the narrative. Giles Bland was in charge of customs collection and had already argued that the Navigation Acts were not properly enforced by the governor. Back in April he had warned the governor that the people were restless and sent him a petition of their grievances, and now he joined Bacon. As Bland himself pointed out to Berkeley, Virginia "affords more then a hundred Thousand Pounds of yearely Revenue to his Majestie." Should Bland persuade His Majesty that Berkeley or his corrupt oligarchy had cost his personal purse, the rebels had hope of England's support of their overthrow of the Virginia government.[25]

But whose version of events would reach England first? While some of Bacon's force successfully seized Berkeley's pride and joy, Green Springs Manor, and some took to redistributing the ill-gotten gains of his friends in Gloucester County, others rode the colony recruiting support. Some marched against the Pamunkey Indians and seized some prisoners. Bland and a mariner named William Carver from the Albemarle border region, however, moved to prevent Berkeley or his supporters' escape to England with any narrative that might paint them the villains to the king. The major disadvantage of the rebel force would now be exposed, for while they could hold the land, they would find themselves weaker on water than Berkeley's side. While Berkeley, who had been hiding on the Eastern Shore, faux-negotiated with Carver, Philip Ludwell, the most haughty of all the oligarchy, seized Bland and the boat. Carver swung, an early martyr.[26]

September 1676 brought a showdown between Bacon and Berkeley, as the latter's navy sailed into Jamestown and the rebels scattered before they could be taken. Many of Bacon's force had gone home after a hot summer's marching. Now, to regroup quickly after receiving the news of the fall of Jamestown, the general needed some alternative tactics. He paraded the Pamunkey captives visibly as they approached the town, to prove his credentials as a man representing the smallholders; he had men kidnap "some of the prime Gent: Women," wives of Berkeley's loyalists, to use them as a human shield; and he made America's first Emancipation Proclamation: like Dunmore a century later, Bacon offered freedom "to all Servants and Negros" who would join up to overthrow Virginia's planter elite. By 1676, on the plantations of Virginia's officeholders, the enslaved outnumbered servants. Join up they did.[27]

Bacon's small force built trenches as fortifications and from those positions easily pushed Berkeley's men out of Jamestown; perhaps few fought with any great passion for the governor. As more Baconites arrived as reinforcements, the planters' army shrank, for most had been "compell'd and hired into his service," and in mid-September, Berkeley retreated to the bay. Then word came that Giles Brent was leading a force from the north on the governor's behalf. Bacon gathered his officers, and the decision was made to destroy Jamestown rather than find themselves trapped in the town. When their soldiers hesitated, Richard Lawrence and William Drummond carried the flaming torches to their own homes. The emblems of the state, the courthouse and the Anglican church, burned as Bacon and his men made their way back to Berkeley's Green Spring.[28]

Brent's force, instead of coming to Berkeley's rescue, "were all run away"; again, the great planters could not summon any deference. They would not fight to save "his [Berkeley's] vallour, or estate."[29] Nowhere in Virginia would the smallholders defend their government. Bacon's men were spread throughout the colony, holding forts and administering an oath of loyalty to the new regime.

But the Chesapeake region was a riverine world, and as the radicals began to believe their dream of a level playing field might really spread across the colony, English ship captains converged in the bay and offered their services to Berkeley. He quickly organized one group to police the York River, and another the James. And at this crucial juncture, Nathaniel Bacon suddenly died. "Verginias foes, to whom for secrit crimes just vengeance owes disarved [deserved] plagues, dreding their just disart [desserts,] Corrupted Death by Parasscellcian art, Him to destroy," the angry elegy read, accusing the oligarchy of creating alchemy to bring down the rebellion.[30]

The rebellion did not end; John Ingram, Lawrence, and Drummond, among others, continued the fight for several more months from their strongholds around the colony. While the Berkeley regime captured Tindall's Point near Jamestown in November, they were pushed back in December along the James and in Gloucester County, which remained in rebel hands. Now Captain Thomas Grantham stepped in to save Virginia for Berkeley. The Englishman played the part of mediator, visiting Ingram's garrison and warning them that a serious force was under sail from England. The rebels would be wise to set down their arms, "lest by persisting in this open Hostility, you force them at last to be sheathed in your own bowels," and let the king judge the merits of the case against Berkeley's management of Virginia. The negotiations continued through the New Year, until Ingram surrendered, presumably with promise of a fair hearing.[31]

Lawrence and Drummond held out on the south side of the York River, less likely to trust Berkeley's word. So too did a group of hundreds of enslaved laborers and servants, to whom liberty was not some vague notion. Grantham conned them into their capture. As Lawrence and Drummond witnessed the rebellion peter out in the threat of the Royal Navy's arrival, they tried to slip away. William Byrd turned in Drummond to save his own skin; the latter was summarily hanged. Richard Lawrence would never be caught. We can imagine that he and his true love, an enslaved black woman, found safety in a frontier space.[32]

The revenge of the Berkeley oligarchy was swift and merciless. Men swung from gallows all over the colony, while the estates of any who had joined Bacon's campaign were seized to the benefit of the loyalists. One proud rebel declared at his trial, "It is well known that I have no kindness for Kings. They have no rights but what they gott by Conquest and the Sword, and he that can by force of the Sword deprive them thereof, has as good and just a Title to it as the King himself." This republican, proven right by William of Orange eleven years later, could not be allowed to live in 1677. Sarah Drummond, on the other hand, lost her husband, but not her fighting spirit. She would sue the Berkeleys and win, regaining control of the property they seized. But despite some effort by the Crown's commissioners investigating the rebellion to draw attention to the worst of the Berkeley-era corruption and taxation, not much eased in the lives of poor Virginians. Married women like Lydia Chisman faced new punishing legislation; any wife who encouraged rebellion would from 1677 on be whipped. (Women had the extra humiliation of being stripped to the waist for such public disciplines.) The right to vote for all freemen was never reinstated, and in sum, "the county elites lost or yielded nothing to the commonalty."[33]

"BUT I . . . AM CONFIDENT of it that it is the mind of this country, and of Maryland, and Carolina also to cast off their governors . . . and if we cannot prevail by arms to make our conditions for peace, or obtain the privilege to elect our own governor, we may retire to Roanoke."[34]

So declared Bacon when the rebellion had begun. Back in the summer of 1676, the radicals of Maryland and the Albemarle had interacted with Bacon, Drummond, and the others. John Culpeper, the young firebrand from Charleston, connected with Drummond, reminding him that he had written in 1667 that Albemarle was attractive to those who were "weary of Sir William's Government." They would offer a safe house to any who needed it. But Fendall and others up in Maryland thought the moment had come to take more deliberate action.[35]

Across the Patuxent River from St. Mary's lay Calvert County, home to another nest of Quakers and democracy. Inspired by Virginia's Declaration of the People, a group of militiamen drew up their own manifesto for the reform of Maryland and Calvert's clique, and quickly built support in the area known as the Clifts. "Never Body was more repleat with Malignancy and Frenzy then our people were about August last, and they wanted but a monstrous head to their monstrous body" was how Deputy Governor Thomas Notley described the popular discontent. The main grievances concerned high and unfair taxes, but especially representation, demanding that all elected representatives be allowed to take their seats, but beyond that they sought a democratic franchise. "The great Clamour is against the greatnes of the Taxes; the debarring of some ffreemen who have nothing to Entitle themselves to a being in this Province, from voting in the Choice of the Delegates for makeing of the Lawes, & lastly that those poore ffreemen are Obliged to pay taxes equall with the rich." Maryland's poll tax had been means-tested before 1650, but no longer. And while at first it was small—in 1663 it amounted to 25 pounds of tobacco per worker—in 1675 the levy soared to 165 pounds each, with an increase in 1676. This had been approved after the disenfranchisement of so many.[36]

On September 3, "with fforce & Terror of Armes" sixty men gathered, led by William Davis and others, determined to press the governor and the Council to grant their demands. This was not in secret. Notley sent them a message, trying to defuse the situation. He offered to have their grievances discussed at the next Assembly, but given the success of the rebels in Virginia, the men of the Clifts would not settle so easily. Notley fumed, "they did from thence march away with drummes beateing & Collours flying . . . though they have since with drawne & dispersed themselves & lye lurkeing till they can find a fitter Opportunity to worke Out their wicked & malitious designes."[37]

Notley had to admit that Davis and his allies had touched a nerve; the following day, he offered a general pardon to anyone but the leadership who might stand down. Gerard's sons-in-law on Wicomico Creek were not involved with this uprising, but they observed with empathy:

> Witness the Insurrection at the Clifts occasioned by his Lordspps
> Writts of Elleccon comanding Four Representatives for each County
> to be elected as an Assembly out of which Four, his Lordspp afterwards called only two that he thought most fitt for his Interest to be an
> Assembly who laid the greatest Levy upon the People that ever was
> laid in that Province. Which they refused to pay as not being laid
> by their legall Representatives and for which three of them were
> condemned and two of them executed.[38]

Davis and another ringleader, Pate, were caught and quickly hanged, for Notley, too, had learned from Virginia that such sedition must be nipped. Should the men of the Clifts ally with Fendall and his democrats, let alone the rebels to the south, rule by the planter elite of the Chesapeake stood in serious jeopardy. Notley did not dare call for elections.

While he pondered the construction of control mechanisms, the news came of Bacon's death, followed soon by reports that an English armada had set sail. The tide turned in Berkeley's favor. Notley could breathe. He issued a Remonstrance addressing the grievances, claiming that defense costs necessitated the levies, while "the mutiny & Rebellion of Davis & his Complices" only made costs soar. He denied that any of the taxes enriched officials. As for the recent disenfranchisement of the landless freemen, "what man in England can be admitted to the Election of Parliament men that hath not a visible Estate in land or Goods?" But even this he would discuss with Baltimore. A more equitable tax burden he dismissed. "But put the case itt be hard the poore ffreeman should pay as much for his head, as the Rich man doth for his owne head." Notley considered the question ridiculous. Why would Maryland be different than anywhere else in the English Empire? He finished with a warning that any public disturbances would not be tolerated. Given the summary executions of Davis and Pate, this could not be ignored. Notley would not let Maryland go the way of "the distressed & miserable Condicon of our Neighbour Colony torne in peeces under the maske of publique Reformacon & ease from taxes."[39]

For the Levelers of Maryland, who sought to give landless men a say in their own government, this was another blow and demanded a fresh approach. The king and Parliament would support Baltimore's social hierarchy—they were sending an armada to Berkeley's aid—but perhaps an appeal on religious grounds might work. Oppression of poor people in England or Virginia little troubled the aristocrats. But oppression by a Catholic was another matter. To this end, they framed a pamphlet, *Complaint from Heaven*, presenting Baltimore's regime as a papist oligarchy willing to use the assistance of Indians to subjugate Protestant Englishmen. Surely Parliament would intervene against "the Cabinet of Popish Maryland"? The pamphlet charged Baltimore with murder, responsible for all the deaths inflicted by Indians over the past few years, but also addressed the "great taxes" that lined the pockets of his cronies; like those imposed by Berkeley, the levies supposedly provided for defense, but "little or nothing came forth." Corruption rather than mismanagement accounted for such failures. Meanwhile the people of the Whorekill had suffered terribly when his troops had been forced to "leave poore weemen with child naked, to the mercy of a desperate hard winter when no botes nor reliefe could com to them."[40]

The author, often suspected to be Fendall himself, cited various laws of the Assembly and explained to the audience how the Calverts manipulated elections and offices, and "the poore Country payes every time," not merely in defense levies, but in sinecures. "An item for chancellors fees; item secretary fees etc: and the more Assemblies the oftener it goes about, all dae thy nothing els, but augment fees upon fees." The *Complaint* argued that all was underlaid by Baltimore's putting his own authority over that of the king. The Charter had authorized Baltimore to civilize the Indians, "not to make himselfe . . . an absolute prince over the King's freeborn Subjects off England." Not that most Maryland settlers had fine lineage: "Wee confess a great many of us came in servants to others, but wee adventured owr lives for it, and got owr poore living with hard labour out of the ground in a terrible Willdernis." Yet the Catholic grandees seized lands to establish towns, "without commons or possibility for poore people to live in." Echoing the Diggers of the English Revolution as they decried enclosures, the *Complaint* called out the process of primitive accumulation, whereby the few seized land and kept others, who might otherwise have grown their own food, poor and dependent. The papist Baltimore rewarded those Protestant

"Turne-Coates" who sold out their fellow settlers, such as Notley, "for having bespoke the said 2 shilling custo pr hogshead to my Lords Heyre . . . and made it hereditary appears now owr own Deputy's Deputy Governor."

Citing the era of Ingle, when the proprietor was forced to bear the costs of government in peace and war, the author of the *Complaint* explained how that act was repealed, leading to levy after levy, taking money from the colonists and placing it in the hands of the Calverts. Referencing the execution of Davis, done "onely to terrify others," the writer poured scorn on the "paternall" remonstrance. Baltimore and his Council "make us and owr wyffs and children crye, flye, trye, pye, paye, suffer and curss you for it." The people were willing to pay any taxes actually necessary for the country, but not "to maintain my Lord and his Champions in their prince-ship." Here, he echoed Bacon's anger at Berkeley's "juggling Parasites." Despite all the levies, life in Maryland remained precarious, with farmers bringing their weapons to their fields in case of Indian attack, something the "Grandees about St. Marys" never had to fear. So much for paternalism. Instead they had executed Davis and "prevailed with the Virginians to hange their best comon wealths men." So the plea to England: "Our great King and Parliament . . . are wee Rebells because wee will not submit to their arbitrary government and entangle our innocent posterity under that tyrannicall yoake of papacy?"[41]

The *Complaint* fell on deaf ears in London. But Fendall had tapped into a motivating tool for those Marylanders who might be deferential to the class status of the Calverts, or merely frightened of their power. Fighting papists, especially those who appeased Indians, could be sold as a patriotic act rather than a rebellious one. Overthrowing the government if it was Catholic, he argued, could be defended in England, while Bacon's Rebellion could only be interpreted as sedition against a royal governor. So Fendall adapted his rhetoric. For the next fifteen years, the radicals of Wicomico Creek would entangle their democratic aspirations for self-government and a wide franchise with religious justifications. Between allegiance to the identities of class or race lay that of faith. It was a very powerful inducement.

Notley, however, could report that he had pacified Maryland. He smugly judged himself a better ruler than Berkeley, for although the Virginia governor retook the reins, "I feare the warme weather when it comes may produce another swarme, that may have as venomous stings, as the late [traitors] had. . . . There must be an alteration though not of the Government yet in the Government, new men must be put in power, the old ones will never agree with the common people, and if that be not done, his Majtie in my opinion will never find a well setled Government in that Colony."[42]

Southward, the Albemarle settlers had quickly squelched a couple of law and order types who had tried to impose a regime similar to the planter oligarchies of Maryland and Virginia. In the fall of 1675, Thomas Eastchurch had claimed the governorship, established a Council including a newcomer named Thomas Miller, locked up John Jenkins, and instituted tax collection. After helping her husband elude trial, Johanna Jenkins combined with George Durant and John Culpeper to plot how to rid Albemarle of the new men. With popular support, "Generalissime" Jenkins sent Eastchurch and Miller packing, Miller to Virginia to face trumped-up charges of treason, and Eastchurch to England, where Miller soon joined him.[43]

Meanwhile, as the events in Virginia unfolded, Culpeper and others escorted Miller to Virginia for his trial, contacting the leadership of Bacon's Rebellion, for Drummond had been a friend to Albemarle. Bacon knew that the Great Dismal Swamp would prove too formidable a barrier for Berkeley's forces, and so with the rebellion strong in the counties along the southern border, he reminded his forces that Carolina would be a safe place. Indeed, as the Royal Commissioners reported in July 1677, "not only men's Servants, butt also Runaway Rouges and Rebells fly to Carolina on the Southward as their common Subterfuge and lurking place; and when wee remanded some of the late Rebells by letters could not have them sent back to us."[44] Jenkins was not going to extradite his fellow democrats.

The residents of Albemarle, under Jenkins, were not subject to the corrupt fees and the heavy tax burden of their neighbors; the only "tax" they normally paid was owed to the king, in the form of an export custom duty on tobacco. (The rebels of Virginia's Lower Norfolk County had declared such duties a burden, and their request for an exemption from customs brought the response that it was "wholly mutinous to desire anything contrary to his Majesties Royall pleasure and benefitt.")[45] The rather mutinous Albemarle people, however, avoided paying those duties in collaboration with half a dozen traders from Boston whose small vessels could navigate the dangerous slipping sands of the Outer Banks waterways and who happily smuggled the tobacco to customers abroad. Appointed customs officials, such as Valentine Bird, winked at boats coming in and out. As all within the community benefited, no matter their economic or political position, and with the proprietors' attention remaining firmly fixed on Charles Town, no one had feared any change in their business practices.[46]

But in London, Miller and Eastchurch impressed upon the proprietors that power in their colony now lay in the hands of disreputable men who conspired with New England men. They talked their way into government posts with lucrative fees. Bacon's Rebellion had been crushed by the time Miller made his way back to Albemarle in the summer of 1677. Eastchurch delayed his arrival when he met and decided to woo a rich widow in the Caribbean. He deputized Miller as governor in addition to the role of customs collector. Upon his landing, Miller showed his official papers and seized the reins of power. Assessing a heavy poll tax, as in the colonies to the north, he grabbed enormous amounts of tobacco, goods, and monies in the name of the king and for his administration of the colony. He also refused to call an Assembly, but if he thought that prevented the people of Albemarle from organizing protests, he was much mistaken.[47]

Jenkins, his Maryland ally William Crawford, Culpeper, and others planned the overthrow of Miller. George Durant spent the fall of 1677 in England, but sailed back on December 1 with one of Albemarle's favorite New England traders, Captain Zachariah Gillam. Gillam carried weapons as well as other trade goods, and with his help and that of other traders, the residents burst first into the home of Timothy Biggs, one of Miller's deputies, and then into Miller's house, and seized all the records of his office and the men themselves, locking them on Gillam's boat.[48] There they wrote their version of Bacon's Declaration:

The Remonstrance of the Inhabitants off Paspatancke to all the Rest of the County of Albemarle.

3 DECEMBER 1677.

First the occasion of their secureinge the Records & imprisoning the Presidt is, that thereby the Countrey may have a free parlemt & that from them their aggreivances may be sent home to the Lords, wch are breifely these;

In the first place (omitting many hainous matters) hee denied a free election of an Assembly and hath positively cheated the Countrey of one hundred and thirty thousand pounds of Tobacco which hath raised the levie to two hundred and fifty pounds of Tobo per head more then otherwaies it would have beene besides neer twenty thousand pounds of Tobo charge he hath brought upon us by his pipeing guard & now Capt. Gillam is come amongst us with three times the goods hee brought last yeare but had not beene two houers on shore, but for the slip of a word was arrested for one thousand pounds sterling & many affronts and indignities thrown upon him by ye Presidt himselfe, in somuch that had hee not beene earnestly perswaded by some hee had gone directly out of the Countrey and the same night (about midnight) hee went aboard with a brace of pistolls and presenting one of them cockt to Mr Geo. Durants breast & wth his other hand arrested him as a Traytour and many other Injuries, mischiefes and grievances hee hath brought upon us, that thereby an inevitable ruein is comeing (unlesse prevented) which wee are now about to doe and hope & expect that you will joyne with us therein, and subscribe this 3d day of 1ober 1677.[49]

The Remonstrance defended the rebels' decision to seize Miller. This declaration emphasized representation first and foremost. Miller had denied them a "free election" and a "free parlemt." Without the approval of an Assembly, Miller had set a colony-wide levy of 130,000 pounds of tobacco, plus an extra tax to pay for his "pipeing guard," or his enforcers. This fell heavily on the residents, a material example of the difference made by losing representative government. Miller had also confronted Gillam and Durant, popular figures in the Albemarle community.

The Remonstrance went out to the various precincts of Albemarle, calling for support from the people, and demanding that any other men who had served as Miller's officers should be brought by delegates for a "free parlemt" to a "Generall Meeting." As delegations arrived over the next fortnight, they stopped at Crawford's home in Pascotank precinct, "Craford vowing and swearing that if any came to oppose them or relieve us yt they would stand by each other to ye last dropp of blood and that if any dyed to bee sure wee that were their prisonrs to dy first."[50]

Crawford, "one of the chief contrivers as well as acters in this Rebellion," had been ready to fight for Fendall's republican rebellion in 1660; seventeen years later, he wanted his parliamentary government and still saw no reason to pay customs to a king. The Marylanders wanted to be rid of an aristocratic proprietor, and Virginians wanted a vote for the free but landless. Albemarle had succeeded in achieving these goals in practice. No property qualification prevented a North Carolinian man from voting; unlike the Calvert family, no proprietor of Carolina ever visited, not even Berkeley. Only Thomas Miller stood in the way of a de facto republic, given the distant and intermittent rule of the Lords Proprietors.[51]

Richard Foster led the group from Currituck, out on the Banks, where "by a shout of one and all cryed out wee will have noe Lods noe Landgraves noe

Cassiques we renounce them all and fly to the King's protection soe downe went ye Lords Proprietrs for about halfe an owre," recounted the arrested customs officer. Just as in Maryland, North Carolinians revealed that they paid no deference to aristocrats of any title. Foster suggested that they keep their leveling tendencies under wraps, and so the group concentrated on the priorities for their representatives, who received "instructions from ye Rable how they should prceed att thier assembly wch was, first absoelutely to insist upon a free traid to transport their tobacco where they pleased and how they pleased without paying any duty to ye King; . . . they should bring ye said Miller to a tryall for severall odious crymes they then contrived to tax him wthall one espeacially for cheating the Country of 135,000 lbs of Tobacco." They would not tolerate taxation without representation, whether in the form of customs or levies.[52]

The delegations of the five precincts assembled with their prisoners at Durant's home in Perquimans precinct, some greeted by the booming guns of Gillam's boat. Gillam and other traders also brought the rum for the celebration of democracy's return. Aware of how the English powerful reacted to any questioning of their authority in the aftermath of the Cromwellian era, again Miller and his deputies were charged with treacherous talk. But it was the rebels who had no time for those who inherited their status and power. Miller would later complain, "the rabble . . . upbraided his Majtys proclamations and Lds Proprs authority, and there Lordshipps much threatened also by the sd Culpeper, Durant, Craford especially the said Craford said . . . that if ye Govr came among them there or the Lords either, they would serve them ye same sauce or words to that purpose." Crawford had rallied to arms to support Fendall in 1660, and had not mellowed in the years since. With the officials locked up, with the authorizations and seals of government back in Jenkins's hands, the crowd reconstituted their Assembly—a unicameral parliament with no executive—and court system. With Jenkins and Crawford among the justices, Durant served as attorney general, and the crowd selected a jury for the trial of Miller. Many called for the death penalty, uttering "threats vows and bloody oathes of stabbing hanging, pistolling or poisoning," but before the sentencing, a messenger arrived from Virginia. Eastchurch had landed, and some friends of Miller had made it to Virginia to warn him what was afoot.[53]

By the end of 1677, Bacon's Rebellion had been over for a year, and the revenge exacted upon those who had temporarily overthrown Berkeley had been severe. Eastchurch might easily drum up support from the Virginian gentry, still rankled that so many of their "renegades" had escaped to

Albemarle. Would the Great Dismal prove enough of a barrier? This could be the end of the career open to talents. Those who had suffered through years of Chesapeake indentured servitude would not surrender meekly. A border guard set off to hold the line. Crawford and the other precinct representatives wrote to the Virginia government, on behalf of "The almost Unanimous Inhabitants," explaining that Miller and Eastchurch were the problem. The deputy governor there in Berkeley's absence, Herbert Jeffreys, had enough on his plate, and as Eastchurch fell ill with a fever and died within weeks, the Albemarle rebels won. One last place sheltered the Levelers.[54]

With Miller and his deputies imprisoned in log houses, Culpeper became the chief customs officer, and Albemarle settled down, for the Assembly met again in spring at the home of John and Johanna Jenkins. But Timothy Biggs escaped. He was on his way to London to tell the proprietors, so the Assembly sent an agent ahead to counter his story, Gillam paying his expenses and following soon after with Durant. Jenkins "put yr Country in a military posture to oppose all till ye return of ye agents," but in the meantime, the New England boats could continue to trade, and the "sundry fugitives" from Bacon's Rebellion could continue to avoid handing over their tobacco to pay local government fees.[55]

Durant, understanding that the proprietors had nothing to gain or lose from customs duties, proved more savvy than Biggs, who was quickly silenced by the lords, despite his warning that Albemarle posed an enormous threat to the stability of the masters of the entire Atlantic seaboard, such as "New England, New Yorke, Maryland & Virginia by servants, Slaves & Debtors flying thither." Jenkins and the rest would offer sanctuary to all, even "idle debters, theeves, negros, Indians and English servants," declared a representation presented to the proprietors. But the proprietors' interests now lay in South Carolina, and as the king might pull their charter for the southern portion of the grant if he thought his customs were in jeopardy, the lords wanted the news from North Carolina kept under wraps. They found a new investor named Seth Sothell who was willing to travel to Albemarle, and appointed him as governor. Sothell's ship was taken by Turkish pirates. Albemarle remained free.[56]

Biggs tried to take charge of customs collection upon his return in early 1679, but Culpeper would not back down, posting a notice on the court door that "therefore whoever shall enter or cleare with [Biggs] thinking they have done their duty therein he or they may be hereby informed that I will make seizure of them & bring them to tryall according to Act of Parliament." The proprietors appointed a local man, John Harvey, as governor in Sothell's place, and despite an escape by Miller and a series of legal moves by him to bring the rebels to justice, for now the refuge stood. When Culpeper and Gillam were arrested and tried a year later, Shaftesbury himself stepped in to testify in Culpeper's defense, successfully shutting the matter down. Biggs pleaded vainly for Virginia to send a force. But no one would help defeat this democratic rabble, with "their industrious labor to be popular." No potential profit merited the effort, not yet.[57]

In Maryland, on the other hand, authorities would continue to try to suppress the radical movement. In the spring of 1679, a warrant went out for Fendall, accusing him of "Divers false malitious and scandalous reports touching his Lspp: the Rtt Honblec the Lord Propry of this Province." He readied for another attempt to bring down the proprietary and replace it with a more representative system. "Now the time was come and he would right himself for that the times were now Difficult and troublesome, and he should find Disaffected psons enough at the Cliffes & the Eastern Shore that would stand by him," he told his neighbors, for Fendall understood the geography of politics in Maryland. The troublesome times were a reference to the Popish Plot gripping England in late 1678. Five Catholic peers, charged with conspiring to depose the king, were thrown in the Tower of London, as rumors spread throughout the country. By August 1679, twenty-two Catholics had been executed. The anti-Catholic fervor was duly noted by Fendall, for if his dream of a parliamentary democracy in Maryland now seemed utopian and unlikely to motivate his fellow colonists, the lesson that the power of anti-Catholicism might be harnessed to the same effect was reinforced. Hearing that the Calverts had been made aware of his inflammatory rhetoric against them, Fendall found a hiding place, and despite the warrant, he was not caught.[58]

Bacon's Rebellion had failed, and the Virginian oligarchy reasserted control. But in the colonies around them, in backcountry creeks and swamps, the concepts of meritocracy and democracy refused to die. Baltimore still feared Fendall and Gerard's family, calling them "Rank Baconists" and suspecting them of "tampering to stirr up the Inhabitants of Maryland and those of the north part of Virginia to mutiny" in 1681. The relentlessness of revolutionary ideas continued to frighten the powerful on both sides of the Atlantic throughout the 1680s.[59]

CHAPTER FIVE

Papists in Trouble, 1681–1688

But with all his faults restore us our King,
As ever you hope in December for Spring,
For though the whole world cannot show such another,
Yet we'd better by far have him than his brother.

—ANDREW MARVELL, "The Statue in Stocks-Market"

The 1680s saw the tensions between Crown and Parliament continue in England, while in the American colonies, the Commonwealth men of Maryland would not surrender to the Calvert oligarchy who controlled the best lands and the political offices. Ironically, Chesapeake tobacco grown by poor farmers and servants offered Charles and James Stuart a means to absolutism; if colonial customs duty money flowed into the kings' countinghouse, they need never call Parliament. So they sent military officers to the colonies to enforce the Navigation Acts. Those acts pushed the poor white settlers of America to the brink of financial ruin; their Cromwellian attitudes pushed them toward rebellion. The higher-ranked planters in Virginia and Maryland contended with a weak infrastructure to contain such restlessness. Their solution was to find a new source of labor and to legislate a new system of human classification.

THE POET ANDREW MARVELL, like John Milton, had admired and worked for Cromwell and after the Restoration served as a member of Parliament. Forced to choose between two evils, Marvell opted for Charles II over his brother James ("we'd better by far have him than his brother"), for the only thing worse for England than an absolute monarch was a Catholic absolute monarch. The popularity of Marvell's satiric pamphlet *An Account of the Growth of Popery and Arbitrary Government*, despite extensive attempts by the Crown to censor it, demonstrated the fusion in English minds of arbitrary government, France, and Catholicism. Louis XIV, the Sun King, stood as the epitome of that indivisible trio. The Popish Plot was eventually revealed to be false, but not before Irish Catholic archbishop Oliver Plunkett was hanged, drawn, and quartered for supposedly plotting a French invasion of England. Ireland's Catholics, already considered barbaric, would be so much more dangerous with French support. The anti-popery fervor bled into the constitutional tension. Most did not fear Rome nor concepts of transubstantiation; they feared a king like Louis, who would rule without any input from the people. As Charles II aged without a legitimate heir, his brother James, Duke of York, stood in line, holding rosary beads. His conversion to Catholicism was no longer a secret by the mid-1670s.[1]

Leadership in Parliament of the group gradually coalescing under the name "Whigs" fell to Shaftesbury, one of the Carolina proprietors. An earlier struggle to ensure that James's daughters had a Protestant education had failed. Now, Shaftesbury organized the parliamentary opposition to introduce three successive Exclusion Bills, designed to exclude James from the line of succession. This would mean that upon Charles's death, the throne would pass either to Charles's illegitimate son, the Duke of Monmouth, or to James's eldest daughter, Mary, who had wed the staunchly Protestant William of Orange. The Exclusion Crisis in England raged from 1679 to 1681, as anti-popery reached its height there, with competing campaigns in the streets and in a pamphlet war. Parades marked the anniversary of Protestant Queen Elizabeth's coronation, burning the pope and cardinals in effigy. But the Stuarts had plenty of power and patronage to wield. Charles prorogued Parliament again and again to prevent passage of any act of Parliament excluding his brother, only lending further weight to the argument that the obedience to clerical authority demanded by the Catholic Church translated to an end to the parliamentary system of governance. However, rigorous censorship limited the propaganda the Whigs could distribute. Counterattacks portrayed them as revolutionaries who would destroy the country with another civil war. Shaftesbury was sent to the Tower for treason; as the royalist Tories maneuvered control of local governments and law enforcement, he went into exile in 1682. James's succession was secured.[2]

The Stuart brothers learned their lessons. The threat to royal power was real. They must stamp out all vestiges of Cromwellian or Leveler thought and expand their income by creating a revenue stream from colonial trade to prevent the need to call any potentially republican Parliaments. During the 1670s, the brothers had not merely strengthened the mercantilist Navigation Laws, but also granted broader powers to the East India Company and the Royal African Company. These business companies had plenipotentiary powers in Asia and Africa, permitting them to conquer territory and establish courts there in the name of the king, so long as they delivered to him a percentage of the profits from spices, fabrics, gold, silver—and human slaves. Officers of Crown or corporation were empowered to show no mercy; the savage brutality that accompanied England's theft of the world's people and commodities over the next two centuries was unleashed in full now. Tens of thousands of Africans in the 1680s and 1690s suffered the Middle Passage, to die from overwork and malnutrition on Caribbean sugar, Chesapeake tobacco, and South Carolinian rice plantations. Millions would follow in the eighteenth century.[3]

All of this was made possible by the investment in and development of the British navy, both merchant and military, and as the empire expanded, the financial sector, whose center shifted from Antwerp in the Netherlands to London in the late seventeenth century. The Royal Greenwich Observatory opened in 1675, to pinpoint longitude for better navigation. The Royal Navy blurred the line between private and public, protecting English merchants as it simultaneously protected the royal treasury's interests through customs enforcement. Manned increasingly by impressed sailors, the ships themselves were a microcosm of the brutal hierarchical empire. Marcus Rediker describes the grim reality of Britannia's glory: "For sailors, the press-gang represented slavery and death: three out of four pressed men died within two years, with only one in five of the dead expiring in battle. Those lucky enough to survive could not expect to be paid." Authority over proprietary and charter colonies emanated from the throne, through a board or committee (whose name changed many times, such as the Council for Trade and Plantations or the Lords or Board of Trade, as they figured out the imperial administrative structure), not Parliament.[4]

The early 1680s also witnessed attempts by colonial governors to flush away all democratic ideology in the English-speaking world through a reassertion of hierarchical right, tight judicial discipline, and direct rule from London. Even the traders of New England were to be brought under the Crown's thumb. Edward Cranfield, sent to New Hampshire as governor in 1682, suspected that all Puritans were Roundhead republicans who needed to be brought under control. His initial efforts to try smugglers ran aground on the rocks of juries who, like so many other colonial juries, refused to convict anyone for breaking laws they felt to be unfair. An attempt to overthrow Cranfield in January 1683 failed, but gradually his persecution of Puritan preachers would build resentment throughout New England. In Bermuda, a royal governor would be saved by ship captains, as Berkeley had been a few years before in Virginia, from a populace "wholly averse to Kingly Government" who demanded a commonwealth. Algernon Sidney and other republicans in England were executed in 1683, accused of the Rye House Plot, a treacherous conspiracy to restore the Commonwealth at home. The repression, which saw no interruption from one Stuart brother to the next, confirmed to democrats around the Atlantic world that Catholic kings were absolutist kings.[5]

Charles II died in February 1685, and James II assumed the throne, a professed Catholic monarch. Many in England were revolted at the idea, and some supported Charles's illegitimate son, the Duke of Monmouth, as successor. His attempt to raise a popular army to take the Crown failed in June, in the face of James's professional troops. The Tory gentry were torn. Loyal always to the two pillars of order, monarchy and the established church, they hated the notion of a Catholic king, but they knew from the experience of the 1640s that overthrowing a king might easily spawn Levelers and their dangerous ideas of equality and rights to representation. As it stood, James was an old man. His daughter Mary had married her Dutch Protestant cousin William. They would wait out James's reign, convinced that it would be short.[6]

With the Monmouth rebellion crushed, James's first message to the people of Maryland signaled his priorities by informing them that he expected them to understand and strictly observe the "Principall Laws relating to the Plantation Trade." A few months later, his cousin Louis revoked the Edict of Nantes, ending almost a century of toleration for the Calvinist Huguenots, who fled France by the hundreds of thousands, carrying the message that a Catholic king automatically meant absolutism. James foolishly did nothing to correct that feeling, now widespread through the Atlantic world. As his biographer describes, "Government for James was a one-way process: the king commanded, the subject obeyed." Buoyed in his faith by his survival of the Exclusion Crisis and by his inheritance of the throne, he believed himself destined to restore England to Catholicism, not by force but through toleration that would produce mass conversion.[7]

Edward Randolph had brought quo warranto to the Massachusetts Bay Colony in 1684, revoking their charter, and James restricted the Puritans further, by creating the Dominion of New England. Combining the separate colonies into one entity served the empire more efficiently. After a half century of self-government, the Yankees lost their representative assemblies. With dizzying speed, James would move to incorporate New York and New Jersey into the Dominion under the uncompromising authority of Sir Edmund Andros, a military officer whose family had been staunchly loyal to the Stuarts throughout the Interregnum.[8]

Meanwhile in North Carolina, Seth Sothell, finally ransomed from the Turkish pirates, took the reins of government. Sothell set about bribing a few planters with massive tracts of land and installed them as his Council and magistrates, pushing George Durant out of power. The regime change shocked Albemarle, as harsh punishments meted out in court included estates seized, physical tortures, and longer servitude. The sanctuary reeled, but without John Jenkins, who had died shortly before Sothell's arrival, they struggled to find an organized answer. And when James doubled the duty on tobacco in 1685, no spot of ground on the globe seemed safe from the imperious greed of the Stuarts.[9]

So the most ferocious democrats of all took to the sea. While the merchant elite of port towns in other Quaker-dominated colonies had sponsored pirates for decades, the Chesapeake had been mostly off-limits, as Virginia's status as a royal colony and the Calverts' hierarchical attitude had together prevented pirates finding a safe place to trade and to rest. Carrying currency of all kinds and untaxed goods, pirates found a welcome in North Carolina, however, for pirates' political economy matched that of many who had run there from the rigid Cavalier colony. The pirates of the Caribbean struck back at the empire in small ways and large, in real ways and symbolically. Flying the flag of no nation, they recognized no hierarchy of lineage, for their captains were popularly chosen; they rejected the horrific discipline of the Royal Navy, inflicting pain only on cruel shipmasters. The buccaneers met with their fellow Levelers in Albemarle's dockside taverns, flamboyantly challenging the pomp of empire with their tricorn admiral hats and stolen shirts of lace, breaking the spell of rank and deference such accoutrements purportedly cast. When the open slave trade made them supporters of law and order in colonial harbors, the great planters of Charles Town turned against pirates. Stede Bonnet and Blackbeard would finally be caught in North Carolina waters, but by officials from the neighboring colonies.[10]

While Andros began his campaign to rein in smuggling in the northern colonies, Baltimore appointed his nephew to the post of customs commissioner for Maryland. That would not satisfy James. Even a Catholic proprietor earned no quarter. By early 1687, the king's imperial bureaucrats launched quo warranto proceedings to revoke the Maryland Charter and bring the whole stretch of America's coast north of Virginia into the Dominion and under the direct rule of his most loyal military officer. Enough customs duties, and James might never have to call Parliament at all. Instructions went out to every colony to suppress all pirates.[11]

THE 1680S saw the struggle against absolutism in England carried over to Maryland and North Carolina. In Maryland, Bushwood continued to be a locus of resistance, as the Gerard sisters' husbands, John Coode, Kenelm

Cheseldyne, and Nehemiah Blakiston, stepped to the forefront. The threat to autonomy was two-pronged: Catholic Calverts and Catholic Indians.

The latest Lord Baltimore, Charles Calvert, lived in Maryland and presided over the government personally. Like King Charles, he continuously prorogued any meeting of the Assembly through the years of the Exclusion Crisis, but the appearance in August 1681 of Oneida and Onondaga representatives intent on attacking the Piscataway and asking for Maryland's neutrality meant that he needed to renew various taxes and militia laws in preparation for whatever might follow. But he faced a problem of appearances. He also needed to dispel the rumors that Fendall was right about a Catholic-Indian conspiracy, for to preserve peace, it was important that Baltimore make a pact with the Iroquois, and that would leave him vulnerable to Fendall's accusations.[12]

Anti-popery on both sides of the Atlantic in this era reflected a greater fear of France's armed forces than of the theology of Rome. And the French maintained positive relationships with Indians further north. Complicating the picture, however, local Indians such as the Piscataway and Nanticoke had made their peace with the Maryland settlement. And most worrisome of all—to every white settler in North America—were the Iroquois, who were not allied with the French, but whose raids southward kept all on edge. After the French had successfully repelled them from Canada in the 1660s, the Iroquois, the most powerful group east of the Mississippi, officially allied with the English in 1675 and absorbed the rest of the Susquehannocks they had defeated, boosting their population and territory. While groups further north in Massachusetts had suffered defeat in King Philip's War, and Bacon's Rebellion took an enormous toll on Virginian groups, the Iroquois recovered. Understanding that they retained the upper hand, the Five Nations negotiated from a position of strength and never conceded their right-of-way in any colony.[13] When they planned attacks on Maryland-allied Indians, Lord Baltimore and his Council found themselves caught in the middle of a delicate and dangerous diplomacy. They showed no real loyalty to Maryland Indians and would not protect them, but they had no trust for the Iroquois either, even if they were officially English allies. Baltimore figured that the Iroquois would turn on the white settlements of Maryland and Virginia after they had "subdued, conquered and destroyed" the local Indians. So he had to work with them in an attempt to control their incursions into his colony. Fendall and Coode would continually try to exploit that situation to paint a picture of a Popish Plot in Maryland: Calverts and Indians working together to keep Maryland's poor Protestants from any say in their own governance.[14]

In March and April 1681, Fendall, always aware of political and potentially constitutional developments in England, thought that the Exclusion Crisis might be the end not only of James, but of Catholic rulers in the British Empire. He encouraged some neighbors to ignore the levies, for, he argued, Baltimore would soon be removed from power. Fendall claimed that the Iroquois, in particular the Seneca, were planning an attack in collaboration with Baltimore and the Council and that it was time for the Protestants of Maryland to rise and reclaim their government. All that was required was the seizure of the governor and his Council, for few would defend them. At first Fendall proved unable to recruit enough supporters—the fear of charges of treason was real, given the fate of Bacon's men—but the murder of six settlers at Point Lookout by unidentified Indians in early May provided evidence that his suspicions, "the Papists joineing with the Sinniquo," were not without grounds. By the summer, rumors flew that in fact the victims had been killed by Catholics. "It was not Indians but people of their own Physiogmony or complexion dressed up in Indian habitt," went the story. Fendall and Coode spread the idea in Virginia, too.[15] Fendall was seized and locked up, but supporters gathered in July "with . . . swords, pistols Gunns and other weapons as well offensive as defensive in Warlike manner" to break him out of prison. His brother headed to Virginia to drum up more men. They were unsuccessful, and the leader of Fendall's supporters, George Godfrey, a local justice of the peace and militia officer, also found himself on trial for mutiny. The Council, furious that Coode sat as a member of the Assembly, issued a warrant for him in September, and throughout October collected depositions, but such was the level of support for Fendall that he had a steady stream of visitors while imprisoned.[16]

That fall, the Lower House of the Assembly immediately locked horns with their Catholic proprietor over authority and representation. With the spouses of the Gerard sisters, Coode and Cheseldyne, taking the lead and claiming "full power & Authority given [them] by the Freemen," the delegates demanded that all constituencies have their four delegates, and that "upon Serious Examination of the best Records and Authorities of the Customs and usages of the Commons house of England (the only Rule to walk by) Do Nemine Contradicente Vote that it is the undoubted Priviledge of this house that the Speaker of this house issue his Warrants that Writts of Election of Members may issue forth to fill up the Vacant Places of those that are Dead Since the last Sessions."[17]

Baltimore's reaction was predictable; he ridiculed the idea that the Lower House had control over elections. "His Majesty hath the Sole Power to Dispose of his Conquests upon terms he Pleases, is not Tyed to take the Parliaments Consent," he argued, comparing his position to that of the monarch in England, and "he Hath granted his Lordship a Patent with Several Powers and Priviledges." But the Maryland Commons would not concede their liberties easily. "If the Word Conquest intends that we are Subject to Arbitrary Laws and Impositions," they responded, it would be interpreted as an attack on their "Inherent Right yea and Birth right."[18] Once the writs had gone out, the fight continued over whether "So Scandalous a Person" as Coode should be allowed to keep his seat in the Lower House. His colleagues stood by him, arguing that in order to dismiss him, they would have to try him themselves. Baltimore balked at that, but did send a deposition quoting Coode as saying "he cared not a fart" for one councilor and "cared not a Turd for the Chancellor [Baltimore's uncle Philip Calvert] nor the Governor neither." This was to no avail; the delegates insisted on Coode's right to his seat. The struggle for power between Maryland's Lord and Commons continued the whole session.[19]

The trials of Fendall, Coode, and Godfrey began in mid-November in the provincial court, with the Council as the justices. Charges against Fendall included his threats against his judges, the councilors. Fendall conducted his own defense, revealing himself to be a smart and educated man, well informed as to legal procedure. He began by refusing any Catholics as jurymen. He argued that he had not been presented with the evidence against him—eyewitness testimony—before the trial began, but the justices argued that Fendall would only have thwarted justice "by your Influence upon the people in that County." Certainly, some people the Council expected to testify against Fendall suddenly claimed that they had never heard Fendall say any mutinous words. Others swore that for the previous two years, Fendall had predicted the imminent fall of the Calverts. "No Baltemore will be Proprietary here long so you need not fear; land enough here in a short tyme," he had told them, indicating a better distribution of wealth once the aristocrats were out of power. Testimony, even for the prosecution, made it clear that Fendall had widespread support around the colony. As other witnesses came forward, Fendall questioned their reliability. William Boyden was a co-conspirator who once had offered to bring a troop of at least forty men to Fendall's aid, who now Fendall claimed, "to slip his own neck out of the collar lays it upon others." Fendall pointed out flaws in some of the more damning testimony; the lack of precise dates prevented him from producing an alibi. Witnesses called for his defense portrayed the prosecution witnesses as having a personal vendetta against Fendall, such as Izabell Bright, who, it was claimed, had referred to Fendall as a "knave and Rogue and Madam Fendall as salt whore and salt Bitch," because she had economic grievances against him.[20]

In the end, the jury found him guilty of seditious words but not of action. However, the trial had broadcast the level of popular support for Fendall, and so the court sentenced him to a fine and banishment, taking time to emphasize how moderate this was, as they might have assigned him "boaring of the Tongue, cropping one or both Ears," or other such painful and permanent disfigurement. Coode, still an elected member of the Assembly, was acquitted by his jury of charges of seditious speech made at Blakiston's house. Coode had boasted that he could command a force "when he pleased" to take land from the Catholics, and the jury claimed that they felt the words had been said in jest. Coode claimed that he had only accidental encounters with Fendall. The justices warned Coode to "keepe a Guard upon your Tongue." While they took his threats seriously, they knew, too, of the level of his popular support, given the Lower House's relentless defense of him through September. Rumors flew that his brother-in-law Cheseldyne had organized 500 men in Virginia, ready to ride upon his signal if "Capt Fendall or Capt Coode should doe otherwise than well upon their tryall."[21]

George Godfrey did not command the same degree of support, for the jury found him guilty of mutinous speech. The following day, the magistrates sentenced him to death, but Baltimore commuted the sentence to life in prison. Fendall left for Virginia, and Baltimore warned that he might exploit "the discontented party in Virginia to stir up another rebellion there." Trouble would certainly come to that colony by the spring of 1682.[22]

"TOBACCO IS MOST DAMNABLE Low both here and in holland . . . would Even hardly Cleare itselfe," complained a Maryland trader from London in late 1681.[23] Sixty years of experimentation of agricultural technique in the Chesapeake had brought substantial gains. Given the differences between Europe and America, farmers measured yields not in bushels by acre, but in bushels by laborer, for land was not the crucial factor in determining profit. All depended on the workforce one could exercise. Productivity had soared over the decades, with the average worker harvesting almost four times the amount of Orinoco tobacco his peer would have done in the 1620s, despite the intensive demands of the crop. Planters had learned to grow maize and to allow livestock to forage, easily providing the household sustenance while most of the labor remained dedicated to the cash crop. This had produced a surplus. Elite planters could make an income on the larger volumes they produced, but by 1680 the "good poor man's country" had disappeared. The availability of servants had shrunk, and only the rich could afford to purchase the enslaved.[24]

The glut of tobacco kept prices low and continued to impoverish the small-scale tobacco farmers in Maryland, Virginia, and North Carolina. No group was hit harder than poor smallholders in Virginia, where taxation to serve the planter elite had lessened little since Bacon's Rebellion. With royal governor Lord Culpeper temporarily out of the colony, the lieutenant governor erred by calling an Assembly to meet in Jamestown in April. All the Lower House delegates were "big with expectation to enact a Cessation" of tobacco planting for a year, to allow the price to climb. But shortly after their arrival in town, word came from England that they were to be prorogued until the fall. The delegates were asked to make one decision: whether the two companies of soldiers stationed in Virginia since the upheavals of Bacon were to be disbanded or continued at the expense of the Virginia taxpayer, for the Crown would no longer pay the bill. To the dismay of the councilors, the burgesses of the Lower House privately talked on the matter for four days, coming to no agreement, and it was widely believed that they actually continued to debate how to bring about a colony-wide cessation. They voted to make the journal of their meeting public, so that the voters might see how they tried to enact legislation, but were prevented by the higher authorities.[25]

When the residents of Gloucester County, one of the last places to surrender to Berkeley's forces during Bacon's Rebellion, heard that their Assembly had been prorogued, they took matters into their own hands. A Virginia official noted that "Bacon's Rebellion had left an itching behind it." Encouraged by the clerk of the House of Burgesses, at the end of April, they broke into companies of at least twenty and began to systematically destroy the tobacco plants. (They may have been "scraping" the seedling beds; typically the seedlings were transplanted to the fields in May and June. This would have made the task much quicker and easier than working their way across whole fields.) Starting on their own farms to demonstrate that they were neither rioters nor thugs, they "voluntarily destroyed their owne and then joyned forces and . . . cut up all plants wherever they came." For about three days, the teams moved through the county, until the lieutenant governor heard the news and dispatched the Gloucester Militia Horse and Foot to repress the mutineers. By May 8, two ringleaders had been imprisoned and the others had surrendered and promised to stop. But the elite remained very nervous. "It's to bee feared the contagion will spread," admitted one, because the small farmers are "soe now sunk to nothing that their low estate makes them desperate." Baltimore had portrayed Virginia's farmers as "ripe and ready for another Rebellion as ever they were" the previous summer, and now the grandee understood that "only destroying Tobacco-plants will not satiate their (it's to be feared) rebellious appetites." The "mutinous tempers" of the unpaid soldiers "double our apprehensions."[26]

He was right to worry. New Kent County farmers picked up where Gloucester men had left off, and the farmers of Middlesex County also moved quickly through their region, until by May 18, Baltimore had sent militia to the Potomac, to ensure that the mutiny did not spread to Maryland, for he believed as many as 500 armed "rabble" might be involved. However, by the end of the month, the uprising had been crushed. Estimates by the major planters put the losses at anywhere between 6,000 and 10,000 hogsheads (perhaps seven million pounds of tobacco).[27] One of the more vigorous government agents found his own crop destroyed "out of spight," according to Lord Culpeper, who sent a report the following January to the Committee for Plantations. Culpeper had to search for a 1337 statute that would allow him to charge the ringleaders with treason rather than rioting, for the latter charge, which carried only fines and imprisonment, would actually cost the government, "for scarce one of them was worth a farthing . . . and there are in effect noe prisons but what are soe easily broken." He worked hard to find juries to convict three and had two hanged at their own county courthouses as deterrents to their neighbors. "Having soe fully asserted the Dignity of the Government," he coolly decided to pardon the third, a teenager, in a gesture of power.[28]

Some unruly women had tried unsuccessfully to sustain the plant-cutting riots when the men were suppressed by authorities. "The women had so cast off their modesty as to take up the hoe that the rabble were forced to lay down," a disgusted Virginia official reported. The Gerard clan would not surrender, either. Coode and Cheseldyne continued to be elected as representatives through the 1680s and continued to contest Baltimore in the Assembly, refusing to admit councilors wearing swords as symbols of their status into the Lower House, for example, and demanding electoral reforms to guarantee that the voice of the people would be heard. They were often joined by the Rousby men, Christopher and John, who also fought the authority of the Calverts.[29]

Christopher Rousby in particular had frustrated Baltimore for several years, for he had secured an appointment directly from London as customs official, keeping the office out of the hands of the proprietor's oligarchy. Letters from both Rousby and Baltimore in 1681 to Crown customs officials accused and counter-accused each other, Rousby charging that Baltimore sought only to put his kin and in-laws into the position, while Baltimore claimed that Rousby uttered such seditious and insolent remarks about James and other aristocrats as "greate men are greate knaves and Turne Coates and begin to pisse backwards," in addition to carrying himself with too much "pride" and publicly announcing his "hatred to Kingly Government." Given their backgrounds, probably all the charges were true. But Rousby went to London and defended himself vigorously against the "feigned and contrived" allegations that bore no specifics nor evidence. Gerard Slye, Susannah Gerard's son, who had traveled to England with Rousby, testified on his behalf. Rousby turned the tables on Baltimore, who was "severely reprehended" by the Lords of the Treasury for his handling of customs prior to Rousby's appointment. He also received a letter asking about his "partiality to Papists."[30]

Baltimore, forced to apologize for his mistakes and lack of oversight on customs collection, fumed at the republican, but another issue consumed his time. The Pennsylvania Charter appeared to grant some of Maryland (actually current-day Delaware) to William Penn, whose agent immediately told the affected residents not to bother paying Maryland taxes. The boundary line dispute festered for several years, and Baltimore finally sailed to England in 1684 seeking resolution. In the absence of the proprietor, any remaining traces of deference evaporated. "There is little difference betweene him [Baltimore] and a fart. . . . What are the Calverts? My family is as antient as the Calverts," declared one disgruntled farmer, while a dissenting carpenter refused to give a new Anglican minister access to the church. Others refused to show any respect to the councilors, "a Company of Chimney Sweepers." And then came word that Fendall was on a ship on the Potomac.[31]

Somehow, despite the order to the sheriff to "press boate and hands" to apprehend Fendall, he escaped arrest and disappeared again. The tension among the besieged Council grew, until one day in November, Colonel George Talbot's rage at the insolence of Rousby exploded in violence. On board the *Quaker*, commanded by Captain Thomas Allen, Talbot, Baltimore's surveyor-general and one of his inner circle, stabbed the customs official to death with a dagger to the chest. Allen's crew seized Talbot and locked him in irons. When the Council brought a warrant for Talbot's arrest, Allen refused to recognize their authority. Supported by Nehemiah Blakiston, Allen scorned the proprietor's sovereignty; "he valued him noe more then another mann." Perhaps Blakiston warned him of the murderer's close connections to the government of Maryland and the unlikelihood that Talbot would be duly punished. Some days later, Allen delivered the prisoner instead to the royal governor of Virginia.[32]

To the great dismay of the Maryland Council, Governor Francis Howard upheld Allen's decision and refused to extradite Talbot. However, as his predecessor Lord Culpeper had predicted, no secure prison existed in the Chesapeake region. Talbot's wife organized a party to free him in February. The hue and cry went up to recapture the fugitive, but Talbot found a safe hiding place with friends at first and then moved to his own home. His friends on the Council did not exert themselves for the recapture of the murder suspect.[33]

The Maryland Council's willingness to let a murderer go free reached the ears of officials across the Atlantic. Blakiston had assumed the role of customs collector after Rousby's death and complained to the London authorities that the Council treated the king with "disrespect and contempt." They had "conspired" to free Talbot, and Blakiston added that they would not cooperate with him in his collection of custom duties, thus cheating the king of thousands of pounds. (The son of the regicide obviously cared little for the coffers of a Stuart; he sought only to discredit the Calvert aristocrat's hold on power in Maryland. Baltimore emphasized that point in his defense, sarcastically remarking, "It were to be wished that Mr Blackiston had at all times expressed his loyalty to the King.") But as North Carolina's rebels and Rousby himself had discovered a few years before, only one colonial issue won the attention of powerful men in England: any failure to collect His Majesty's duties. With the royal authorities' full attention on them, Talbot's councilor friends were forced to ensure that he turned himself in and then tried their best to protect him by suggesting St. Mary's City for his trial. Howard would have none of that, and by the summer, Baltimore wrote from England that they had best surrender him to the Virginia authorities. Eventually he was found guilty and sentenced to death, but received a pardon from the king.[34]

James's imperial administration's attempts to tighten control over the colonies met with mixed success. The discipline consequential to any disrespect of the new Catholic king would not be gentle. But when a group of Maryland men raised their glasses to Monmouth, two juries in a row would not convict them. In some of the neighboring colonies, the power struggle moved in the Tories' favor. In North Carolina, Sothell's corrupt regime enriched themselves with huge grants of land, even a few who had been players in the rebellion for a "free parlement" in 1677. Not everyone would play along, though. George Durant remained an active opponent. Most Quakers still refused to take oaths. Those runaways could still hide along the Outer Banks, harvesting beached whales and sheltering pirates. And more and more of the small planters escaped having to pay the king's duties by diversifying their household economies, replacing tobacco with hogs as their cash "crop."[35]

Many of the Virginia elite, like the Tories in England, welcomed the fresh emphasis on status and lineage. Already, the office-holding elite had more slaves than servants, acquired through privateering, through trade directly with Caribbean islands or through Dutch connections. And now, as the Royal African Company expanded operations, the ships of the Atlantic slave trade were beginning to stop in the ports of the mainland colonies. As each year brought them more opportunities to enslave their labor force, the gulf widened between the big planter oligarchy and the poor freemen.[36]

Although some had been raised in Anglican homes where no contention arose about inherited privilege on any basis, other settlers who had been friendly to the republican cause shifted in their political philosophy. The area settled by the original Ingle's rebels, the Northern Neck of Virginia, housed a group that had offered a safe place for Gerard and Fendall over the years. There, the workforce had remained mostly white servants, long after the sweet-scented tobacco region along the York, Rappahannock, and James Rivers had converted to slavery. John Washington, married to Anne Gerard (and, after her death, to her sister Frances) and thus another brother-in-law to Coode, Cheseldyne, and Blakiston, died in 1677. His son Lawrence along with Nicholas Spencer and the Lee family emerged as the great planter elite of the Northern Neck over the course of the last two decades of the seventeenth century. When the enslaved workers of the Northern Neck planned an uprising in 1687, the principles of equality in law and government the planters' parents had treasured ran into an economic and psychosocial challenge. They had grown accustomed not merely to a comfortable lifestyle for the time, but to an inflated status. The powerful seduction of separating themselves within their society—the lure of exclusivity—led them to turn not only on Africans, but on their fellow white Virginians. By the 1680s, only slavery made great wealth possible in Virginia. Tobacco prices stayed low, and when King James increased his cut, profit margins shrank so that a great volume was required. Those profits had to be supplemented by the perks of office-holding, through which they could gouge the smallholders, to engender enough money to fund the conspicuous consumption of luxury items that inspired jealousy in their neighbors and self-satisfaction in themselves. Any talk of "rights," any attempt to shake the system, threatened their vanity.[37]

What they told themselves so that they might sleep at night as they sold out the ideals of their parents and neighbors we cannot know, but probably included some platitudes about law and order working for the greater good. Perhaps they bought into the concept of the natural aristocracy—"some are just born superior to others." But once they whelped even one less than exceptional child, the notion of "natural" would run headlong into and need to be merged with the older sense of lineage and breeding to protect their legacy of power and privilege. Horsemen like Virginia planters certainly believed in breeding for faster, fancier animals: thoroughbreds. Yet their own humble lineage taught that quality "blood" might be found anywhere. And so, the particularly American version of hierarchy began to gel over the course of this generation, twisting material desires into a convenient blend of faith, science, and philosophy. Any white blood had the potential for greatness. The potential had to be confined to white blood to maintain a hold on African labor, and to justify the seizure of Indian land. Race replaced the European sense of "class": the inescapable hierarchy of lineage. Eventually they would search the Bible for Old Testament passages that endorsed their worldview, ignoring the big stories of God's spectacular vengeance on Egyptian enslavers and focusing instead on the curse of Ham.

When reality confounded the new religion of white supremacy, when enslaved people grabbed any opportunity to exercise personal autonomy, especially when they demonstrated economic initiative, or when white women found black men irresistible, the fallacy of the philosophy lay bare. Such realities had to be shut down. In 1687, those Northern Neck slaves who had used the cover of a funeral to gather together to plan the overthrow of their planters, "with a designe of Carrying it through the whole Collony of Virginia," shone a spotlight on the gaping holes in the racial argument currently under construction. They desired liberty and equality, and they showed the same qualities of intelligence and courage as any in the governor's cabinet. The governor thus issued a proclamation prohibiting "any Solemnity or Funeralls for any deceased Negroes."[38]

In 1681, Maryland's Lower House had passed one important measure at Baltimore's request, enforcing more strongly a limit on freedom for some. An Act concerning Negroes and Slaves confirmed the lifetime and hereditary status of slavery, "as theire fathers were," as had been enacted in 1664, and distinct from Virginia's 1660 decision to make freedom dependent on mothers. That law, however, had punished white servant girls who had married enslaved men by enslaving them too, for the husband's lifetime.[39] Masters then began to *encourage* such matches—the Assembly noted that the marriages happened "sometimes by the Instigacon procurement or Conievance of theire Masters Mistres or dames"—especially of those recently arrived who might be kept ignorant of the statute and find themselves working for many years beyond their original indenture. Then came Eleanor Butler, known as Irish Nell, Baltimore's servant girl, who promptly fell in love with Charles, a slave on another plantation. Baltimore stood to lose her service to Charles's master, so he warned her that she and her children would lose their liberty, but she declared she would "rather have Charles than have your lordship."[40]

Baltimore had the law changed, although it would not apply retroactively to Nell. It seemed to the men of the Assembly that white women needed to be controlled, for their "Lascivious & Lustfull desires" would lead to "Inconveniencys Controversys & suites" over the status of the children born from intermarriage with any black man. In an effort to ensure that masters would no longer try to enslave the white women under their authority, any master of a white servant woman who married a slave would lose her service and would be fined 10,000 pounds of tobacco. The woman and children would be emancipated, however. The tie between slave society and patriarchal society could not be spelled out more clearly. The onus was not on the white woman to control herself, but on her master.[41] And so we see another small brick in the transition from class to race as the fundamental determinant of rights, let alone status, placed in the structure of Maryland society. Just as lower-class white men defended vociferously their right to representation, they sentenced the children of enslaved black men to hereditary bondage.

Legislation provides a window into actuality, of course. Miscegenation had been illegal since the 1660s, but not stringently enforced. As was the case for white indentured servants, African men outnumbered black women for several decades, giving women choices among suitors. Had servant women not been choosing black men as their partners, there would have been no need for such a law. Plenty of people of different races found each other attractive. In Somerset County, at least ten free black men had white wives. Irish Nell remained enslaved and bore Charles eight children. But as the big planters made the switch to the slave society over the last decades of the seventeenth century, they "had come to understand the utility of whiteness." Such mixed-race children became an issue. They threw a wrench into tidy classification of humans by race. So as the construction of race moved forward, planters and Enlightenment philosophers developed the concept of fractions of blood until eventually one drop of African blood determined one's fate in southern colonies. Indians would hear themselves described as "half-breeds" and "quadroons." This line of thinking progressed as economic needs dictated. Pushed by planters who moved to Maryland from Barbados, carrying with them ideas about controlling one's labor force tested in the killing fields of the sugar islands, the slave code took form. By 1692, the Maryland legislature more universally punished any sexual interaction between any white woman and any black man. Planter men had free license to rape enslaved women, of course, and made their peace with enslaving and selling their own children for money for the next two centuries. For the next twenty-five years, Virginia's planter elite, and those in Maryland and South Carolina, would build a slave code, addressing each problem, patching each hole in their argument by closing off, one by one, every opportunity for black women and men to challenge racial hierarchy, in the hope that the superiority of white blood might appear unquestionable.[42]

But frontier regions like Somerset County, where Quakers and Anthony Johnson had set up home, remained "free soil" for decades longer, for the first generation to witness the elite's machinations did not wholly buy into their ideas about racial hierarchy. "Emmanuel a negro" joined with white servants to defy their master in 1684, as servants and slaves had joined forces in Bacon's Rebellion. Throughout the eighteenth century, fewer families there would be counted as members of the elite class than anywhere else in Maryland.[43] Gradually, though, as they realized the fate that would befall their children, white women would ever more rarely risk sexual interactions with black men anywhere in the American colonies.

MEANWHILE IN ENGLAND, James II alienated the group he needed most: the Tories. By constantly pushing for toleration for Catholics, and through actions such as appointing over eighty Catholics as army officers in this era of rabid anti-popery, he drew the opposition of even the most ardent royalists. Then, after proroguing Parliament, he tried to control elections in an effort to pack the next Parliament with men willing to overturn the legislation penalizing Catholics. All this further cemented the correlation of Catholicism with absolutism in the minds of Englishmen. Still, comfortingly, Mary awaited the throne—until the news came in late 1687 that James's younger wife was expecting a child. If the baby was a boy, he would leap over his sisters in the line of succession. Through the spring, rumors circulated that the pregnancy was false and just a papist trick to bring in a male child to keep the Crown for the Catholics. But on June 10, 1688, a new Catholic heir to the throne of England was born. He would never become James III. His birth illuminated how flexible notions of divine right, hereditary monarchy, and patriarchy were for the English in the seventeenth century.[44]

CHAPTER SIX

Religion Is but Policy, 1689–1699

> Had not brave Orange come,
> We had been quite undone . . .
> Now Protestants eyes are ope
> And Popery has had its scope
> So their next turn will be the Rope
> For Tyburn is waiting still
> Some of their blood to spill
> Their old Roguery to fulfill
> For they have run out their race
> And now to their soul disgrace.
> Their Rogueries known and will be show[n]
> When Parliament takes its place.

By the late 1680s, faith in the dream of a republic and a democracy faded around the Atlantic world. To believe it possible was utopian thinking. The suppression of dissent by the Stuarts had been so successful that now the best one could hope for was a Parliament that held some power of the purse, and some representation for commoners. And even that watered-down dream seemed to be drifting out of reach in the summer of 1688. Every decision of James II emulated the Sun King. As even the Tories of England despaired of their monarch, the colonists in the Americas hated the tightening of state control over their assemblies and their trade. The absolutism of a Catholic king—and of the Catholic proprietor of Maryland—appeared to be confirmed in perpetuity with the birth of the young prince. What could be done? Around the Atlantic world, a revolution took different forms. The radicals of the Chesapeake seized the opportunity.

In England, young Prince James had been born in the middle of another constitutional storm. In an effort to pack Parliament with supporters, his father had declared "Indulgence" for Catholics and Dissenters, allowing them to hold public office. He decreed that the Indulgence Declaration should be read from every pulpit in England during May 1688. Seven Anglican bishops decided to make a stand. In their petition, they claimed that they must be excused from reading the Declaration, and essentially argued that the king could not unilaterally overrule parliamentary law—a bold challenge to arbitrary government. Precedent was in James's favor, but popular opinion was not.

While the bishops were arrested for seditious libel and locked in the Tower, supporters ensured that their petition circulated widely with its overlapping arguments about Catholicism and an end to parliamentary rights. Over the next few weeks, the bishops took on heroic stature around England, and in the midst of the furore, the new heir to the throne was born. The trial was a one-day affair, with an acquittal issued the following morning. The national celebrations at the bishops' victory far exceeded those for the birth of the royal baby. The not guilty verdict and the public reaction to it sent a clear message about the popularity of the king and his son.[1]

Protestants on both sides of the English Channel looked on in fear as James II and Louis XIV moved toward a military alliance. James's elder daughter Mary, until the moment of the prince's birth set to become queen, was married to her cousin William of Orange, stadtholder, or governor, of the Protestant Dutch Republic. William had developed into the hero of Protestantism in the European context of the tyrannical Catholic Louis. Even before the baby had taken Mary's place in the line of succession, William began to build a fleet for the invasion of England. However, he needed the assurances of leading Englishmen that James would be unable to defend his authority. Those assurances were offered earnestly a week after the birth of the prince. The army had no loyalty to the king who had thrust Catholic officers upon them. When Louis turned his forces east against German opposition, the Dutch had their moment of opportunity. William assured the Dutch parliament, the States General, that he did not intend to usurp the English throne, but to preserve the freedom of Parliament, and that he had the support of the people.[2]

Issuing a declaration addressed to the people of England in October, William repeated that he came only to reinstate the liberties of Englishmen from the machinations of James and his evil advisers. Citing the moves against the Church, the universities, the army, the judiciary, and the electoral process, William claimed that he sailed at the behest and on behalf of Parliament. He landed at Torbay on November 5, the national day of celebration of the 1605 failure of Catholics to blow up Parliament.[3]

The Glorious Revolution has often been described as a coup, because the usual story describes how, after powerful players in England approached Prince William of Orange and offered him the throne, he arrived on the coast of England in November and was welcomed into London before Christmas. James was permitted to flee the country, as none of his subjects, especially those serving in his military forces, would support him. More recent work has emphasized how revolutionary the events of 1688 actually were, with much violence in Scotland and Ireland, but also more popular action in England than has previously been noted.[4]

In the colonies, too, people grabbed the opportunity to restore the apparatus of self-government from James's generals. Although the stories of the overthrow of the Dominion of New England, of the Leisler rebellion in New York, and of Maryland's Protestant Associators are well known, the actions extended south into Virginia and North Carolina, too. The colonial democrats did not win a perfect commonwealth, but the successes were sweet to Fendall's group from Bushwood who had declared their republic in 1660. Thirty years of struggle culminated in the overthrow of arbitrary government.

Historians discuss the events in Maryland in religious terms; the antipopery rhetoric of those in opposition to Baltimore has been emphasized over the grievances about representation and democracy.[5] But only when we grasp that "Catholic" operated as a synonym for arbitrary, for aristocratic, for antidemocratic in the late seventeenth century do we understand the motives of the rebels. They were not crazy; both James and Baltimore sought absolute control of their fiefdoms. Baltimore's Council for the past two decades had been Catholic and/or the proprietor's kin by lineage or marriage. They had attempted to protect a murderer among them. And the final deputy governor, President William Joseph, was a Catholic who declared to the Assembly in the fall of 1688 that kings were appointed by God and that their recent refusal to sign the oaths of allegiance to Baltimore was "Rebellion." The Calvert oligarchy was real, not a conspiracy theory.[6]

Joseph's high-handedness would cost his boss dearly. The Lower House finally conceded the oaths of fidelity, but their resistance had shaken the Council. In January 1689, as the first news of the William and Mary usurpation reached the Americas, the Maryland Council called for all the public armaments to be brought in from the surrounding regions to the Calvert seat at Mattapany. They claimed that they were in need of repair, but the message was clear all the same; the arms would be redistributed to those trusted to "faithfully serve the King your Lordship and the Country." Given the semiconstant rumors of Indian attack, perhaps the recall might have been considered prudent, but the promise to redistribute the arms only to those considered loyal to Baltimore was clearly political and one more example of the lengths to which his clique would go to preserve their power. The arms had arrived by March 10. James had fled his throne some twelve weeks earlier.[7]

Two weeks later, just across the Virginia line in Stafford County, Parson John Waugh of Overwharton parish, old friend of Thomas Gerard and witness to his will, told his parishioners that Seneca Indians were massing in Maryland, readying to attack the Protestant settlers of the entire region. The Seneca apparently knew more of British developments than many colonists, for "they did heare the Englishmen in England had cut off their Kings head and that there were abundance of Dutchmen comeing in." As the story circulated, promulgated by Waugh from his pulpit, French Catholic Indians, with the full cooperation of Baltimore's Catholic Council, would soon slaughter Protestant settlers, so those Protestants had better prepare for war. Frontier families fortified themselves, but their friends over the Maryland line had no munitions. As the rumors flew back and forth across the colonial border, the French-backed Seneca army swelled to 10,000 men. Apparently their ally in Virginia was Giles Brent, a Catholic man originally from Maryland. Waugh railed against the Catholic alliance of Indian and French, who would violently seize control if the Protestants were not stalwart defenders of liberty.[8]

What has become known as Parson Waugh's Tumult was the beginning of the Glorious Revolution, American-style. Already in the Caribbean, the news of the end of the Stuart Catholic dynasty had provoked unrest in Barbados. There the local threat was not French-backed Indians, but so many miserable indentured Irish servants whose Catholicism made them very suspect and left their masters vulnerable. The lieutenant governor acted quickly, however, to arrest a Catholic official and assured the security of the government. The response of the officials on the mainland was not so wise. From Massachusetts to North Carolina, colonists who had treasured their independence or who had long struggled to win it determined that they would ensure that the removal of the Stuarts would guarantee their right to a say in their own governance.[9]

Although the Northern Neck had sheltered radicals from Ingle's and Fendall's rebellions for decades, the turn to enslavement of their labor force enriched some of the families of the area, separating them materially from their neighbors. The Lees, Spencers, and Allertons retained the desire to be masters of their own domains, but now also masters of others. Their self-interest lay not in democratization of the power structure, but in maintaining the hierarchy of the planter elite in Virginia and in law and order that would protect their property rights. They could not permit the disorder that would ensue from Waugh's admonitions to the small farmers to arm themselves, nor for Brent to be attacked. Bacon's Rebellion remained much too fresh a memory. So they intervened, having Brent's house searched to demonstrate that he had no stockpile of weapons or ammunition. Brent moved to a friend's house to stay, but soon "the Rabble" besieged that house. The movement spread. Waugh declared, "Being no King in England, there was no government here." As in Bacon's Rebellion, what began with hostility toward Indians blossomed into a questioning of elite rule.[10]

The disorder almost immediately seeped into southern Maryland, and by March 24, Henry Jowles wrote to councilor William Digges, "the onely person left wee can trust," describing the "greate uproar and Tumult" set in motion by the news that the Indians had been encouraged to attack the settlements by another councilor, Henry Darnall. Sworn depositions claimed that an Indian "war captaine" had named Brent in Virginia and Darnall in Maryland as ringleaders of the conspiracy, who "had hyred them." This had been the design behind the calling in of the public arms from the counties. Jowles, a local militia officer, sent a boat to Mattapany for those munitions "which were taken from us." The second letter accompanying the boat addressed Joseph. If he did not send the arms, the militia would "hold themselves betrayed by your honour to the Comon Enemy."[11]

Joseph dispatched the munitions, with an oath that "by all that is sacred in heaven or on Earth wee will stand by you and by all the English . . . with our lives and fortunes." Darnall set off to personally protest his innocence, while William Digges, too, rode to meet Jowles, finding, to his alarm, "a hundred men in Armes exercising." Planters close to the Stafford County line reported the sounds of "drums and vollyes of shott."[12]

Within a few days, it became clear to Digges that the originators of the fear were Waugh and others "of the meanest quality." The class warfare underlying the unrest was real. If the elites did not settle the affair fast, they feared that these farmers would "pillage and plunder the people Especially such as had anything to loose." Joseph repeated his story in several letters that the Indian scare was a ruse to justify theft, this despite sworn affidavits that "Easterne shoare Indians" had been the origin of the fear. The councilors quickly corresponded with Virginia planters to cooperate in quelling the storm. Visits to the Piscataway fort and "all the woods between Patuxon and Potomack" found no Seneca army.[13]

The Virginia planters declared William of Orange to be the rightful king on April 27, hoping to quiet the fervor. But in June, a crowd forcibly freed men arrested for spreading the original rumor of a Catholic and Indian plot. Nicholas Spencer agreed with the Maryland Council that class unrest underlay all the commotion in northern Virginia; their personal property was at stake should small farmers exploit the turmoil over the rightful king of England to bring about a greater democracy. The immediate interpretation of the planter elite in both Virginia and Maryland of the unrest was to equate more power in the hands of the people with "plunder." Their assumptions about the purpose of politics—to enrich those who held the reins—tell us more about them than about those beneath them on the social ladder. As we shall see, when Baltimore's councilors lost that power, there was no pillaging of their estates.[14]

Waugh was arrested and brought to Jamestown to publicly apologize and promise obedience to the authorities. But Joseph and the rest of Baltimore's Council, perhaps hoping that James would retake his crown, delayed any public announcement about the monarchy. They were not alone in such a response. James's men in many of the American colonies were loath to accept that a second king had been deposed in their lifetime.[15]

Sir Edmund Andros, James's appointee as political and military commander over the Dominion of New England, sat on the news of the new crowned heads for too long. There, again, the French Indians seemed close to their borders, and the administration's efforts at peacekeeping often appeared to the Massachusetts colonists more like alliance-building. At the moment that most small farmers of the Chesapeake accepted that the Iroquois were not about to join Lord Baltimore in a papist rebellion against their Protestant king, the Puritans to the north took forcefully to the streets of Boston to proclaim that the reign of James and his imperious officials had come to an end. On April 18, led by a carpenter and a "long-time troublemaker," the movement started, not from Boston gentlemen, but from "the rabble" of the city streets, and was carried forward by the arrival of crowds from the surrounding countryside. They "came armed into the town in the afternoon, in such rage and heat, that it made us all tremble . . . for nothing would pacify them but he must be bound in chains." Andros and Edward Randolph, the hated customsman, were imprisoned. The old Puritan governments were back in place in several New England colonies by early May, as if the Dominion had never happened. Opponents of the restoration of self-government decried the activists as "levelling," "democratical," and in search of "an Oliverian republic." The Navigation Acts were suspended in practice, as smugglers and pirates again plied the waters of Massachusetts Bay.[16]

With Andros locked up, his deputy governor in New York, Francis Nicholson, faced his own rebellion without instruction from his superior. It came in the form of a list of grievances from Long Island, grievances against taxes to support an oligarchy. New Yorkers had a shorter history of self-governance than their northern neighbors; the Dutch had not allowed any input from their settlers. But the English takeover had eventually led to an Assembly, which first met in 1683 and wasted no time in drawing up a "Charter of Libertyes and Priviledges," providing for no taxation without representation, a wide franchise for fair representation, and religious toleration. The Charter never was enforced, but the democratic tendencies of the settlers were in no doubt. Now, their hopes of representative government, coupled with the fears of Catholic Indians, led them to declare that James's officials had no legitimacy. Nicholson attempted to bring in the militia to quell dissent, but that backfired on May 31, as the militia mutinied. Jacob Leisler emerged as a leader of the popular movement, and Nicholson fled. The king rewarded the latter with the position of lieutenant governor of Virginia.[17]

June saw the formation of a democratic style of government. A Committee of Safety took over the reins as they awaited orders from the new Protestant monarchs, with Leisler confirmed as commander in chief. In the spring of 1690, he issued writs of election for an Assembly, but although he had mass support from working people, ethnic differences between Dutch and English settlers, as well as the opposition of merchants, obstructed the creation of a united community. Leisler also hoped to unite colonists across colonial boundaries, writing to the new governments in New England. He found a receptive audience in John Coode.[18]

As the Dominion of New England evaporated in April and May, William Joseph of Maryland somehow still failed to see the writing on the wall. The messenger from Baltimore had died before he could tell them to make the declaration of William and Mary, but instead of taking that initiative, Joseph delayed the meeting of the Assembly until October and made no proclamation. Through May and June, Coode and the other husbands of the Gerard sisters aligned with militia officer Jowles to plan the end of the Catholic oppression of Maryland. The oblivious Council thought the country was "all quiet" until a message arrived in the middle of the night of July 16 that Coode "was raising men up Potomack." Two days later, his force, now swollen by men from neighboring counties carrying the public arms, took the courthouse. Although Digges had called up a militia, they refused to defend him, and Coode forced Digges to surrender the government records. Other councilors meanwhile were mustering men around the colony, but met with the same response—the militia were on Coode's side. As his army reached 700, with Jowles as second-in-command, Coode commandeered "great guns" from a ship in the harbor and threatened the Council at Mattapany. With trumpet sounding, he sent in the Declaration and demanded "the imiediate Surrender of the Garrison together with all the Arms Amunicon and all Manner of Warlike provisions whatsoever therein." With no chance "of quieting or repelling the People thus enraged," Baltimore's government ended on August 1, without a shot fired.[19]

John Coode, widower of Susannah Gerard, ally of Josias Fendall, now held power in Maryland. Like the revolutionaries of eighty-seven years later, he felt that the situation demanded that the new Protestant Association explain their actions, so with his brothers-in-law Blakiston and Cheseldyne and others, he composed their Declaration. All was couched in terms of loyalty to William and Mary, arguing that Baltimore had ignored that his Charter placed allegiance to the Crown above allegiance to him. The charges against the proprietor's administration moved seamlessly between Catholicism and corruption—"Churches and Chappels . . . are erected and converted to the use of popish Idolatary and superstition. Jesuits and seminarie priests are the only incumbents . . . as also the Chief Advisers and Councellors in affaires of Government, and the richest and most fertile land sett apart for their use and maintenance." The insurgents' objective was "to defend the Protestant Religion among us, and to protect and chelter the Inhabitants from all manner of violence, oppression and destruccon." The failure of the Council to declare the new monarchs for months after the other colonies was telling. In fact, "solemn masses and prayers are used . . . for the prosperous success of the popish forces in Ireland and the French designs against England." William had declared war on France.[20]

This was no republican statement, but in Maryland what mattered now was democracy in practice, not whether or not Britain had a king or a commonwealth. The Associators issued the writs for an election of "a full and free Assembly," to meet within a month. No Catholic could hold office, but local Protestant sheriffs and justices should continue their management at the county level. They jailed a few noncooperating officials, while the Council sought escape from the colony. Around the colony, people had to decide whether to back the revolutionary regime without knowledge of the action in England and Ireland. A clear class difference emerged. Letters to Baltimore, full of outrage, disclosed again and again that only "the better sort" would not participate in the new Assembly, while "the giddy and besotted multitude" followed Coode and chose delegates "of no commendable life and conversation." One loyal supporter recommended amnesty for all but the ringleaders, to "reduce the people to their obedience," and Baltimore needed to act fast. Along with their expressions of disgust, however, they noted that Coode was the representative of the majority. And one opponent claimed that Coode compared himself to Masaniello.[21]

Masaniello was a leader of a 1647 revolt of the poor in Naples that began as riots born of excessive taxation on food and developed into a campaign against aristocratic rule, succeeding in the very short term in getting equal representation in the government for those at the bottom. That Coode chose him as his role model and not Cromwell of the same era speaks to how his focus was now on democracy rather than republicanism. Unlike Cromwell, Masaniello was a Leveler. Coode made no attempt to become an autocrat. The Associators Convention met promptly in August, and with Cheseldyne as Speaker, voted to continue temporary laws. There would be no executive branch. And they set the lowest levy in a long time, for the excessive costs of "70 or 80 thousand pounds of tobacco for the Charges of his Lordship's Councell & deputie governors" were eradicated. Local courts carried on conducting most of the colony's routine business over the fall of 1689. Coode, now serving as commander in chief of the armed forces, corresponded with England and other colonies on their behalf, including Leisler of New York. They maintained a friendly correspondence especially about mutual concerns for defense against the French and Indians.[22]

In England, as soon as Baltimore became aware of the summer events, he sought help to reclaim his authority, but the Committee for Trade and Plantations did not leap to his defense. Even before the rebellion, they had recommended that proprietary colonies Maryland, Pennsylvania, and Carolina come "under a nearer dependence on the Crown." They questioned why the monarchs had not been proclaimed in Maryland. Although Baltimore produced paperwork explaining how he had sent an undelivered order in February, in January the committee decided upon a full investigation before they would restore his control. Having also read the Declaration, they ordered that "the Present administration" remain in command of Maryland's government. The official blessing of William himself, dated February 1, left no further gray area: "We do further authorize and impower you to continue in our name your care in the administration of the Government." Most importantly, enforcement of the Navigation Acts, and thus collection of the king's revenue, should command their full attention.[23]

Before the rebels had received this news, however, Baltimore's representatives in Maryland further played into the hands of the rebels. Members of his Council had been on the run since the overthrow of their regime, spotted in Pennsylvania and Virginia as they sought a route to England. On the night of January 3, 1690, Baltimore's stepson Nicholas Sewall secretly made his way to his Maryland home. The Convention's customs official, John Payne, found out and tried to board his boat for inspection, but fearing capture, Sewall's crew shot Payne and ran to Virginia. Duplicating the murder of Rousby by Talbot, the old regime had placed themselves as opponents of the king's customs collector. Coode demanded that the Virginia authorities return the culprits for their trial. The Virginians arrested the men, but proved reluctant to hand them over to a rebel government. But Coode could now report to London that it was the rebels who defended the king's purse and Baltimore's councilors who killed a second customs officer.[24]

The second meeting of the Maryland Convention in April 1690 put executive power in the hands of a Committee of Twenty, with two delegates from each county, to run the colony between meetings of the Assembly. Coode, Blakiston, and Cheseldyne were the first three names on the list. Yet, true to political principle, the committee had little power. The first serious challenge they faced came in June in the person of Baltimore's agent, James Heath. Heath demanded Baltimore's personal property and the share of export revenues traditionally granted to the proprietor. What should they concede? After some deliberation, the committee allowed that Baltimore could have any bills and bonds in his name in the government offices, but he would not get Mattapany House back, for that was a government building, not his personal property. Of course, Heath could assume possession of any crops and livestock on the surrounding plantation, but the committee was not responsible for any missing animals. Perhaps ex-councilors Darnall and Sewall had removed some of the stock, they suggested. Naturally, Heath was furious, composing in response a statement accusing Coode of embezzlement and tyranny, among other crimes. It was clear that Crown officials in Whitehall would have to decide the financial settlement of Baltimore's estate, public and private. Coode and Cheseldyne sailed to England in July, as the official agents of the colonists, and Blakiston stepped into the leadership role in St. Mary's.[25]

Over the winter, the arguments raged back and forth to the Committee for Trade and Plantations about the merits of Baltimore's regime pre-rebellion and about his rights as a private property owner in Maryland. Coode and Cheseldyne mounted a formidable defense of the rebellion, detailing the various decisions by Baltimore that had caused friction with the Lower House for decades. Whether those arguments truly persuaded the Crown authorities, or whether their general inclination for tighter royal control of the colonies won the day, we cannot know. Certainly, Charles II, James II, and William had in common the desire for Navigation Acts enforcement. Coode could point to the murder and subsequent coverup of not one but two different customs officers by Baltimore's closest confidants. On March 12, 1691, King William revoked the Charter given the first Lord Baltimore and brought the "Province of Maryland under our immediate care and Protection." He would appoint a governor, of course, but the rule of the Calverts was over.[26]

The planter elite had effectively silenced Parson Waugh in Virginia, and that colony escaped any further unrest. But in North Carolina, where arbitrary rule for several years by a new proprietor named Seth Sothell had subjugated the Levelers and Quakers, they rose again to exploit the revolutionary moment of 1689. Sothell was no Catholic, and the Albemarle movement had no element of anti-popery at all. As the men of Albemarle might have explained to those in Maryland, corruption could spawn from all faiths. Sothell had persecuted George Durant, seizing his lands. Little documentation has survived to explain the events of the late summer and fall; but we know that those whom Francis Nicholson, the new governor of Virginia, described as "the Mob" imprisoned Sothell, accusing him of "unjust and arbitrary actions," and banished him. The Lords Proprietors in London, conscious of royal scrutiny of the American colonies, suspended him from office and appointed a prominent Virginia planter, Philip Ludwell, governor in his place.[27]

When Ludwell's authority was challenged in the summer of 1690, he appealed to Nicholson for help. Having learned his lesson in New York, Nicholson had been given a second chance as a colonial administrator. He sent Ludwell to England, writing ahead of him to the Committee for Trade and Plantations that he had settled the political scene. Nicholson could not afford to be seen as weak again, but the uncertainty of the political structure in Maryland and North Carolina threatened Virginia, for "here is in this Country a great many idle & poor people that would be ready to follow their neighbours." Ludwell appointed Thomas Jarvis as a deputy governor of North Carolina, unaware that Jarvis had run away from Maryland with John Jenkins in the aftermath of Fendall's Rebellion in 1658. Albemarle's reins were back in the hands of a commonwealthman. And as he never crossed the Great Dismal Swamp, Ludwell had no idea that now residing in Perquimans County, sheltered by Jarvis, was the old radical himself, Josias Fendall.[28]

Nicholson continued to plead the dangerous conditions along the American coast. In his eyes, there was a great deal too much democracy. Leisler had swung from the gallows, but North Carolina still offered a safe haven for escaping "Servants Debtors and Slaves." The Quakers of Pennsylvania, given their "pernicious principles," might ally themselves with the French. With Maryland in the hands of Coode in 1691, such places were "fatall examples" for Virginians. And he noted that the colonial democrats were not isolated, discrete communities. The Fendall's Rebellion network now stretched north and south along the American coast. "For in all these parts they correspond very much one with another."[29]

THE MOVEMENT FOR a democratic republic along the Chesapeake's waterways had endured for almost fifty years by the summer of 1691. Born in the days of Ingle's Rebellion and forged at the table of Susannah Gerard in Bushwood, Maryland, the faith in the rights and abilities of commoners to rule themselves never ebbed. Pope and Sturman, Gerard and Fendall, Jenkins and Jarvis, Bacon and Culpeper, Coode and Cheseldyne: with feisty women maintaining their network, their perseverance over the decades stands as the truest militancy.

The restoration of the Albemarle democracy proceeded under Jarvis until his death in 1694, and he was followed into office by Thomas Harvey, whose earlier marriage to Johanna, the widow of John Jenkins, gives some indication of his political attitudes. With self-government, a wide franchise, and religious toleration, Albemarle in the 1690s saw none of the unrest of previous decades. Their victory was closer to total than that of the Gerards in Maryland; no authoritarian Englishman sat in the governor's chair, Edward Randolph's rants about the free movement of pirates and smugglers had no impact, and the Church of England received no mandatory tithes. They paid no quitrents, little customs, and small levies. No Indian trouble disturbed them. But the grandees would eventually emerge.[30]

Maryland's story was a little more mixed. Edward Andros, who had firmly controlled the Dominion of New England for the Stuarts, took over as temporary governor in 1693, immediately dissolving the Assembly. When the king appointed Nicholson for a longer term, Andros returned to Virginia. Now the Chesapeake was supervised by experienced military officers, and not just any officers, but those who had presided over the hated Dominion and tried to cover up the overthrow of James II. Had the Glorious Revolution been for nought?[31]

Nicholson's appointment began in the fall of 1694. This was a man who would brook no more of the provincial disobedience and disregard for proper class deference. Troublemakers needed to be identified and curtailed. And the source of all trouble in Maryland had been the Gerard clan. Seeking to establish his authority over the popular locals, he called for an accounting of the revolutionary years, demanding to know where the public arms had been distributed and about the handling of any taxes. Blakiston had just died. His widow, Elizabeth Gerard Blakiston, Coode, and Cheseldyne were on the defensive. A year later, they had collected and presented all the paperwork to clear themselves of any wrongdoing. But Coode saw the writing on the wall: that Nicholson viewed his leadership in the community as a threat to central power. "Let me have agen the papers delivered in Councill about Surrender of Mattapany wch thinke my selfe unsafe in being with out," Coode wrote, for the official surrender of Baltimore's Council protected his status as the leader of a revolution that had fought for the present king.[32]

Coode's prescience became apparent in 1696, when Nicholson felt secure enough in his position to make his move against the republican democrat. Informers told him that Coode was stirring up people, educating them about good government, and trying to build a movement that would restore the kind of representative democracy Maryland had enjoyed under the Committee of Twenty. Nicholson wanted the radical removed from the House of Burgesses. The charges shifted as the governor sought any means to oust Coode. It began with an accusation that Coode was a minister, because those who had held religious office could not serve in the Lower House. Coode had been an Anglican priest when he arrived in Maryland in 1672, but since his marriage to Susannah Gerard had not served in that capacity. It was widely accepted in the seventeenth century that clergy should be devoted to spiritual, not temporal, affairs. Nicholson would not let him be sworn in. Coode's colleagues defended him vociferously, as they had fifteen years before. "We humbly acquaint your Excellency that we find the said Lieutenant Col. John Cood is a member of this House duly Elected that he hath sate in the General Assemblies of this province for almost twenty years together . . . we humbly conceive our Selves proper Judges of our own members and therefore have resolved that the said John Cood is Legally qualified to sit as a member of this House."[33]

Infuriated by this response, Nicholson sent for the lawyers of St. Mary's to come immediately to the Council, seeking proof that Coode's background as a minister in England would prohibit him from service, "whether a Priest can dispriest himself." Coode's colleagues meanwhile resolved that they would do no government business "till the House was full." The lawyers, including Cheseldyne, had to agree that legal precedent worked against Coode, for Holy Orders left "an Indeleble Character stamped upon" those who had ever been ordained. But the Lower House again voted that he was qualified.[34]

Now Nicholson turned his wrath on Coode, calling him "so . . . wicked scarce to be parrelled in the Province . . . his Factious contradictory Spirit in all manner of Business . . . whether he has not at this present Cost the County more Tobacco then Perhaps he is worth or ever will do them good." The argument went back and forth from House to Council for four days. Even when a committee reported that Coode had undoubtedly served as a minister in both England and Maryland, the burgesses stood by the man who had always been willing to speak truth to power, to organize them, and to risk his neck in a leadership role for his community's rights to a just and representative government. Nicholson shamed them into at least launching the governmental affairs—they were spending the people's money while in session—and searched for witnesses who would testify against Coode on other matters.[35]

Once he had found one man willing to depose that Coode had committed blasphemy, Nicholson summoned the men who were in the vicinity at the time of the alleged crime. (The irony of accusing him of blasphemy while at the same time pursuing his downfall through his position as a religious minister appears to have been lost on Nicholson; he wanted to rid himself of the troublesome priest, by any means.) This would be grounds for removing Coode from his position as a militia officer. Three of the men could recall "nothing material." But the others provided some very interesting reports.[36]

At Mrs. Proctor's Annapolis tavern, in conversation with a local Catholic, Coode was reported to have dismissed Christianity altogether, declaring "all Religion to be a Sham," arguing the unlikelihood "of God Almighty's Genereateing a Son," "That the Priests of both the Churches, Roman and Protestant were Rogues and that it was all one to serve God or the Devill, for Religion (said he) is but policy." Several witnesses deposed that he said, "All Religion lies in Tullies Offices."[37]

"Tully" referred to Marcus Tullius Cicero, philosopher of the Roman Republic, who, in the fall of 44 B.C.E., wrote *De Officiis*, having been pushed out of political office as Caesar, Antony, and Augustus struggled for control of the state. *De Officiis* takes the form of a letter to Cicero's son, advising him on becoming a virtuous man. Known by the early seventeenth century as "Tullies Offices," the work had been very popular among the well-educated of England through the Tudor and Stuart dynasties. While England's universities still would not waste money on books for their libraries, experts estimate that about 70 percent of Cambridge students owned a personal copy.[38]

The essential wisdom from "Tullies Offices" taught that the most noble profession was public service. The expedient and the virtuous need not be at odds. Justice required placing the public good over the private. That such lessons needed no grounding in Christian scripture or theology was inherent in the date of its first publication.[39] Other writings by Cicero included *The Republic*. Cicero scholar Raphael Woolf tells us we should not confuse terms used by Cicero, such as "republic" and "democracy," with the meanings those words convey to the modern reader. For "republic," "commonwealth is probably the most literal equivalent in English that still captures the distinctly political sense of the Latin phrase." The one common and crucial component of all Cicero's teachings about good government was equality of all classes before the law. "Cohering around what one might call a principle of transparency," Cicero argued that "states rot from the head down," and even the most virtuous of men must be checked by accountability for their decisions in government.[40]

Coode was teaching the people of Maryland that justice was not "Equally & impartially administred" under Nicholson. They had thought that the dismissal of Catholics from office would have brought an end to arbitrary government, but time had revealed the opposite, for Andros had instantly shut down the Assembly. What made Coode so especially dangerous was that, despite his own status as a wealthy landowner, he attempted to educate others. For Nicholson got wind of the fact that Coode was "writing or having such sort of Booke or pamphlets, which may prove of more dangerous consequence to those persons, in whose hands such writings may chance to Come." "Tullies Offices" removed the Anglican pulpit's efficacy as a means of telling people that God's will was that they be obedient and know their place—the Anglican cosmology of the planter class currently taking shape throughout the Chesapeake region. Nicholson ordered the seizure of all papers in Coode's home, authorizing the sheriff to "break open lock, trunck, Chest . . . and take into his possession all small pamphlets, writings and papers & close seal them up in a bagg, together with a Catalogue or List of all his other Books."[41]

The censorship reminds us that Coode was right. Books about commonwealths and constitutions might be fine in the hands of gentlemen in Cambridge or on Virginia plantations—those we would come to call Enlightenment scholars—but such questioning of power and hierarchies could not be tolerated among the lower classes. There, egalitarian thought might be seen as a termite, eating away at the structure of planter power. This was what the planter class meant by law and order, by stability—the repression of ideologies that might shake the foundation of their privilege. Public education represented a real and present danger. Coode's desire to share what he was learning through his studies reminds us of the freedom of the 1640s, as preachers and soldiers alike spread knowledge throughout the Atlantic world. The cheap press had produced thousands of broadsides, full of news, satire, and song. Education on a democratic scale led to a republic, a commonwealth without Star Chamber, where people would demand that the "greatest he" should have no more say than the poorest. But there was no press in the 1690s Chesapeake.[42]

The House of Burgesses finally had to concede that Coode could not be a member, and he left. Understanding that Nicholson would not be content until he was entirely silenced, Coode ran to Virginia that fall, and despite the governor's pleading with Andros to arrest him, Coode remained sheltered by friends in the Northern Neck for at least two years. But he remained a threat to Nicholson, for Coode spent his time in Virginia penning an attack on the governor and his arbitrary ways. Proclamations pinned to every place of public gathering threatened prosecution to anyone who might harbor Coode and offered a lucrative twenty pounds sterling reward for his apprehension. No one turned him in.[43]

The storm blew in again in the fall of 1698. Again, "great disturbances . . . fomented by divers wicked persons . . . especially by John Cood" showed that the royal regime did not satisfy all the Protestants of Maryland. Finally, though, Nicholson caught some of the troublemakers. He arrested and imprisoned the next generation of the Gerard clan, Gerard Slye, son of Susannah Gerard and Robert Slye, for causing public commotions, and for "abusing and reviling" Nicholson. The governor proved amenable to forgive Slye as a misled man, if he would "deliver up all Papers." Sheriffs pulled in other friends of Coode from the days of the Revolution, Philip Clark and Robert Mason, in hope they could deliver Coode and the offending writings. These papers turned out to be a rough draft of "Articles of Charge against his Excellency," handed over by Slye to secure his own release from prison. Nicholson led a grand jury to indict Coode in absentia for "endeavaouring . . . to excite & stir up his majestys liege people within this province to rebel against his Majestys Govr." Nicholson sent angry messages to Andros all fall, pressing him to find and arrest Coode, who had found refuge in Virginia and continued to communicate with Maryland. Andros, no friend to Nicholson, sent all the admittedly "extraordinary" documents related to Coode back to the authorities in England, but made no fresh attempts to arrest him.[44]

Many people in Maryland, despite their great respect for Coode, were unable to expend the same level of energy and risk-taking necessary to maintain his degree of militancy, for allies like Clark, Slye, and Mason suffered badly at the hands of Nicholson. The Lower House successfully intervened on Clark's behalf, but his prosecution had a chilling effect nonetheless. At this moment, Nicholson's machinations against his rival Andros succeeded, and in December 1698, Nicholson moved to Virginia to assume that more lucrative office. From there he issued a new decree against his indefatigable enemy, his fury displayed in the personal nature of his attack, claiming Coode to be "a deformed pson his face resembleing that of a Baboone or Monkey Clubfooted his feet Standing inwards one to the other and a Notorious Coward." But Coode held the loyalty of his neighbors and quickly moved back to Maryland.[45]

The new royal governor was Nathaniel Blakiston, grandson of the regicide. He had not grown up in Maryland with the Gerard clan, but was a nephew of Nehemiah and Elizabeth Gerard Blakiston, and the family's anti-autocrat philosophy showed in his decisions. He had, however, served in the West Indies in both military and political office, so he was no rebel. The governor pardoned Clark and Mason. He clearly respected the powers of the Lower House and government at the local level. He advised Coode to surrender to the justice system for his blasphemy, but Coode took his time, demonstrating the boundaries of real power in the colony. His trial that summer kept Nicholson from further interference. A jury convicted him of blasphemy, but not of rebellion, and sentenced him (probably the usual penalty for blasphemy, the boring of the tongue with a red-hot iron), but in the fall, the justices asked Blakiston to suspend "the execution of the Corporal Punishments . . . upon consideration of his service done on the Revolution," and the Council agreed unanimously. Coode never even paid the fine. He lived quietly under Blakiston, who reduced public taxation and relaxed enforcement of many laws. But when another officious royal governor arrived from England, Coode would again take a seat in the legislature in 1708, shortly before his death.[46]

The men of the Revolution of 1689 limited royal control through an Assembly with a strong sense of self through the 1690s. They protected Coode. They severely limited plural office-holding. Quakers in the community held out against church establishment. However, as those public representatives grew wealthier on the black backs of those they had purchased and enslaved, their dedication to the principle of equality waned. Now they would manipulate the meaning of liberty to include only those of European origin. Cheseldyne enslaved at least a dozen people. Nehemiah Blakiston's widow,

Elizabeth Gerard, remarried, and together they purchased eleven people. By 1708 even Coode's estate included seven enslaved people.[47] As the seventeenth century gave way to the eighteenth, power in Maryland and North Carolina became ensconced in the elite planter class, as in their neighbor Virginia. Some would describe this development as "maturation" or "stability," but it would seem a step back from what Coode offered—a democratic republic, only achieved almost ninety years later and preceded and accompanied by the enslavement of hundreds of thousands.[48]

The repression of Coode and his ideas reveals how democracy threatened elite power on the eve of the eighteenth century. Throughout the British Empire, High Tories would strike back, seizing power in Britain, and using establishment of the Anglican Church to bring their distorted version of order—like an old feudal triangle of wealth distribution and power—to the globe. Establishment meant the prohibition of dissenters of all stripes from the political system, in places like Maryland and North Carolina. It meant a rigid system of racial hierarchy in the American colonies, for acceptance into the southern planter elite demanded conformity.[49] The pulpits issued a theology of knowing one's place, that God had willed that one remain in the condition in which one was born. To resist authority on earth was to challenge His authority in heaven.

The dissenters, freed by the English Revolution to interpret the Bible for themselves, had emancipated thought for the English-speaking world in the second half of the seventeenth century. The lowly Christ, who washed the feet of the disciples, who preached in the Sermon on the Mount that it was the meek and the poor who were God's chosen: this was the God of the dissenting. Essentially revolutionary in its overthrow of the notion that God looked with favor upon the rich, it moved the religious and political worlds closer together.

A few like Coode moved through and beyond the religious sphere and into a republican philosophy that needed no God to defend its righteousness. Equal justice marked a virtuous society. Coode had witnessed how Baltimore's justice system had tried to allow Talbot, the murderer of Rousby, to escape punishment. That seemed like Catholic justice, but even after the Protestant Revolution, Nicholson would use the justice system to try to silence dissent. Thus it was not only or necessarily the theology of Catholicism that led to arbitrary government. Master Tully taught before the birth of Christ that the best society depended on equality before the law.

Military men like Andros and Nicholson, planters like William Byrd II in Virginia, Caleb Dorsey in Maryland, Thomas Pollock in North Carolina—all shared a vision of the "best society" that contrasted sharply with that of Coode. Their best society would be governed by the best people, and the best people were themselves and their children. Even self-made men who might at first have resented those born to privilege accepted the concept of hierarchy of birth when their sons were born. Intermarriage of elite colonial children mimicked that of aristocratic matches in Europe. They would create a governing class, an elite of unlimited wealth, groomed for leadership. This required the repression of dissenting theologies, of preachers who might draw attention back to the lowly Christ, let alone classical philosophy and the critical thinking it provoked. Education must be limited; access to pulpits must be limited; access to justice must be limited. If lower-class whites demanded justice, they would be reminded how lucky they were. When blacks demanded justice, they could be killed.[50]

John Coode's education and desire to educate others represent the last gasp of the seventeenth century—on land. There were Levelers yet, at sea, on board pirate boats, thwarting the Royal Navy: stealing their money and flaunting their disrespect. Men of all colors sought to establish another order. Their days were numbered, too.[51]

Conclusion

The group of people connected by the family of Thomas and Susannah Gerard, clustered in a few square miles on either side of the Potomac in St. Mary's, Charles, Westmoreland, and Stafford Counties, fought for fifty years to build a representative democracy with free white male suffrage. Joined by thousands of others in Virginia and North Carolina, risking their lives and livelihoods for a Leveler republic, they claimed again and again that "the poorest he" should not be taxed without representation. They believed that class status at birth did not determine one's ability and should not determine one's civil rights or political ambition. Spreading out around the Chesapeake region, they sought safe places away from state infrastructure to practice self-government, thwarting the old regimes where power resided only in the hands of the well-connected few.

These radicals developed alliances that crossed traditional demographic categories. Women played leading roles. Although there is no evidence that these women argued for their own franchise, there is every reason to believe that most of the men whose names are attached to this movement followed the lead of their wives. Women taught men to question traditional sources and customs of authority, and women organized men to realize change. At moments in the story, enslaved and free black people fought with the rebels, and Indians lived peacefully alongside them. These groups would not see personal or collective gains, but fought for the best possible outcome from the options of that moment. Each person understood that rule by English kings and lords, or the Chesapeake planter elite, would not be in their best interest.

Some players surprise us. Thomas and Susannah were wealthy and well connected, Josias Fendall owned thousands of acres, and John Jenkins and George Durant would grow relatively rich. Yet they adopted political positions to empower others, risking their fortunes in the process. Fendall would lose almost everything. A governor once seized Durant's entire estate. So what drove them to continue fighting? They had lived through a king beheaded and a society run by artisans. True believers in republican ideas, they grasped what Thomas Paine would explain a century later. "No one by birth could have a right to set up his own family in perpetual preference to all others for ever. . . . One of the strongest natural proofs of the folly of hereditary right in Kings, is that nature disapproves it, otherwise she would not so frequently turn it into ridicule, by giving mankind an ASS FOR A LION. . . . A French bastard landing with an armed Banditti and establishing himself king of England against the consent of the natives, is in plain terms a very paltry rascally original. It certainly hath no divinity in it."[1] No publishers existed in the seventeenth-century Chesapeake to capture a pamphlet like *Common Sense*, but we can suppose that among John Coode's papers lay similar reasoning. Royal Governor Nicholson was smart enough to have them burned.

However, political principles rarely lie far from economic concerns. When it served their purpose, seventeenth-century radicals in the colonies would declare their devotion to the king. Sometimes the more immediate enemy was Lord Baltimore or William Berkeley or Seth Sothell. The man directly in front of them, preventing their participation in deciding on how much the people would pay in taxes to support his lifestyle, was the one who had to be dealt with. Philosophical purity to republicanism would hamper the overthrow of the proprietor or governor, because perhaps the Crown might help in ousting him, as William of Orange did when he ruled in favor of the Protestant Associators in 1691. Philosophical purity is a luxury not afforded many on the front lines of oppression. Pragmatic, compromising solutions offered to ease the economic burden, and people with little power in the face of a mighty empire chose them.

But a nastier compromise must damage their historical reputation. In their attempt to overthrow the British hereditary class system, they acquiesced to the continuation of lineage in a different form. Race, a relatively new concept, substituted as the category to determine even an opportunity to have a say in government. This was not unquestioned in the seventeenth century, when many indentured servants saw little difference between themselves and the Africans working alongside them. Bacon issued an emancipation declaration, and black and white fought together for the overthrow of Berkeley. Along Maryland's Eastern Shore, free black and mixed-race marriages highlighted the equality of all men in real terms. We cannot accept arguments about the inevitability or unconscious development of slavery in the colonies.

Over a couple of generations, the republican radicals along the banks of the Potomac, including the ancestors of George Washington, decided where to stand on lineage as determinant of one's access to power. In Ingle's time, they fought as Levelers. By 1690, they fought exclusively for white men. And another generation later, some would fully embrace the old class *and* racial hierarchies, marrying to join the rich and dominant political class, comparable to the regimes of Baltimore and Berkeley. That was a lucrative decision; "from 1711 on, the wealth of the richest 5 per cent really ballooned," writes Maryland's economic historian. In 1776, they accepted that to maintain their wealth in slaves, they must combine with poor white men to defeat the British. They conceded in principle, if very little in practice, the equality of lower-class whites to ensure their participation in the War for Independence. Through that war, the planter elite continued to manipulate racial antagonisms to preserve their political control for another century. And poor whites accepted the racial hierarchy to preserve their relative status.[2]

Gender, an ancient concept, also continued as a system of political, legal, and social inequality *within* the race and class structures. Relative positioning fluctuated; Mary Beth Norton has demonstrated how "rank trumped gender" in the seventeenth century, when Lady Berkeley made decisions for and commanded deference from white men in a lower class. Kathleen Brown has shown us how gender influenced the creation of the social construct of race. Slavery and patriarchy mutually reinforced the ability of a few to grow both rich and powerful, putting the hard and dirty work on the backs of others, exploiting their labor in households and plantations, on ships, and, later, in factories.[3]

Nonetheless, the Gerard network's fight to overthrow the old class system in the colonies should be seen in the same light as suffragists and civil rights activists of the modern period. While we might wish that our forebears could have reasoned or empathized their way through to the fullest vision of human equality, we should celebrate all who faced down severe repression in their attempts to remove even one brick in the wall of inequality. The maintenance of resistance is exhausting. Protest movements demanding an extension of rights to new groups of Americans eventually provoke backlash. Egalitarians often end up fighting their neighbors as well as the powers that be, for disquiet in the streets and in the courts is upsetting. But this is the most American behavior of all—using one's freedom to work toward the altering or abolition of any system of government that is not serving the ends of the "Safety and Happiness" of all.

As the seventeenth century gave way to the eighteenth, the struggle for a real democracy waned. Southern planters—including some descendants of the Gerard network, corrupted by wealth and status—hitching their power to racist ideology to counter class antagonisms, wore down their opposition with a relentless campaign, absorbing the rebellions and the protests and the dissent. They would buy off some of their poor neighbors with a system of racial hierarchy aimed at both African and Indian, silence others through church establishment, and push the fiercest radicals west to the frontier. Divided by race, those at the bottom found no common ground for a commonwealth.

Some historians have seen the onset of the Georgian era as the coming of stability and a civil society from an era of disorder. Those who sought the equality of all, although they succeeded for short spells in North Carolina, lost altogether or settled for less. But "law and order" is the rallying cry of the fascist, not the democrat. It is not disordered to fight for the equality of all; we should consider such action the most civilized. "Barbarous" is better applied to the inhumane treatment of others—not the actions of rebellious servants. There has been little less civilized in American history than the selling of people, naked on auction blocks, to the highest bidder.[4]

So the attention paid to the lineages of southern planters, still sometimes heralded like nobility, is misplaced when we seek heroes from our past. While the lineage of that Maryland gentry can be charted through two women—Henrietta Maria (named after Charles I's Catholic queen) Neale Bennet Lloyd and Jane Lowe Sewall Calvert—another lineage, that of the radicals, can be traced from Susannah Snowe Gerard. The concept of equality in the South—even white male equality—is better traced through Bushwood than Monticello.[5]

"Ideas that are defeated often seem to disappear, but more often they persist, deep beneath the surface, slowly shifting the plates above," James Kloppenberg notes.[6] The Sons of Liberty and the North Carolina Regulators—dissenters from Anglicanism—would fight again for equality before the law generations later. By that time, racism had had generations in which to seem natural to whites who had lived in slave societies. While the American Revolution would lead to the end of slavery in half of the new nation, where slavery did not form the bedrock of their communities, the three-fifths compromise at the Constitutional Convention founded a nation of liberty upon slavery. Starting with the descendant of the leader of Ingle's Rebellion, slave-owning president after slave-owning president governed until only devastating war would bring an end to the selling of people.

When we think of American revolutionaries, our minds tend to 1776 and a declaration penned by a southern planter, from a breed of men who envisioned themselves as the aristocracy of the colonial world. Those men wanted independence from Britain so that they might rule. But the 1770s push for a republic founded on social equality, just like the 1650s effort, came not from those types, but from the recently arrived landless immigrants, the dockside laborers of the port cities and the small farmers of the back country who would refuse to fight in a Continental Army that did not stand for their equality before the law and equality of opportunity for their children. Those revolutionaries made it clear that they would not stoop and bow for any other American. Their seventeenth-century antecedents were the regicides in England and the republicans in Maryland and North Carolina. The Gerard network deserves a prominent place in the political history of the United States.

Notes

Abbreviations

AM   Maryland State Archives
CRNC Colonial Records of North Carolina
EBBA English Broadside Ballad Archive, University of California at Santa Barbara
NCSA North Carolina State Archives, Raleigh

Introduction

1. Kloppenberg, *Toward Democracy*, 4.

2. Carla Pestana's *The English Atlantic in an Age of Revolution* examines the Interregnum period throughout the Atlantic region, including Africa and the Caribbean. She usefully sets some of the Maryland rebellions in this wider context, but the scope of work does not allow for an in-depth look at activists. John Donoghue, in *Fire under the Ashes*, does follow a network of activists moving between London and New England. He shows us how radical ideas circulated in the Atlantic in the era, highlighting how one neighborhood sent out people who struggled for egalitarian ideals, even confronting slavery. The anti-Catholicism tied into their political ideology compromises the message. Donoghue's and Pestana's works conclude before we can see the longer-term effects of the radical ideas, especially in the southern colonies. David Lovejoy, *The Glorious Revolution in America*, is an excellent telling of that part of the story through several colonies, yet he does not explain John Coode. Peter Linebaugh and Marcus Rediker, in *The Many-Headed Hydra*, enlarged our perspective to show us working people of every gender, color, and degree of freedom intent on extending their autonomy in the colonial era. The threat this underclass posed made them a "many-headed hydra," an ever-looming threat to authority, not a docile mass that elites might ignore as they argued about government among themselves. This thesis is well supported in the records of the Chesapeake in the seventeenth century.

3. Riordan, *Plundering Time*; Rice, *Tales*; Carr and Jordan, *Maryland's Revolution of Government*.

4. I am indebted to the genealogical websites created by the Milam family of Virginia and the Combs family, and to the descendants of George Durant and of John and Johanna Jenkins, especially Billee Stallings, for their laborious research.

5. Ahnert and Ahnert, "Protestant Letter Networks in the Reign of Mary I," 1–33.

6. "The sex ratio was six men to a woman in the 1630s and three men to a woman by mid-century and after." Carr, "From Servant to Freeholder," 26.

7. Hailwood, "'Come Hear This Ditty.'"

8. Brewer, "Slavery, Sovereignty, and 'Inheritable Blood,'" 1038–78. I agree fundamentally with Brewer that there existed a "parallel logic" in the late seventeenth-century

Atlantic world, whereby the proponents of hereditary power in terms of monarchy and aristocracy bought most fully into the idea that slavery was hereditary.

Chapter One

1. Antoinette Sutto's excellent work, *Loyal Protestants and Dangerous Papists* (2015), examines in full the fluctuating relationship between church and state in seventeenth-century Maryland. Sutto argues that the degrees of loyalty to England and to the Stuarts shown by Maryland practitioners of the many shades of Christianity were "a long awkward negotiation." Baltimore's policy of toleration, seen in its seventeenth-century context, is not a modern, secular policy. This book will focus on the organization and strategies of popular politics in the shadows of that negotiation. For included in the debate over the proper roles of Crown and confessional should have been another—local power. And that debate that happened on the ground was less theoretical or theological and more pragmatic. The protagonists were consistent about one thing—increasing their control over their own lives. When a republic was possible, they were republicans. When it was not, they would praise a king to secure his assistance in overthrowing an aristocrat. When it helped, they would claim that Catholicism was tyranny, even if their spouse was Catholic. John D. Krugler, in *English and Catholic*, makes a case that the success that the original Calvert had in balancing his political and material success with his Catholicism in England allowed him to pursue an extension to the colonies.

2. Puritans portrayed Catholicism, or "popery," as an opposite rather than a different branch of Christianity. In their eyes, the acceptance of the authority of a man, the pope, an authority supported by ritual and a mythology of saints and relics, marked out popery as the realm of the Anti-Christ. Authority emanated solely from God, explicitly described in Scripture, they believed. The Catholicism of England's enemies, the Spanish, French, and Irish, linked the spiritual to the political. Peter Lake, "Antipopery: The Structure of a Prejudice," in Cust and Hughes, *Conflict in Early Stuart England*. Some of the most important literature on the reign of Charles I includes Lockyer, *The Early Stuarts*; Cust, *Charles I*; Hill, *A Century of Revolution*; Kishlansky, *A Monarchy Transformed*; Russell, *The Fall of the British Monarchies, 1637–1642*.

3. Krugler, *English and Catholic*, 7–9; Land, *Colonial Maryland*, 4–6; quote from Osgood, *The American Colonies in the Seventeenth Century*, 59; Farrelly, *Papist Patriots*, 49–50.

4. James Horn, "Servant Emigration to the Chesapeake in the Seventeenth Century," in Tate and Ammerman, *The Chesapeake in the Seventeenth Century*, 54; Carr, "From Servant to Freeholder," 26.

5. AM 1: 2–9, 170; AM 4: 37, 46, 54; Jordan, *Foundations of Representative Government*, 1, 19–22, 35–36. Jordan's detailed examination of the Maryland Assembly in the 1630s and 1640s shows how politically conscious these freemen were, with "an avid interest in the English political scene and similarly intensive debates in Maryland on many of the same subjects," 29–31.

6. AM 3: 89–90.

7. Snyder, *Brabbling Women*; Julie Crawford, *Mediatrix*, 2–10; Patricia Crawford, "Piety and Spirituality," in Dinan and Meyers, *Women and Religion*. Works that examine

the lives of women of this era in Maryland include Meyers, *Common Whores, Vertuous Women, and Loveing Wives*; Carr and Walsh, "The Planter's Wife"; Mary Beth Norton, "Gender, Crime and Community," in Henretta, Kammen, and Katz, *The Transformation of Early American History*.

8. Jordan, *Foundations of Representative Government*, 14; Russell Menard, "Immigrants and Their Increase," in Land, Carr, and Papenfuse, *Law, Society, and Politics*, 92–93; James Horn, "Adapting to a New World," in Carr, Morgan, and Russo, *Colonial Chesapeake Society*, 153–56. I am indebted to the generation of Maryland social historians, especially Lois Carr, Lorena Walsh, and Russell Menard, whose painstaking and masterful scholarship on the social, economic, and demographic history of this region grounds all my research.

9. Wareing, *Indentured Migration and the Servant Trade*, 142–44; Revel, "The Poor Unhappy Transported Felon's Sorrowful Account"; AM 10: 213–15; 49: 318–19.

10. Lorena Walsh, "Community Networks in the Early Chesapeake," in Carr, Morgan, and Russo, *Colonial Chesapeake Society*, 219–39. Walsh's article is a jumping-off point for my work here; I wanted to see whether there were political ramifications for the powerful in this lack of deference. The small radius for connections that she mapped also proves very important in this story.

11. Horn, "Adapting to a New World," 148–59.

12. Rice, *Nature and History in the Potomac*, 92–96. Rice gives a full description of the ecological and political environment of the Potomac region at the moment of contact, including the territories of the Iroquoian Susquehannocks and the Piscataways, Chopticos, and Wicomocos. Fausz, "Merging and Emerging Worlds," in Carr, Morgan, and Russo, *Colonial Chesapeake Society*, 51–72; Sutto, *Loyal Protestants and Dangerous Papists*, 37–44, 53–56.

13. Barry, *Roger Williams*, 42–78. For the fullest treatment of the entire British Atlantic world's interaction with the English Civil War, see Pestana, *The English Atlantic*.

14. Robertson, *Tyrannicide Brief*; Viswanathan, *Masks of Conquest*. Viswanathan explores how the academic discipline of English literature in India in the nineteenth century was "a vital, active instrument of Western hegemony in concert with commercial expansion and military action," 166–67.

15. The literature on the English Revolution is enormous. Recent overviews include Braddick, *God's Fury*; Hirst, *England in Conflict*; Kennedy, *The English Revolution*; Woolrych, *Britain in Revolution*.

16. Robertson, *Tyrannicide Brief*, 46–48.

17. Scottish National Covenant, February 37, 1638.

18. Braddick, *God's Fury*, 134–41, 196–208; Robertson, *Tyrannicide Brief*, 71.

19. Kishlansky, *Monarchy Transformed*, 147–49; Woolrych, *Britain in Revolution*, 209–13.

20. Braddick, *God's Fury*, 210, 243–46, 353–54.

21. Hill, *The World Turned Upside Down*, 57–63.

22. Kloppenberg, *Toward Democracy*, 50–54. For example, the British royal family learned an important lesson from the life and death of Diana Spencer; next time a charming and photogenic young woman might marry into the royal line, they should embrace and support her. In an age of mass-media celebrity, such a person would bolster their popularity and allow the Windsors to hold onto their assets.

23. *AM* 1: 29, 40–41, 89, 130, 142–43. Attorney, in this case, meant a representative in court when Gerard was unable to attend, rather than someone of legal training. It demonstrates a relationship of trust and respect between these men.

24. Riordan, *Plundering Time*, 28–29, 90–97, 103, 124–27. Riordan's book gives a thorough explanation of the background tensions among powerful people in Maryland, including the Susquehannocks, that contributed to the course of events in the 1640s.

25. Riordan, 29.

26. *AM* 4: 231–34.

27. *AM* 4: 235–61.

28. Riordan, *Plundering Time*, 150–59.

29. Riordan, 161–65.

30. *AM* 4: 458–59.

31. Riordan, *Plundering Time*, 172–86.

32. Riordan, 186–96. William Berkeley, governor of Virginia, would later plunder the estates of the rebels of 1677 and defend his actions by citing the actions of Charles I during the Civil War. Webb, *1676*, 107.

33. *AM* 4: 376; Riordan, *Plundering Time*, 198–217.

34. *AM* 3: 173. The "Petition" has not survived. Farrelly, *Anti-Catholicism in America*, 21.

35. *AM* 3: 174–76; *AM* 4: 394, 453; Riordan, *Plundering Time*, 274; Carr, "From Servant to Freeholder," 43.

36. *AM* 1: 239; *AM* 3: 171, 220.

37. *AM* 3: 174; *AM* 4: 357–59; Norris, *Westmoreland County Virginia*, 105–7; Beitzell, "Thomas Gerard and His Sons-in-Law," 202.

38. Eliga Gould, "Revolution and Counter-Revolution," in Armitage and Braddick, *The British Atlantic World*, 222–25.

39. Goodwyn, *The Populist Moment*, xviii–xx.

40. Lutz, *Documents of Political Foundation*, 233.

41. *AM* 1: 239–40; Riordan, *Plundering Time*, 258–68.

42. *AM* 1: 209.

43. Billings, *The Old Dominion in the Seventeenth Century*, 353–55; *AM* 3: 175–79.

44. *AM* 3: 182.

45. Riordan, *Plundering Time*, 278–81.

46. *AM* 1: 213–33, 267–70; 3: 211–13; 4: 321–24.

47. Norris, *Westmoreland County Virginia*, 149–53; Eaton, *Historical Atlas of Westmoreland County*, 59–69.

48. Robertson, *Tyrannicide Brief*, 71–100.

49. Mendle, *The Putney Debates of 1647*.

50. Manning, *Far Left in the English Revolution*, 31–79; Kloppenberg, *Toward Democracy*, 51, 107–114.

51. Mendle, *The Putney Debates of 1647*, 14–15.

52. Manning, *1649*, 13–48.

53. Robertson, *Tyrannicide Brief*, 140–87; Foster, *The Long Argument*, 148–50; Peacey, "Blakiston, John," *Oxford Dictionary of National Biography*.

54. Robertson, *Tyrannicide Brief*, 198–205; Manning, *1649*, 44–45.

55. Robertson, *Tyrannicide Brief*, 208–9.

56. Manning, *1649*, 201–15.

57. Manning, *Far Left in the English Revolution*, 59–61; Hill, *The World Turned Upside Down*, 234–50.

Chapter Two

1. "Commonwealth" is a term that had different connotations in different eras. Alexander Haskell's 2017 work *For God, King, and People* shows that at the turn of the seventeenth century it might be used interchangeably with "kingdom." Focusing on Virginia, he explains how the purpose of an Atlantic colony had not been fully worked out by 1607 and that the moral component, or God's mission for Englishmen, still factored into how colonizers and colonists envisioned their polity. "A fragile combination of self-righteousness and moral and legal ambiguity at the heart of Tudor and early Stuart colonization in America . . . gave not only Virginia but also the colonies that followed immediately in its wake a taut and mercurial atmosphere in which worldly and godly tendencies competed . . . for primacy" (21). For those living through the Revolution, however, "commonwealth" became associated with republic. The religious aspect remained entirely in flux.

2. *AM* 1: 217–29. Because of Greene's veto, the bill with its Remonstrance was not recorded, unlike the other less offensive acts. *AM* 1: 232–33.

3. *AM* 1: 215, 226–27, 238–39.

4. *AM* 3: 201; Steiner, *Maryland under the Commonwealth*, 10.

5. *AM* 1: 238–43; Jordan, *Foundations of Representative Government*, 52–53.

6. *AM* 3: 267–68.

7. *AM* 1: 245–46. Krugler, *English and Catholic*, 247, claimed that the act "freed the human spirit from the shackles of tradition." But the act's partner, prohibiting critique of Baltimore, puts the level of freedom of expression in context.

8. *AM* 1: 248–49.

9. *AM* 1: 264–69. Sutto, *Loyal Protestants and Dangerous Papists*, 62, suggests that Baltimore was angry at the Jesuits rather than the Ingle rebels, but no one had less influence on Maryland colonists at this moment than Catholic priests.

10. *AM* 3: 243–44.

11. *AM* 1: 273, 287–88.

12. *AM* 3: 275–76; "The Lord Baltemore's Case, 1653," in C. Hall, *Narratives of Early Maryland*, 173.

13. *AM* 3: 280.

14. "Virginia and Maryland, or The Lord Baltamore's Printed Case Uncased and Answered, 1655," in C. Hall, *Narratives*, 219; "Babylon's Fall, 1655," in C. Hall, 236.

15. *AM* 3: 311–12; "Virginia and Maryland," 224–25.

16. *AM* 1: 340–47.

17. *AM* 3: 315. Anne Arundell was the wife of a Calvert. The Puritans referred to their county as Providence, however.

18. Carr, Menard, and Walsh, *Robert Cole's World*, 123–24.

19. "Babylon's Fall," 239.

20. Heamans, "An additional brief Narrative," 140–53; *AM* 10: 433–34.

21. Hammond, "Hammond versus Heamens," 236–61; Heamans, "An additional brief Narrative"; "Babylon's Fall," 239–43.

22. Owen Stanwood, "Catholics and Protestants in Early America," in Beneke and Grenda, *The First Prejudice*, 220. As Stanwood explains, anti-Catholicism had a patriotic element as well as a democratic element. The French surrounded the English in America from Acadia to Louisiana.

23. Hammond, "Leah and Rachel," 1656, in C. Hall, *Narratives*, 304.

24. Hammond, "Leah and Rachel," 304–5; Luke Barber to Cromwell, April 13, 1655, in C. Hall, *Narratives*, 264; "Babylon's Fall," 242–44; Heamans, "An additional brief Narrative."

25. Hammond, "Hammond versus Heamens"; Heamans, "An additional brief Narrative."

26. *AM* 10: 422–34.

27. *AM* 10: 463.

28. *AM* 3: 323–35.

29. Russell Menard, "British Migration to the Chesapeake Colonies," in Carr, Morgan, and Russo, *Colonial Chesapeake Society*, 104, 121; Pestana, *English Atlantic*, 183–85; Wareing, *Indentured Migration and the Servant Trade*.

30. *AM* 3: 325.

31. *AM* 3: 354–57; *AM* 41: 565.

32. Hill, *The World Turned Upside Down*, 72.

33. *Christian Faith and Practice in the Experience of the Society of Friends* (London Yearly Meeting, 1960).

34. Neill, *The Founders of Maryland*, 142; Graham, "Meetinghouse and Chapel," in Carr, Morgan, and Russo, *Colonial Chesapeake Society*, 259; Carroll, *Quakerism on the Eastern Shore*, 9.

35. Archaeologists from St. Mary's College are leading the way in the research into the area on either side of Wicomico Creek, where Fendall, Slye, and Gerard lived and plotted. See King, Flick, and Bauer, "Lord Baltimore and the Politics of Landscape"; Strickland and King, "Josias Fendall's Dwelling Plantation"; King, Baumler, Coogan and Strickland, "In Search of Thomas Gerard."

36. Jourdan, *Abstracts of Charles County*; Maryland Archives, Land Office Patent Records, S-920-7, Book Rx, 29(b), 150(b)–151, 93(a); Skordas, *The Early Settlers of Maryland*; Lorena Walsh, "Community Networks," in Carr, Morgan, and Russo, *Colonial Chesapeake Society*, 233–38.

37. Coombs, "The Phases of Conversion," 343, 355.

38. Robert Slye, by 1662, was the only slave owner in the region. Whether any enslaved person worked in the house in 1659 we cannot know. Walsh, *Motives of Honor*, 192. A neighbor would pay one of Slye's slaves in 1663 for treating his sick child.

39. *AM* 20: xiv.

40. Ulrich, *Good Wives*, 9; Ulrich, *A Midwife's Tale*, 79–87; Ahnert and Ahnert, "Protestant Letter Networks in the Reign of Mary I."

41. *AM* 1: 381–82.

42. *AM* 1: 383; Jordan, *Foundations of Representative Government*, 66–70; Horn, "Adapting to a New World," in Carr, Morgan, and Russo, *Colonial Chesapeake Society*, 147–57;

Lois Carr and Lorena Walsh, "Changing Lifestyles and Consumer Behavior," in Carson, Hoffman, and Albert, *Of Consuming Interests*; Menard, "From Servant to Freeholder," 37–64; Henry M. Miller, "An Archaeological Perspective on Diet," in Carr, Morgan, and Russo, *Colonial Chesapeake Society*, 185–95; King, Flick, and Bauer, "Lord Baltimore and the Politics of Landscape," shows how the next Calvert to govern Maryland would deliberately build brick houses spread throughout the colony to display power and inculcate deference.

43. *AM* 1: 387–88.

44. *AM* 1: 388.

45. *AM* 1: 388–91.

46. *AM* 1: 391; *AM* 3: 387.

47. *AM* 41: 427–28.

48. Hutton, *The Restoration*, 71; Sharp, *In Contempt of All Authority*, 220–56.

49. Hutton, *The Restoration*, 85–118.

50. *AM* 41: 427–29.

51. *AM* 3: 387, 392–95, 397–98.

52. James, *The Lower Norfolk County Virginia Antiquary*, 3: 103.

53. *AM* 3: 396; *AM* 41: 428–29.

54. *AM* 53: 49–53.

55. *AM* 3: 396–99.

56. *AM* 3: 400–402; *AM* 41: 447–50; *AM* 53: 107–8.

57. *AM* 41: 448–49.

58. *AM* 41: 449–50.

59. *AM* 41: 427–29.

60. *AM* 3: 405–7.

61. *AM* 41: 484.

62. *AM* 41: 447–50; *AM* 1: 402.

63. *AM* 41: 470, 492, 509, 511; *AM* 3: 445.

64. *AM* 53: 161, 174.

65. King, Flick, and Bauer, "Lord Baltimore and the Politics of Landscape."

66. *AM* 53: 306–7; Harrison, *Landmarks of Old Prince William*, 38; Norris, *Westmoreland County Virginia*, 5–9, 38–43; Fischer and Kelly, *Bound Away*, 74.

67. Batts was Francis Yeardley's interpreter. *AM* 10: 347; "Francis Yeardley's Narrative of Excursions into Carolina, 1654," in Salley, *Narratives of Early Carolina*, 25–26 (hereafter "Francis Yeardley's Narrative"); Dorman, *Westmoreland County, Virginia*; Nugent, *Cavaliers and Pioneers*, 299, 331, 392, 442.

Chapter Three

1. "Proceedings in York County Court," 28.

2. "Proceedings in York County Court," 29–30.

3. Snyder, *Brabbling Women*, 2, 35–36.

4. "Proceedings in York County Court," 30–31.

5. "Proceedings in York County Court," 34–37.

6. Billings, "A Quaker in Seventeenth-Century Virginia," 132–33, fn17.

7. Powell, *Dictionary of North Carolina Biography*, 2: 107–8; Billings, *Sir William Berkeley*, 165; Webb, 1676, 5, 69.

8. Swanson, *A Golden Weed*, 36–37.

9. Billings, *The Old Dominion in the Seventeenth Century*, 167–72.

10. Billings, *Sir William Berkeley*, 202–3.

11. Billings, *The Old Dominion in the Seventeenth Century*, 77; Neill, *Virginia Carolorum*, 296–99. John Porter's son was to fight for Quakers and "their dangerous tenents" in North Carolina a half century later. See McIlvenna, *A Very Mutinous People*, 126–50.

12. Torrence, *Old Somerset on the Eastern Shore*.

13. *AM* 10: 347.

14. "Francis Yeardley's Narrative," 25–26.

15. "Francis Yeardley's Narrative," 25–29; Fox, *A Collection of Many Select and Christian Epistles*, 2: 55; John E. Byrd and Charles L. Heath, "Tuscarora Settlement Patterns," in Blanton and King, *Indian and European Contact*.

16. *AM* 10: 351.

17. "Francis Yeardley's Narrative," 26–27; McIlwaine, *Minutes of the Council*, 505; Billings, *Sir William Berkeley*, 77; Cumming, "The Earliest Permanent Settlement in Carolina," 82–89; Butler, "The Early Settlement of Carolina," 20–28.

18. Neill, *Virginia Carolorum*, 305–6; Neill, *The Founders of Maryland*, 142; Deed from King Kiscutanew to Nathaniel Batts, September 24, 1660, Nathaniel Batts Papers, NCSA; *CRNC*, 1: 19. Durant genealogists also suggest he may be related to a famous Roundhead, pastor to the Long Parliament, John Durant.

19. Billings, *Sir William Berkeley*, 135–62; Butler, "The Early Settlement of Carolina."

20. *CRNC*, 1: 45.

21. *CRNC*, 1: 33–34, 64–65. Jarvis's grant is lost.

22. "Drummond to Dear Friend, Sept. 1666," in Billings, *Papers of Sir William Berkeley*, 293–95; McIlvenna, *A Very Mutinous People*, 86.

23. Thompson, "The Thief, the Householder, and the Commons," 253–80.

24. Billings, *Sir William Berkeley*, 166. The republicans had a network as richly connected as the planters. Bushrod found his sanctuary in Nomini Bay, purchasing George Durant's tract there in 1665. Nugent, *Cavaliers and Pioneers*, 442.

25. *CRNC* 1: 45, 51.

26. Meanley, *The Great Dismal Swamp*; Cecelski, *The Waterman's Song*, 3–5; Merrens, *Colonial North Carolina*, 90–91.

27. Rutman and Rutman, *A Place in Time*, 65–69.

28. Rutman and Rutman, 40–44.

29. Rabushka, *Taxation in Colonial America*, 233, 263; McIlvenna, *A Very Mutinous People*, 90.

30. *CRNC* 1: 100; Neill, *Virginia Carolorum*, 229.

31. *CRNC* 1: 156–57.

32. Powell, *Ye Countie of Albemarle*, 3–8; *CRNC*, 1: 175, 764.

33. Powell, *Ye Countie of Albemarle*, 6–12.

34. Powell, 55–64.

35. Billings, *Sir William Berkeley*, 150–51, 186–88.

36. *AM* 2: 43–44, 143.

37. Billings, *Sir William Berkeley*, 192–93.

38. *AM* 2: 66; 5: 18; "Drummond to Dear Friend, Sept. 1666."

39. Nuala Zahedieh, "Economy," in Armitage and Braddick, *The British Atlantic World*, 55–56; Billings, *Sir William Berkeley*, 141–46.

40. Powell, *Ye Countie of Albemarle*, 39–41; *CRNC* 1: 181.

41. Kloppenberg, *Toward Democracy*, 152–59; Wilson, *The Ashley Cooper Plan*, 57–63. Locke drew up the Fundamental Constitutions for the proprietors, serving more as an attorney than as the author of the ideas. Brewer, "Slavery, Sovereignty, and 'Inheritable Blood,'" 1044, 1052.

42. *CRNC* 1: 259; *CRNC*, 2nd ser., 7: 339–41; Powell, *Ye Countie of Albemarle*, 54.

43. Fischer, *Suspect Relations*, 44–45; *CRNC*, 1: 215–18.

44. McIlvenna, *A Very Mutinous People*, 41–44.

45. Grimes, *North Carolina Wills*, 472–74.

46. Northampton Oath, March 1652, signed by Horsey, in Wise, *Ye Kingdome of Accawmacke*, 139–53. Wise explains the oath as the work of disaffected royalists, but there is no mention of the king, and in fact its authors name Parliamentary Commissioner Richard Bennett as their choice for governor of Virginia, not Berkeley.

47. Russo and Russo, *Planting an Empire*, 90, 109; Perry, *The Formation of a Society*, 214–20.

48. Deal, *Race and Class*, 116–17; Colonel Edmund Scarburgh's Report of His Proceedings at Annemessex and Manokin in October 1663, in Torrence, *Old Somerset on the Eastern Shore*, 388–91, 44–54.

49. Carroll, *Quakerism on the Eastern Shore*, 35.

50. *AM* 5: 411–18.

51. Headley, *Married Well and Often*, 147.

52. Beitzell, "Thomas Gerard and His Sons-in-Law," 203.

53. Norris, *Westmoreland County Virginia*, 37–38; *AM* 22: viii; *AM* 60: preface, 42.

54. *AM* 23: 443.

55. Baldwin, *The Maryland Calendar of Wills*, vol. 1, 76–77.

56. Billings, *Sir William Berkeley*, 221–27; Billings, *The Old Dominion in the Seventeenth Century*, 321.

57. Billings, *The Old Dominion in the Seventeenth Century*, 326–29.

58. *CRNC* 1: 259, 288; Sirmans, *Colonial South Carolina*, 31; McIlvenna, *A Very Mutinous People*, 48–49.

59. See Fischer, *Suspect Relations*; Hawks, *History of North Carolina*, vol. 2, 338–39.

60. Wood, *Strange New Land*.

61. Breen and Innes, "*Myne Owne Ground*"; Deal, *Race and Class*, 225–26.

62. Fischer, *Suspect Relations*, 48.

63. K. Brown, *Good Wives, Nasty Wenches*, 132–33, 143–46.

64. Fischer, *Suspect Relations*, 15–16.

Chapter Four

1. *AM* 2: 168–69, 175–77; 5: 77–78.

2. Jordan, *Foundations of Representative Government*, 84.

3. AM 2: 354–56; Jordan, *Foundations of Representative Government*, 85–87.

4. Devalinger, "The Burning of the Whorekill, 1673," October 1950; AM 5: 136.

5. Tarter, *The Grandees of Government*, 5, 26, 39.

6. Billings, *A Little Parliament*, 88–106.

7. Webb, *1676*, 220–21; Tarter, "Bacon's Rebellion," 17; Oberg, *Samuel Wiseman's Book of Record*, 209–12, 222, 246.

8. Morgan, *American Slavery, American Freedom*, 238; Webb, *1676*, 12–13; Oberg, *Samuel Wiseman's Book of Record*, 246.

9. Rice, *Tales*, 5–7.

10. Rice, 19–23.

11. Rice, 30–32; Billings, *Papers of Sir William Berkeley*, 498–99.

12. Billings, *Papers of Sir William Berkeley*, 486–87, 491–93, 497–98, 507.

13. Oberg, *Samuel Wiseman's Book of Record*, 145–47.

14. Tarter, "Bacon's Rebellion," 24–25.

15. Rice, *Tales*, 44–48; Billings, *Papers of Sir William Berkeley*, 536–37.

16. Billings, *Papers of Sir William Berkeley*, 520–21, 537; Tarter, "Bacon's Rebellion," 25; Rice, *Tales*, 49–50.

17. Billings, *Papers of Sir William Berkeley*, 523–24; Andrews, *Narratives of the Insurrections*, 96; Rice, *Tales*, 116.

18. Tarter, "Bacon's Rebellion," 26; Billings, *Papers of Sir William Berkeley*, 507.

19. Billings, *Papers of Sir William Berkeley*, 537.

20. Hening, *Statutes at Large*, 2: 341–65; Rice, *Tales*, 67–69.

21. "Thomas Mathew's Narrative,' in Andrews, *Narratives of the Insurrections*, 28–32.

22. Tarter, "Bacon's Rebellion," 28–31; Billings, *Papers of Sir William Berkeley*, 537.

23. Tarter, "Bacon's Rebellion," 32; Billings, *Papers of Sir William Berkeley*, 536–37, 582; Webb, *1676*, 5, 69; Washburn, "The Humble Petition of Sarah Drummond," 354; Snyder, *Brabbling Women*, 35; Susan Westbury, "Women in Bacon's Rebellion," in Bernhard et al., *Southern Women*, 30–46; Coombs, "The Phases of Conversion," 346–50.

24. Bacon, "Proclamations of Nathaniel Bacon,"55–63.

25. Billings, *Papers of Sir William Berkeley*, 464–65, 487–91, 515–16. At the Restoration, Parliament granted Charles II "poundage" for life, an increased duty on colonial imports and exports, including tobacco, for his personal income. Rabushka, *Taxation in Colonial America*, 237–38.

26. Rice, *Tales*, 83–87; Webb, *1676*, 53–56.

27. Rice, *Tales*, 89–92; Andrews, *Narratives of the Insurrections*, 66–69, 135; Coombs, "The Phases of Conversion," 349–53.

28. Rice, *Tales*, 94–96; Andrews, *Narratives of the Insurrections*, 135.

29. Andrews, *Narratives of the Insurrections*, 73.

30. Rice, *Tales*, 99–101; Andrews, *Narratives of the Insurrections*, 75.

31. Rice, *Tales*, 105–11; Grantham, *An Historical Account of Some Memorable Action*.

32. Rice, *Tales*, 114–17; Andrews, *Narratives of the Insurrections*, 96.

33. Rice, *Tales*, 117, 127; Tarter, "Bacon's Rebellion," 33–34; Wertenbaker, *Virginia under the Stuarts*, 204; Norton, *Separated by Their Sex*, 28–31; Snyder, *Brabbling Women*, 38; Mary Beth Norton, "Gender, Crime, and Community," in Henretta, Kammen, and Katz, *The Transformation of Early American History*, 140.

34. Webb, *1676*, 70; Rice, *Tales*, 121.

35. Andrews, *Narratives of the Insurrections*, 7, 145.

36. *AM* 5: 153–54; 15: 131, 137; Neill, *Virginia Carolorum*, 299; Rabushka, *Taxation in Colonial America*, 259–60.

37. *AM* 5: 143; 15: 128–29.

38. *AM* 8: 225.

39. *AM* 15: 137–40.

40. *AM* 5: 134–36; Graham, "Popish Plots," 197–216.

41. *AM* 5: 134–49.

42. *AM* 5: 153–54.

43. *CRNC* 1: 259, 287–90. Rankin, *Upheaval in Albemarle*, tells the story admittedly "heavily on the side of the proprietary faction," opposed to the rebellion. There are no footnotes. McIlvenna, *A Very Mutinous People*, 46–70, recounts the tale in greater detail than here.

44. *CRNC* 1: 235, 269; Oberg, *Samuel Wiseman's Book of Record*, 177.

45. Oberg, *Samuel Wiseman's Book of Record*, 249; Rabushka, *Taxation in Colonial America*, 237–38, 263.

46. *CRNC* 1: 244–45.

47. *CRNC* 1: 248–49, 278, 287–88.

48. *CRNC* 1: 248–49, 279–80, 287–88.

49. *CRNC* 1: 248–49.

50. *CRNC* 1: 280.

51. *CRNC* 1: 228, 258.

52. *CRNC* 1: 272–73.

53. *CRNC* 1: 272–74, 280–82.

54. *CRNC* 1: 274, 283, 288, 298.

55. *CRNC* 1: 272–74, 282–83.

56. *CRNC* 1: 248, 261, 288. The decision of the proprietors is set in the fuller context of English politics in McIlvenna, *A Very Mutinous People*, 60–69.

57. *CRNC* 1: 242, 256, 275–77, 296; McIlvenna, *A Very Mutinous People*, 65–69.

58. *AM* 15: 244–49; Kenyon, *The Popish Plot*, 180.

59. *AM* 5: 281.

Chapter Five

1. Patterson et al., *The Prose Works of Andrew Marvell*, 2: 197–207; Farrelly, *Anti-Catholicism in America*, 62–63.

2. Timothy Harris, "The British Dimension," in Claydon and McBride, *Protestantism and National Identity*, 143–56; Timothy Harris, "The Leveller Legacy," in Mendle, *The Putney Debates of 1647*, 219–40.

3. V. Brown, *The Reaper's Garden*; Davies, *The Royal African Company*, 63–74, 97–104; Lawson, *The East India Company*, 42–50; Rediker, *The Slave Ship*.

4. Michael Braddick, "The English Government," in Canny, *The Origins of Empire*, 286–308; Linebaugh and Rediker, *The Many-Headed Hydra*, 151.

5. Stanwood, *The Empire Reformed*, 27–47.

6. Miller, *The Glorious Revolution*, 1–10; Harris, "The Leveller Legacy," 231–36.

7. *AM* 17: 392–98; Miller, *James II*, 122–27.

8. Lustig, *The Imperial Executive in America*, 25–30.

9. McIlvenna, *A Very Mutinous People*, 71–76.

10. Hanna, *Pirate Nests and the Rise of the British Empire*, 174–75, 366, 389; Rediker, *Villains of All Nations*.

11. *AM* 5: 424–25; 17: 401, 541–42; *CRNC* 1: 354.

12. *AM* 7: 109.

13. Richter, *The Ordeal of the Longhouse*, 135–37; Dennis, *Cultivating a Landscape of Peace*, 270–71.

14. *AM* 5: 281.

15. *AM* 5: 312–14, 321, 331; 17: 50–56.

16. *AM* 5: 332–333; 7: 112–13; 17: 30–31, 48.

17. *AM* 7: 123.

18. *AM* 7: 117–27.

19. *AM* 7: 135–38, 160–61, 181–84. Future governors would exert themselves to exclude Coode from the Assembly through the 1690s and beyond.

20. *AM* 5: 312–24.

21. *AM* 5: 327–32; 70: 104. A decade later, Coode would demonstrate that it was no joke.

22. *AM* 5: 332–34, 351.

23. *AM* 5: 307.

24. Walsh, *Motives of Honor*, 22, 144–47, 182–83, 198–200.

25. Billings, *The Old Dominion in the Seventeenth Century*, 349–53.

26. Billings, 349–53; Snyder, *Brabbling Women*, 39; *AM* 5: 281; Swanson, *A Golden Weed*, 32–35.

27. *AM* 5: 357.

28. Billings, *The Old Dominion in the Seventeenth Century*, 353–55.

29. Snyder, *Brabbling Women*, 39; *AM* 7: 348, 407–9, 416–17, 452.

30. *AM* 5: 286–308.

31. *AM* 5: 374–82; 17: 182–85, 264–65, 272, 279–80, 288, 308.

32. *AM* 17: 272, 298–307, 322, 331, 335, 479.

33. *AM* 17: 324, 338, 340–56.

34. *AM* 5: 439–40; 17: 373–78, 410, 425–26, 449–54, 477–81.

35. *AM* 5: 490, 507–12; McIlvenna, *A Mutinous People*, 75–78, 90–91; *CRNC* 1: 350–52.

36. Coombs, "The Phases of Conversion," 335–53.

37. Billings, *The Old Dominion in the Seventeenth Century*, 185–86; Craven, *The Southern Colonies*, 400–405. The five marriages of Frances Gerard Speke Peyton Appleton Washington Hardige contributed to the formation of this elite society. She held enslaved people by 1676.

38. Billings, *The Old Dominion in the Seventeenth Century*, 185–86.

39. *AM* 1: 533–34.

40. *AM Biographical Series*, Irish Nell Butler, SC 5496-000534; *AM* 7: 203–5.

41. *AM* 7: 203–5.

42. K. Brown, *Good Wives, Nasty Wenches*, 126; Menard, "Making a 'Popular Slave Society,'" 377–95; Alpert, "The Origin of Slavery in the United States," 195, 209–11; Men-

ard, "The Maryland Slave Population," 29–54; Menard, *Sweet Negotiations*, 106–19; Morgan, *American Slavery, American Freedom*, 308–15, 328–37; Block, *Rape and Sexual Power*.

43. *AM* 90: 18; Burnard, *Creole Gentlemen*, 6.

44. Miller, *The Glorious Revolution*, 5–11.

Chapter Six

1. Miller, *James II*, 185–87.

2. Miller, 192–93.

3. Miller, 199.

4. Timothy Harris, "Scotland under Charles II and James IV and II," in Harris and Taylor, *The Final Crisis of the Stuart Monarchy*; Pincus, *1688*.

5. Carr and Jordan, *Maryland's Revolution of Government*, 37–45; Sutto, *Loyal Protestants and Dangerous Papists*, 163–74; Hoffman, *Princes of Ireland*, 43.

6. *AM* 13: 150–59.

7. *AM* 8: 56–57, 62–67, 70–72. Sutto's *Loyal Protestants* discusses the power of rumor in an era without newspapers, 129–41. "The Catholic-Indian conspiracy rumor threatened to replace the appointed chain of authority in Maryland. . . . News traveled quickly within the colony and beyond its borders," 140.

8. *AM* 8: 85; Harrison, *Landmarks*, 127–33.

9. Stanwood, *The Empire Reformed*, 86–96.

10. Harrison, *Landmarks of Old Prince William*, 132–33; Holly Brewer, "Subjects by Allegiance to the King?," in Thompson and Onuf, *State and Citizen*, 25.

11. *AM* 8: 70–72, 85–86, 91.

12. *AM* 8: 73–83.

13. *AM* 8: 80–89.

14. Stanwood, *The Empire Reformed*, 108–9; Lovejoy, *The Glorious Revolution*, 263–64.

15. Harrison, *Landmarks of Old Prince William*, 133.

16. Hall, Leder, and Kammen, *The Glorious Revolution*, 38–39, 66; Stanwood, *The Empire Reformed*, 96–98, 136; Andrews, *Narratives of the Insurrection*, 190–210; Lovejoy, *The Glorious Revolution*, 240–49.

17. Lovejoy, *The Glorious Revolution*, 106–21, 251–56.

18. Lovejoy, 274–75, 313–24; Hall, Leder, and Kammen, *The Glorious Revolution*, 99–114.

19. *AM* 8: 114–17, 156–57; *AM* 20: 143–44.

20. *AM* 8: 101–7.

21. *AM* 8: 120–34, 147–49, 158–61; Hoffman, *Princes of Ireland*, 41–45.

22. Carr and Jordan, *Maryland's Revolution of Government*, 65–91; McAnear, "Mariland's Grevances," 398; *AM* 8: 228.

23. *CRNC* 1: 359; *AM* 8: 112–14, 162, 167–68.

24. *AM* 8: 163–64, 166, 171–72, 176–77.

25. *AM* 8: 182–84, 193–99, 207.

26. *AM* 8: 210–36.

27. *CRNC* 1: 359–60, 371.

28. *CRNC* 1: 363–71; McIlvenna, *A Very Mutinous People*, 73–82; Haun, *Old Albemarle County*, 22. Haun's records seem clear that the Fendall family were resident in Perquimans into the 1690s.

29. *CRNC* 1: 371.

30. McIlvenna, *A Very Mutinous People*, 85–87, 97–100, 158–59.

31. *AM* 19: 21.

32. *AM* 19: 25, 40, 143; 20: 142, 172, 213.

33. *AM* 7: 135; 19: 435; 20: 564.

34. *AM* 19: 436–38.

35. *AM* 19: 439, 469, 479–80.

36. *AM* 20: 489–90.

37. *AM* 20: 491–93.

38. Jones, *Master Tully*, 12–15, 114, 131, 163, 198–200.

39. Jones, 44–45, 270.

40. Woolf, *Cicero*, 99–103, 124.

41. *AM* 20: 493, 564; Parent, *Foul Means*, 236–64.

42. Brewer, "Subjects by Allegiance to the King?," 32.

43. *AM* 19: 481; 20: 563–64; 23: 266, 520–23.

44. *AM* 23: 518–31; 25: 4–7, 30–32; *Calendar of State Papers, Colonial Series*, 16: 510–21.

45. *AM* 25: 32; Lustig, *The Imperial Executive in America*, 23; "By His Excellency a Proclamation," February 1699, Maryland Historical Society, MS 2018.

46. *AM* 25: 58, 75, 80, 103; Jordan, *Foundations of Representative Government*, 206–9; Carr and Jordan, *Maryland's Revolution of Government*, 245–47.

47. Carr and Jordan, *Maryland's Revolution of Government*, 202–7, 247–48.

48. David Jordan, "Political Stability," in Tate and Ammerman, *The Chesapeake in the Seventeenth Century*, 243–73.

49. Brewer, "Slavery, Sovereignty, and 'Inheritable Blood,'" 1073–75.

50. Tarter, *The Grandees of Government*, 86; Burnard, *Creole Gentlemen*, 116–17.

51. Carr and Jordan, *Maryland's Revolution of Government*, 215; Linebaugh and Rediker, *The Many-Headed Hydra*, 172–73.

Conclusion

1. Paine, *Basic Writings of Thomas Paine*.

2. Gloria Main, "Maryland and the Chesapeake Economy, 1670–1720," in Land, Carr, and Papenfuse, *Law, Society, and Politics*, 145–46; Holton, *Forced Founders*; Tarter, *The Grandees of Government*; Evans, *"Topping People"*; Parkinson, *The Common Cause*.

3. Norton, *Founding Mothers and Fathers*; Norton, *Separated by Their Sex*; K. Brown, *Good Wives, Nasty Wenches*.

4. Bailyn, *Barbarous Years*.

5. Riley, *Tidewater Maryland Ancestors*, 153–54; Burnard, *Creole Gentlemen*; Bailyn, *Barbarous Years*, 186–90; Carr, Menard, and Walsh, *Robert Cole's World*, 155–57.

6. Kloppenberg, *Toward Democracy*, 4.

Bibliography

Manuscript Archives

Alderman Library, University of Virginia
Archives of Maryland Online
English Broadside Ballad Archive, University of California at Santa Barbara
Maryland Historical Society
Maryland State Archives
Edward H. Nabb Research Center for Delmarva History and Culture
National Archives, London
North Carolina State Archives
David M. Rubenstein Rare Book and Manuscript Library, Duke University

Published Primary Sources

Andrews, Charles. *Narratives of the Insurrections, 1675-1690.* New York: Barnes and Noble, 1943.

Bacon, Nathaniel. "Proclamations of Nathaniel Bacon." *The Virginia Magazine of History and Biography* 1 (1893): 55-63.

Baldwin, Jane, ed. *The Maryland Calendar of Wills.* Vol. 1, *Wills from 1635-1685.* Baltimore: Genealogical Publishing, 1968.

Billings, Warren M., ed. *The Old Dominion in the Seventeenth Century: A Documentary History of Virginia, 1606-1700.* Chapel Hill: University of North Carolina Press, 2007.

———, ed. *The Papers of Sir William Berkeley, 1605-1677.* Richmond: Library of Virginia, 2007.

———. "A Quaker in Seventeenth-Century Virginia: Four Remonstrances by George Wilson." *William and Mary Quarterly,* 3rd ser., 33 (January 1976): 127-40.

Cain, Robert J., ed. *Colonial Records of North Carolina.* Vol. 7, *Records of the Executive Council, 1664-1734.* Raleigh: Department of Cultural Resources, North Carolina Division of Archives and History, 1984.

Calendar of State Papers, Colonial Series

Christian Faith and Practice in the Experience of the Society of Friends. London: London Yearly Meeting, 1960. "Proceedings in York County Court." *William and Mary Quarterly,* 1st ser., 11, no. 1 (July 1902): 34-37.

Dorman, John F., ed. *Westmoreland County, Virginia Records, 1658-1661.* Washington, DC: N.p. 1970.

Fox, George. *A Collection of Many Select and Christian Epistles, Letters and Testimonies.* Vol. 2. New York: AMS, 1975.

Grantham, Thomas. *An Historical Account of Some Memorable Actions, Particularly in Virginia; Also Against the Admiral of Algier, and in the East Indies: Perform'd for the Service of his Prince and Country.* London: J. Roberts, 1716. Eighteenth Century Collections Online: Range 15620.

Grimes, J. Bryan, ed. *North Carolina Wills and Inventories.* Raleigh: Edwards & Broughton Printing Company, 1912.

Hall, Clayton Colman, ed. *Narratives of Early Maryland, 1633–1684.* New York: Barnes and Noble, 1967.

Hall, Michael, Lawrence Leder, and Michael Kammen, eds. *The Glorious Revolution in America: Documents on the Colonial Crisis of 1689.* Chapel Hill: University of North Carolina Press, 2012.

Hammond, John. "Hammond versus Heamens." *Maryland Historical Magazine* 4 (1909).

Haun, Weynette Parks. *Old Albemarle County North Carolina, Perquimans Precinct: Births, Marriages, Deaths and Flesh Marks, 1659–1820.* Durham, NC: Privately published, 1980.

Heamans, Roger. "An additional brief Narrative of a late bloody design against the Protestants in Ann Arundel County Severn in Maryland in the Country of Virginia as also of the Extraordinary deliverance of those poor oppressed people." *Maryland Historical Magazine* 4 (1909).

Hening, William W., ed. *Statutes at Large: Being a Collection of all the Laws of Virginia, from the First Session of the Legislature in the year 1619.* Vol. 2, 1660–1682. Charlottesville: University Press of Virginia, 1969.

James, Edward W., ed. *The Lower Norfolk County Virginia Antiquary.* Vol. 3. Richmond: Whittet and Shepperson, 1901–4.

Jourdan, Elise Greenup. *Abstracts of Charles County Maryland Court and Land Records, Vol. 1: 1658–1666.* Berwyn Heights, MD: Heritage Books, 2007.

Lutz, Donald S., ed. *Documents of Political Foundation Written by Colonial Americans.* Philadelphia: Institute for the Study of Human Issues, 1986.

McAnear, Beverly, ed. "Mariland's Grevances Wiy the Have Taken Op Arms." *Journal of Southern History* 8 (August 1942): 392–409.

McIlwaine, H. R., ed. *Minutes of the Council and General Court of Colonial Virginia, 1622–1632, 1670–1676.* Richmond: Colonial Press 1924.

Milton, John. *The Major Works.* Oxford: Oxford University Press, 2003.

Nugent, Nell M., ed. *Cavaliers and Pioneers: Abstracts of Virginia Land Patents and Grants, 1623–1666.* Baltimore: Genealogical Publishing, 1963.

Oberg, Michael, ed. *Samuel Wiseman's Book of Record: The Official Account of Bacon's Rebellion in Virginia.* Lanham, MD: Lexington Books, 2005.

Paine, Thomas. *Basic Writings of Thomas Paine: Common Sense, Rights of Man, Age of Reason.* New York: Willey Book, 1942.

Parkinson, Robert G. *The Common Cause: Creating Race and Nation in the American Revolution.* Chapel Hill: University Press, 2016.

Patterson, Annabel, Martin Dzelzainis, N. H. Keeble, and Nicholas von Maltzahn, eds. *The Prose Works of Andrew Marvell.* Vol. 2. New Haven, CT: Yale University Press, 2003.

Powell, William S., ed. *Ye Countie of Albemarle: A Collection of Documents, 1664–1775.* Raleigh, NC: State Department of Archives and History, 1958.

Revel, James. "The Poor Unhappy Transported Felon's Sorrowful Account of His Fourteen Years Transportation at Virginia in America." *Virginia Magazine of History and Biography* 56 (1948): 189–94.

Sainsbury, W. Noel, ed. *Calendar of State Papers, Colonial: North America and the West Indies, 1574–1739.* London: Public Record Office, 1860.

Salley, Alexander, Jr., ed. *Narratives of Early Carolina, 1650–1708.* New York: Charles Scribner's Sons, 1911.

Saunders, William L., ed. *Colonial Records of North Carolina.* 10 vols. Raleigh, NC: Hale, 1886.

Shakespeare, William. *Coriolanus.* New York: Simon and Schuster, 2009.

Skordas, Gust, ed. *The Early Settlers of Maryland: An Index to Names of Immigrants Compiled from Records of Land Patents, 1633–1680.* Genealogical Publishing, 2008.

Smith, Nigel, ed. *Poems of Andrew Marvell.* Harlow: Pearson, 2007.

Secondary Sources

Ahnert, Ruth, and Sebastian Ahnert. "Protestant Letter Networks in the Reign of Mary I: A Quantitative Approach." *English Literary History* 82 (Spring 2015): 1–33.

Alpert, Jonathan L. "The Origin of Slavery in the United States: The Maryland Precedent." *American Journal of Legal History* 14 (July 1970): 189–221.

Armitage, David, and Michael Braddick, eds. *The British Atlantic World, 1500–1800.* New York: Palgrave Macmillan, 2009.

Bailyn, Bernard. *The Barbarous Years: The Peopling of British North America; The Conflict of Civilizations, 1600–1675.* New York: Vintage, 2013.

Barry, John M. *Roger Williams and the Creation of the American Soul: Church, State, and the Birth of Liberty.* New York: Penguin, 2012.

Beitzell, Edwin W. "Thomas Gerard and His Sons-in-Law." *Maryland Historical Magazine* 46 (September 1951): 189–206.

Beneke, Chris, and Christopher S. Grenda, eds. *The First Prejudice: Religious Tolerance and Intolerance in Early America.* Philadelphia: University of Pennsylvania Press, 2011.

Bernhard, Virginia, Betty Brandon, Elizabeth Fox-Genovese, and Theda Perdue, eds. *Southern Women: Histories and Identities.* Columbia: University of Missouri Press, 1992.

Billings, Warren M. *A Little Parliament: The Virginia General Assembly in the Seventeenth Century.* Richmond, VA: Library of Virginia, 2004.

———. *Sir William Berkeley and the Forging of Colonial Virginia.* Baton Rouge: Louisiana State University Press, 2004.

Blanton, Dennis B. and Julia A. King, eds. *Indian and European Contact in Context: The Mid-Atlantic Region.* Gainesville: University Press of Florida, 2004.

Block, Sharon. *Rape and Sexual Power in Early America.* Chapel Hill: University of North Carolina Press, 2006.

Braddick, Michael. *God's Fury, England's Fire: A New History of the English Civil Wars.* New York: Penguin, 2009.

Breen, T. H., and Stephen Innes. *"Myne Owne Ground": Race and Freedom on Virginia's Eastern Shore, 1640-1676*. New York: Oxford University Press, 2005.

Brewer, Holly. "Slavery, Sovereignty, and 'Inheritable Blood': Reconsidering John Locke and the Origins of American Slavery." *American Historical Review* 122 (October 2017): 1038-78.

Brown, Kathleen. *Good Wives, Nasty Wenches, and Anxious Patriarchs: Gender, Race, and Power in Colonial Virginia*. Chapel Hill: University of North Carolina Press, 1996.

Brown, Vincent. *The Reaper's Garden: Death and Power in the World of Atlantic Slavery*. Cambridge, MA: Harvard University Press, 2008.

Burnard, Trevor. *Creole Gentlemen: The Maryland Elite, 1691-1776*. New York: Routledge, 2002.

Butler, Lindley S. "The Early Settlement of Carolina: Virginia's Southern Frontier." *Virginia Magazine of History and Biography* 79 (January 1971): 20-28.

Canny, Nicholas, ed. *The Origins of Empire: British Overseas Enterprise to the Close of the Seventeenth Century*. Oxford: Oxford University Press, 1998.

Carr, Lois Green. "From Servant to Freeholder: Daniel Clocker's Adventure." *Maryland Historical Magazine* 110 (Spring 2015): 24-48.

Carr, Lois Green, and David W. Jordan. *Maryland's Revolution of Government, 1689-1692*. Ithaca, NY: Cornell University Press, 1974.

Carr, Lois Green, Russell Menard, and Lorena Walsh. *Robert Cole's World: Agriculture and Society in Early Maryland*. Chapel Hill: University of North Carolina Press, 1991.

Carr, Lois Green, Philip D. Morgan, and Jean B. Russo, eds. *Colonial Chesapeake Society*. Chapel Hill: University of North Carolina Press, 1988.

Carr, Lois Green, and Lorena S. Walsh. "The Planter's Wife: The Experience of White Women in Seventeenth-Century Maryland." *William and Mary Quarterly* 34 (October 1977): 542-71.

Carroll, Kenneth. *Quakerism on the Eastern Shore*. Baltimore: Maryland Historical Society, 1970.

Carson, Cary, Ronald Hoffman, and Peter J. Albert, eds. *Of Consuming Interests: The Style of Life in the Eighteenth Century*. Charlottesville: University Press of Virginia, 1994.

Cecelski, David S. *The Waterman's Song: Slavery and Freedom in Maritime North Carolina*. Chapel Hill: University of North Carolina Press, 2001.

Chernaik, Warren L. *The Poet's Time: Politics and Religion in the Work of Andrew Marvell*. Cambridge: Cambridge University Press, 1983.

Claydon, Tony, and Ian McBride, eds. *Protestantism and National Identity: Britain and Ireland, c. 1650-c. 1850*. Cambridge: Cambridge University Press, 1998.

Coombs, John. "The Phases of Conversion: A New Chronology for the Rise of Slavery in Early Virginia." *William and Mary Quarterly*, 3rd ser., 68 (July 2011): 332-60.

Craven, Wesley F. *The Southern Colonies in the Seventeenth Century, 1607-1689*. Baton Rouge: Louisiana State University Press, 1970.

Crawford, Julie. *Mediatrix: Women, Politics, and Literary Production in Early Modern England*. Oxford: Oxford University Press, 2014.

Cumming, William P. "The Earliest Permanent Settlement in Carolina: Nathaniel Batts and the Comberford Map." *American Historical Review* 45, no. 1 (October 1939): 82–89.

Cust, Richard. *Charles I: A Political Life*. New York: Pearson, 2007.

Cust, Richard, and Ann Hughes, eds. *Conflict in Early Stuart England: Studies in Religion and Politics, 1603-1642*. New York: Longman, 1989.

Davies, K. G. *The Royal African Company*. New York: Octagon Books, 1975.

Deal, J. Douglas. *Race and Class in Colonial Virginia: Indians, Englishmen, and Africans on the Eastern Shore during the Seventeenth Century*. New York: Garland, 1993.

Dennis, Matthew. *Cultivating a Landscape of Peace: Iroquois-European Encounters in Seventeenth-Century America*. Ithaca, NY: Cornell University Press, 1993.

Devalinger, Leon, Jr. "The Burning of the Whorekill, 1673." N.p., October 1950.

Dinan, Susan E., and Debra Meyers, eds. *Women and Religion in Old and New Worlds*. New York: Routledge, 2001.

Donoghue, John. *Fire under the Ashes: An Atlantic History of the English Revolution*. Chicago: University of Chicago Press, 2013.

Eaton, David W. *Historical Atlas of Westmoreland County*. Richmond, VA: Dietz Press, 1942.

Evans, Emory. *A "Topping People": The Rise and Decline of Virginia's Old Political Elite*. Charlottesville: University of Virginia Press, 2009.

Farrelly, Maura Jane. *Anti-Catholicism in America, 1620-1860*. Cambridge: Cambridge University Press, 2017.

———. *Papist Patriots: The Making of an American Catholic Identity*. Oxford: Oxford University Press, 2012.

Fischer, David H. and James C. Kelly, *Bound Away: Virginia and the Westward Movement*. Charlottesville: University Press of Virginia, 2000.

Fischer, Kirsten. *Suspect Relations: Sex, Race, and Resistance in Colonial North Carolina*. Ithaca, NY: Cornell University Press, 2002.

Foster, Stephen. *The Long Argument: English Puritanism and the Shaping of New England Culture, 1570-1700*. Chapel Hill: University of North Carolina Press, 1991.

Goodwyn, Lawrence. *The Populist Moment*. New York: Oxford University Press, 1978.

Graham, Michael. "Popish Plots: Protestant Fears in Early Colonial Maryland, 1676-1689." *Catholic Historical Review* 79 (April 1993): 197–216.

Hailwood, Mark. "'Come Hear This Ditty': Seventeenth-Century Drinking Songs and the Challenges of Hearing the Past." The Appendix.net 1, no. 3 (July 2013).

Hanna, Mark G. *Pirate Nests and the Rise of the British Empire, 1570-1740*. Chapel Hill: University of North Carolina Press, 2015.

Harris, Tim, and Stephen Taylor, eds. *The Final Crisis of the Stuart Monarchy: The Revolutions of 1688-91 in Their British, Atlantic and European Contexts*. Woodbridge, UK: Boydell Press, 2013.

Harrison, Fairfax. *Landmarks of Old Prince William: A Study of Origins in Northern Virginia*. Berryville, VA: Chesapeake Book, 1964.

Haskell, Alexander B. *For God, King, and People: Forging Commonwealth Bonds in Renaissance Virginia*. Chapel Hill: University of North Carolina Press, 2017.

Hawks, Francis. *History of North Carolina*. Vol. 2. Fayetteville, NC: Hale, 1858.

Headley, Robert K., Jr. *Married Well and Often: Marriages of the Northern Neck of Virginia, 1649–1800; Marriages and Marriage References for the Counties of Lancaster, Northumberland, Old Rappahannock, Richmond and Westmoreland.* Baltimore: Genealogical Publishing, 2003.

Henretta, James A., Michael Kammen, and Stanley N. Katz, eds. *The Transformation of Early American History: Society, Authority, and Ideology.* New York: Alfred A. Knopf, 1991.

Hill, Christopher. *A Century of Revolution: 1603–1714.* New York: W. W. Norton, 1982.

———. *The World Turned Upside Down: Radical Ideas during the English Revolution.* New York: Penguin Books, 1975.

Hirst, Derek. *England in Conflict, 1603–1660: Kingdom, Community, Commonwealth.* New York: Oxford University Press, 1999.

Hoffman, Ronald. *Princes of Ireland, Planters of Maryland: A Carroll Saga, 1500–1782.* Chapel Hill: University of North Carolina Press, 2002.

Holton, Woody. *Forced Founders: Indians, Debtors, Slaves, and the Making of the American Revolution in Virginia.* Chapel Hill: University of North Carolina Press, 1999.

Hutton, Ronald. *The Restoration: A Political and Religious History of England and Wales, 1658–1667.* Oxford: Clarendon Press, 1985.

Jones, Howard. *Master Tully: Cicero in Tudor England.* Nieuwkoop: De Graaf, 1999.

Jordan, David W. *Foundations of Representative Government in Maryland, 1632–1715.* New York: Cambridge University Press, 1987.

Kennedy, D.E., *The English Revolution, 1642–1649.* London: Palgrave Macmillan, 2000.

Kenyon, John. *The Popish Plot.* London: William Heinemann, 1972.

King, Julia, Alex J. Flick, and Skylar A. Bauer. "Lord Baltimore and the Politics of Landscape in Seventeenth-Century Maryland." Unpublished manuscript.

King, Julia A., Irene C. Baumler, Christopher L. Coogan and Scott M. Stickland, "In Search of Thomas Gerard: Archaeological Investigations at the Clifton Site Near Bushwood, Maryland." St. Mary's College, Maryland, 2016.

Kishlansky, Mark. *A Monarchy Transformed: Britain, 1603–1714.* New York: Penguin, 1997.

Kloppenberg, James T. *Toward Democracy: The Struggle for Self-Rule in European and American Thought.* New York: Oxford University Press, 2016.

Krugler, John D. *English and Catholic: The Lords Baltimore in the Seventeenth Century.* Baltimore: Johns Hopkins University Press, 2008.

Land, Aubrey C. *Colonial Maryland: A History.* New York: KTO Press, 1981.

Land, Aubrey C., Lois Green Carr, and Edward C. Papenfuse, eds. *Law, Society, and Politics in Early Maryland.* Baltimore: Johns Hopkins University Press, 1977.

Lawson, Philip. *The East India Company: A History.* Harlow, UK: Longman, 1993.

Linebaugh, Peter, and Marcus Rediker. *The Many-Headed Hydra: Sailors, Slaves, Commoners, and the Hidden History of the Revolutionary Atlantic.* Boston: Beacon, 2001.

Lockyer, Roger. *The Early Stuarts: A Political History of England, 1603–1642.* London: Longman, 1989.

Lovejoy, David. *The Glorious Revolution in America*. Middletown, CT: Wesleyan University Press, 1987.

Lustig, Mary Lou. *The Imperial Executive in America: Sir Edmund Andros, 1637–1714*. Madison, NJ: Fairleigh Dickinson University Press, 2002.

Manning, Brian. *The Far Left in the English Revolution, 1640 to 1660*. Chicago: Bookmarks, 1999.

———. *1649: The Crisis of the English Revolution*. Chicago: Bookmarks, 1992.

Matthew, H. C. G., and Brian Harrison, eds. *Oxford Dictionary of National Biography*. Oxford: Oxford University Press, 2004.

McIlvenna, Noeleen. *A Very Mutinous People: The Struggle for North Carolina, 1660–1713*. Chapel Hill: University of North Carolina Press, 2009.

Meanley, Brooke. *The Great Dismal Swamp*. Washington DC: Audubon Naturalist Society, 1973.

Menard, Russell R. "From Servant to Freeholder: Status Mobility and Property Accumulation in Seventeenth-Century Maryland." *William and Mary Quarterly*, 3rd ser., 30 (January 1973): 37–64.

———. "Making a 'Popular Slave Society' in Colonial British America." *Journal of Interdisciplinary History* 63 (Winter 2013): 377–95.

———. "The Maryland Slave Population, 1658–1730: A Demographic Profile of Blacks in Four Counties." *William and Mary Quarterly* 32 (January 1975): 29–54.

———. *Sweet Negotiations: Sugar, Slavery, and Plantation Agriculture in Early Barbados*. Charlottesville: University of Virginia Press, 2006.

Mendle, Michael, ed. *The Putney Debates of 1647: The Army, the Levellers and the English State*. Cambridge: Cambridge University Press, 2001.

Merrens, H. R. *Colonial North Carolina in the Eighteenth Century: A Historical Geography*. Chapel Hill: University of North Carolina Press, 1964.

Meyers, Debra. *Common Whores, Vertuous Women, and Loveing Wives: Free Will Christian Women in Colonial Maryland*. Bloomington: Indiana University Press, 2003.

Miller, John. *The Glorious Revolution*. London: Longman, 1997.

———. *James II*. New Haven, CT: Yale University Press, 2000.

Morgan, Edmund S. *American Slavery, American Freedom: The Ordeal of Colonial Virginia*. New York: W. W. Norton, 2003.

Neill, Edward Duffield. *The Founders of Maryland as Portrayed in Manuscripts, Provincial Records, and Early Documents*. Albany, NY: Joel Munsell, 1876.

———. *Virginia Carolorum: The Colony under the Rule of Charles the First and Second A.D. 1625–A.D. 1685; Manuscripts and Documents of the Period*. Albany, NY: Joel Munsell's Sons, 1886.

Norris, Walter Biscoe Jr., ed. *Westmoreland County Virginia 1653–1983*. Montrose, VA: Westmoreland County Board of Governors, 1983.

Norton, Mary Beth. *Founding Mothers and Fathers: Gendered Power and the Forming of American Society*. New York: Alfred A. Knopf, 1996.

———. *Separated by Their Sex: Women in Public and Private in the Colonial Atlantic World*. Ithaca, NY: Cornell University Press, 2011.

Osgood, Herbert L. *The American Colonies in the Seventeenth Century*, Vol. 2. Gloucester, MA: Peter Smith, 1957.

Parent, Anthony. *Foul Means: The Formation of a Slave Society in Virginia, 1660-1740*. Chapel Hill: University of North Carolina Press, 2003.

Perry, James R. *The Formation of a Society on Virginia's Eastern Shore, 1615-1655*. Chapel Hill: University of North Carolina Press, 1990.

Pestana, Carla. *The English Atlantic in an Age of Revolution, 1640-1661*. Cambridge, MA: Harvard University Press, 2004.

Pincus, Steve. *1688: The First Modern Revolution*. New Haven, CT: Yale University Press, 2009.

Powell, William S., ed. *Dictionary of North Carolina Biography*. 6 Vols. Chapel Hill: University of North Carolina Press, 1986.

Rabushka, Alvin. *Taxation in Colonial America*. Princeton, NJ: Princeton University Press, 2008.

Rankin, Hugh. *Upheaval in Albemarle: The Story of Culpeper's Rebellion, 1675-1689*. Raleigh, NC: Carolina Charter Tercentenary Commission, 1962.

Rediker, Marcus. *The Slave Ship: A Human History*. New York: Penguin, 2007.

———. *Villains of All Nations: Atlantic Pirates in the Golden Age*. London: Verso, 2012.

Rice, James D. *Nature and History in the Potomac Country: From Hunter-Gatherers to the Age of Jefferson*. Baltimore: Johns Hopkins University Press, 2016.

———. *Tales from a Revolution: Bacon's Rebellion and the Transformation of Early America*. New York: Oxford University Press, 2012.

Richter, Daniel K. *The Ordeal of the Longhouse: The Peoples of the Iroquois League in the Era of European Colonization*. Chapel Hill: University of North Carolina Press, 1992.

Riley, George D., Jr. *Tidewater Maryland Ancestors, 1634-1999*. Baltimore: Gateway Press, 1999.

Riordan, Timothy. *The Plundering Time: Maryland and the English Civil War, 1645-1646*. Baltimore: Maryland Historical Society, 2004.

Robertson, Geoffrey. *The Tyrannicide Brief: The Story of the Man Who Sent Charles I to the Scaffold*. New York: Pantheon Books, 2005.

Russell, Conrad. *The Fall of the British Monarchies, 1637-1642*. New York: Oxford University Press, 1995.

Russo, Jean B., and J. Elliott Russo. *Planting an Empire: The Early Chesapeake in British North America*. Baltimore: Johns Hopkins University Press, 2012.

Rutman, Darrett, and Anita Rutman. *A Place in Time: Middlesex County, Virginia, 1650-1750*. New York: W. W. Norton, 1986.

Sharp, Buchanan. *In Contempt of All Authority: Rural Artisans and Riot in the West of England, 1586-1660*. Berkeley: University of California Press, 1980.

Sirmans, M. Eugene. *Colonial South Carolina: A Political History, 1663-1763*. Chapel Hill: University of North Carolina Press, 1966.

Smith, Nigel. *Andrew Marvell: The Chameleon*. New Haven, CT: Yale University Press, 2012.

Snyder, Terri L. *Brabbling Women: Disorderly Speech and the Law in Early Virginia*. Ithaca, NY: Cornell University Press, 2003.

Stanwood, Owen. *The Empire Reformed: English America in the Age of the Glorious Revolution*. Philadelphia: University of Pennsylvania Press, 2011.

———. "The Maryland Disease: Popish Plots and Imperial Politics in the Seventeenth Century." *Occasional Papers of the Center for the Study of Democracy* 4 (Fall 2011): 1–11.

Steiner, Bernard. *Maryland under the Commonwealth: A Chronicle of the Years 1649–1658*. Baltimore: Johns Hopkins University Press, 1911.

Strickland, Scott M. and Julia A. King, "An Archaeological Survey of the Charleston Property: Josias Fendall's Dwelling Plantation." St Mary's College, Maryland, 2011.

Sutto, Antoinette. *Loyal Protestants and Dangerous Papists: Maryland and the Politics of Religion in the English Atlantic, 1630–1690*. Charlottesville: University of Virginia Press, 2015.

Swanson, Drew. *A Golden Weed: Tobacco and Environment in the Piedmont South*. New Haven, CT: Yale University Press, 2014.

Tarter, Brent. "Bacon's Rebellion, the Grievances of the People, and the Political Culture of Seventeenth-Century Virginia." *Virginia Magazine of History and Biography* 119 (2011): 2–41.

———. *The Grandees of Government: The Origins and Persistence of Undemocratic Politics in Virginia*. Charlottesville: University of Virginia Press, 2013.

Tate, Thad W., and David L. Ammerman, eds. *The Chesapeake in the Seventeenth Century: Essays on Anglo-American Society and Politics*. Chapel Hill: University of North Carolina Press, 1979.

Thompson, Peter. "The Thief, the Householder, and the Commons: Languages of Class in Seventeenth-Century Virginia." *William and Mary Quarterly*, 3rd ser., 63 (April 2006): 253–80.

Thompson, Peter, and Peter Onuf, eds. *State and Citizen: British America and the Early United States*. Charlottesville: University of Virginia Press, 2013.

Torrence, Clayton. *Old Somerset on the Eastern Shore of Maryland: A Study in Foundations and Founders*. Baltimore: Regional Publishing, 1966.

Ulrich, Laurel Thatcher. *Good Wives: Image and Reality in the Lives of Women in Northern New England, 1650–1750*. New York: Alfred A. Knopf, 1982.

———. *A Midwife's Tale: The Life of Martha Ballard, Based on Her Diary, 1785–1812*. New York: Vintage Books, 1990.

Viswanathan, Gauri. *Masks of Conquest: Literary Study and British Rule in India*. New York: Columbia University Press, 1989.

Walsh, Lorena. *Motives of Honor, Pleasure, and Profit: Plantation Management in the Colonial Chesapeake, 1607–1763*. Chapel Hill: University of North Carolina Press, 2010.

Wareing, John. *Indentured Migration and the Servant Trade from London to America, 1618–1718: "There Is Great Want of Servants."* Oxford: Oxford University Press, 2017.

Washburn, Wilcomb E. "The Humble Petition of Sarah Drummond." *William and Mary Quarterly* 13 (July 1956): 354–75.

Webb, Stephen S. *1676: The End of American Independence*. New York: Alfred A. Knopf, 1984.

Wertenbaker, Thomas Jefferson. *Virginia under the Stuarts, 1607–1688*. New York: Russell and Russell, 1959.

Wilson, Thomas D. *The Ashley Cooper Plan: The Founding of Carolina and the Origins of Southern Political Culture*. Chapel Hill: University of North Carolina Press, 2016.

Wise, Jennings Cropper. *Ye Kingdome of Accawmacke or the Eastern Shore of Virginia in the Seventeenth Century*. Baltimore: Regional Publishing, 1967.

Wood, Peter. *Strange New Land: Africans in Colonial America*. New York: Oxford University Press, 2003.

Woolf, Raphael. *Cicero: The Philosophy of a Roman Sceptic*. New York: Routledge, 2015.

Woolrych, Austin. Britain in Revolution, 1625–1660. New York: Oxford University Press, 2003.

Index

Made in the USA
Middletown, DE
07 September 2024

60506826R00109